RABBI MOSHE DOMBEY ZT"L MEMORIAL EDITION

שמונה פרקים לרמב"ם

THE 8 CHAPTERS

OF THE

RAMBAM

RABBI MOSHE DOMBEY ZT"L MEMORIAL EDITION

שמונה פרקים לרמב"ם

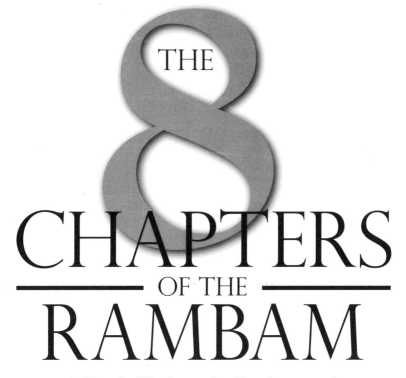

THE 8 CHAPTERS

OF THE

RAMBAM

*A Classic Work on the Fundamentals
of Jewish Ethics and Character Development*

Translation and commentary by
RABBI YAAKOV FELDMAN

A TARGUM PRESS BOOK

First published 2008
Copyright © 2008 by Yaakov Feldman
ISBN 978-1-56871-476-9

The Hebrew text of *Shemoneh Perakim* is that of Rabbi Yosef Kapach, copyright © Mossad HaRav Kook, and is reproduced with permission of the copyright holder.

Published by:
TARGUM PRESS, INC.
22700 W. Eleven Mile Rd.
Southfield, MI 48034
E-mail: targum@targum.com
Fax: 888-298-9992
www.targum.com

Distributed by:
FELDHEIM PUBLISHERS
208 Airport Executive Park
Nanuet, NY 10954

Printing plates by Frank, Jerusalem
Printed in Israel by Chish

בס"ד

שמואל קמנצקי
Rabbi S. Kamenetsky

2018 Upland Way
Philadelphia, Pa 19131

Home: 215-473-2798
Study: 215-473-1212

דפּ בם סיין הנאם ופאלוֹם לֵבֵ

לנֵרֵת הרב האלון ' וטפא
פלענמאן שלוט

פסע רבּציוֹ יֿאֵ האם האמה/... א שאﬥﬧ
בּנקﬡ לﬣﬧﬡﬦﬧ יﬤﬢ מקﬡﬠ לﬧﬧﬨ ששׁשׁﬦ וﬤﬧﬧﬦﬢ
פﬧﬦ﬩ ﬡﬠﬡﬡﬢﬦ ﬧﬦﬢﬡ﬩ﬥ. שﬠﬧﬧﬠ ﬡﬦ ﬡﬢﬥשׁ ﬧﬧ﬩ﬥ ﬧﬨﬠﬧ
ﬧﬧﬦ﬩ ﬡﬦﬥשׁﬧ ﬢﬤﬧﬦ ﬧﬧשׁﬥ﬩ ﬥﬧﬦשׁﬧﬥﬧﬦ ﬥﬧﬧﬡ﬩ ﬥﬦﬧﬢ
ﬥﬧשׁﬧﬢ ﬥﬧﬦﬢﬡ ﬧﬥשׁﬧﬥ ﬧﬨﬧﬦﬧ ﬧﬧשׁﬧﬦﬦﬡﬥﬧﬧﬦ ﬤﬧ
ﬦﬤﬧﬦﬧﬦﬧﬦ.

ﬧﬦﬧﬦﬦ ﬧﬦ ﬧﬥﬧﬧﬦ ﬥﬦﬡﬦﬧﬦ ﬧﬧﬦﬧﬡﬡﬧ ﬢﬦﬧﬦ
ﬧﬧﬨﬦﬧﬧ ﬧﬡﬧﬦﬧﬦ.

דﬧﬧﬦﬧﬦ ﬡﬧﬦﬧﬦﬢ ﬡﬠﬧﬦ

שﬠﬧﬡﬥ קﬠﬦﬦ

D'Var

The D'Var Institute
4 Village Green, Wesley Hills, NY 10952
Box 622, Pomona, NY 10970
1-800-33-TORAH
Fax: 1-866-938-6724

April 2, 2008   BS"D

This letter is to endorse Rabbi Yaakov Feldman's English translation of *Shemoneh Perakim* authored by the Rambam. Rabbi Feldman is known for his translations and books, for writing in a lucid and scholarly fashion. *Shemoneh Perakim* is an important work which until now lacked a scholarly translation. It is an important work which the general English-speaking public had little access to. I therefore endorse its publication. *Yagdil Torah v'yaadir.*

Sincerely,

Rabbi Chaim Friedman
Rosh HaKollel, Kollel Ohr Somayach, Jerusalem

הרב דוב בערל וויין

שדרות בן מימון 15
ירושלים, עיה"ק
טל: 0515-561 (02)
פקס: 1956-567 (02)

2 Nissan 5768
7 April 2008

As in his previous works on *Chovos Halevavos* and *Shaarei Teshuvah*, Yaakov Feldman has succeeded in capturing the essence of a very difficult and erudite work — Rambam's *Shemoneh Perakim* — and presenting it with clarity and verve to the English-speaking reader. The exalted philosophical and spiritual ideas that this great work possesses are of timeless quality and most relevant benefit. Yaakov Feldman has done a great service with his presentation of the Rambam's *Shemoneh Perakim*.

All blessings.

Rabbi Berel Wein

This book is dedicated, with respect and fondness, to

Rabbi Moshe Chaim Dombey, *zt"l*
(*nilb'a* 3 Shevat 5766)

Rabbi Moshe Chaim Dombey was an *ish eshkolos*, a multifaceted Torah scholar whose talents and dedication inspired and touched so many lives:

A pioneer in *kiruv rechokim*, he reached out to his fellow Jews at a time when few believed we could win the hearts and minds of our secular brethren to Torah observance;

A master teacher, he taught thousands of newly observant young men and women the intricacies of halachah, allowing them to build homes imbued with the observance of Torah law;

A talented translator, his works of halachah set a standard for clarity and allowed him to share his expertise in halachah with tens of thousands of readers all over the world;

A founder and manager of Targum Press, his adherence to halachah and business ethics and his *menschlichkeit* in his dealings with others helped create a company that proves that Torah values and business can work in tandem.

Whether in the classroom, in the office, or from his hospital bed, he gave all those privileged to know him a shining example of integrity, clear-sightedness, and rock-solid *bitachon* in Hashem's ultimate kindness.

Shemoneh Perakim was one of the last submitted manuscripts that Rabbi Dombey, *zt"l*, read before his untimely *petirah*. As he did so many times before, he saw the potential of the manuscript and was proud to add it to the list of important Targum Press classics. It is therefore particularly appropriate to dedicate it to his memory.

יהי זכרו ברוך

CONTENTS

Translator's Introduction

Anyone of a sensitive and inquisitive nature has to be overwhelmed in our day and age by the wealth of information available to us about the human situation, the world at large, the cosmos, and more. After all, there isn't a person, place, or thing that hasn't been scrutinized, studied, and peered into inside and out.

As a consequence, we've come to know a lot more about the bustling, jostling, and boisterous world around and within us than ever before. Many have thus become restless and agitated because they are so inundated with data, feelings, and thoughts, which cry out for some sort of bearing and management. After all, few among us can take it all in, yet it's also clear that we will forfeit far too much if we don't take in enough.

It seems the only solution is to somehow or other narrow things down, determine what matters most, what matters less so, and what really doesn't matter at all, and then learn how to apply all that to our lives. And that is where *Shemoneh Perakim* comes in.

For it's my contention that Rambam (an acronym for his name, **Rab**bi **Moshe Ben Maimon**) has provided us herein with a list of priorities, a veritable "guide for the overwhelmed" of any epoch, including our own. It is here that he engages in an early attempt to set order to the grand scheme of things so that we might know what to concentrate upon in the face of it all.

Later works (for example, several parts of *Mishneh Torah*, including

Hilchot Yesodei Hatorah, Hilchot Dei'ot, and *Hilchot Teshuvah*; parts of the Rambam's Commentary on the Mishnah, including the introduction and commentary to *Perek Cheilek*; some of his letters; and several parts of *Moreh Nevuchim*) expanded upon many of the themes offered here. But it was here, in *Shemoneh Perakim,* that Rambam addressed the very most vital existential issues we would all do well to concentrate on, including just who we are, in essence; what is expected of us as Jews specifically as well as what is expected of all human beings; how we are to serve God in the world; and more.

He took the opportunity to delve into all this at this point in his writings because, as we'll find, *Shemoneh Perakim* serves as his introduction to his comments on *Pirkei Avot* ("The Ethics of the Fathers"), and much of all this is touched upon there.

Pirkei Avot is usually taken to be a rather straightforward setting out of many of the moral ideals our Sages held out for us all. Yet as Rambam points out in his introduction to this work, *Pirkei Avot* is clearly something far deeper than that, far more engaging, for our Sages said that whoever wanted to be pious would have to live by its words (*Bava Kama* 30a).

What exactly is piety? Does it come down to otherworldliness, religious zealotry, self-denial, and the like? Can one live in the modern world and be pious? Is there a characteristically Jewish brand of piety or is it a generic type? Are there degrees higher than piety? Why would anyone want to be pious?

To begin with, we'll learn that piety touches upon self-perfection (among other things). But what is self-perfection all about? Any discussion on self-perfection would certainly have to be preceded by an analysis of the "self" in question. What are we, in fact? Are we each a melange of separate independent parts? Or is each individual a "unified field" of sorts, defining the cluster of all of his or her parts (see chapter 1)?

And are we really so in control of our beings that we can perfect ourselves? Aren't there extenuating circumstances and other things out of our control, like our inborn natures? Is there such a thing as predestination, in light of the fact that an All-knowing God would certainly know beforehand if a person is to be good or bad, and could thus force one to act one way or the other (see chapter 2, as well as chapter 8)?

If we imply that we're capable of perfecting ourselves, we must now be imperfect. But how so? What is right about us, and what is not (see chapter 3)? And how do we ever improve ourselves (see chapter 4)?

The subject of prophecy arises at several points in this work, in connection with piety (see Rambam's introduction and chapter 5). What differentiates the pious from prophets? Did Jewish prophets differ from non-Jewish ones, and how so? And if, as we know, Moses was the greatest of prophets, what made him so great? How does that affect our own spiritual station (see chapter 7)?

Hence, we see that *Shemoneh Perakim* touches upon certain deep and vital existential questions it would do us all well to concentrate on if we're ever to live a life of content and challenge, growth and spiritual excellence.

*   *   *

When I first decided to translate and comment upon this dynamic work, I was immediately taken aback by the enormity of the task. Like the author of *Chovot HaLevavot*, Rabbeinu Bachyah Ibn Pakudah, said about himself in his introduction to that book, I too felt ill-equipped for the task and wondered if "I was burdening myself with something that would only demonstrate my limitations" and was "overstepping my bounds."

But as Rabbeinu Bachyah put it, I knew full well that "many good ideas were rejected because of fear," so I too "forced myself to endure the writing of this book and to explain its subject as clearly and vividly as I could."

I drew from others' works, including Rabbi Yosef Kapach's translation from the original Arabic to Hebrew — which serves as our Hebrew text — along with his notes; Rabbi Yitzchak Shilat's later translation into Hebrew with notes, and Rabbi Mordechai Rabinowitz's notes to his *Rambam La'Am* edition. But the ideas contained here are my own and should not be attributed to any of these scholars, for I mainly made use of their syntactic and contextual insights, and most especially of the wealth of Rambam's other writings they directed me to in my own research.

I took certain liberties with the text, including subdividing the chapters for ease of reference and occasionally veering from a literal translation of the text in order to offer a more idiomatic, contemporary translation that is nonetheless true to the original.

I offered notes to the text in the hopes of clarifying Rambam's meaning and to explain the many difficulties, as well as to illustrate my point that his messages are essential for us in our own day and age. And I provided a synopsis of the original text itself at the end of each chapter for review.

Several of the more difficult ideas called for a longer, more technical explanation; and certain themes presented here were presented in Rambam's earlier and later works and called for some comparison and contrast to what is said here. These explanations and analyses are included in the supplementary notes at the end of the book.

The Hebrew text of *Shemoneh Perakim* is taken directly from the edition translated from the original Arabic and edited by Rabbi Yosef Kapach, *z"l*, published by Mossad HaRav Kook, Jerusalem. I would like to gratefully acknowledge the permission and cooperation of Mossad HaRav Kook, particularly Rabbi Yosef Movshovitz, in this project. I also wish to acknowledge the gracious cooperation and assistance of Judaica Press, Inc., for the use of material that they had originally designed for this book.

I want to thank my children, Nechama, Aryeh, and Dina; and my beloved wife, Sara, for her comments, insight, encouragement, and life-partnership.

Lastly, I thank God Almighty for allowing me the strength, time, resources, and all else it took to produce this work.

שמונה פרקים לרמב״ם

THE EIGHT CHAPTERS OF THE RAMBAM

הקדמה

INTRODUCTION

ע״ו

W E'RE PRESENTED HERE WITH *a beguiling statement of purpose: These eight chapters serve as an introduction to a work so full of meaning and so challenging for most that we could hardly plumb its depths without these introductory chapters. It's as if Rambam were promising to take us through a room so dark and even so daunting that we'd have to use a very powerful and precise light to see our way through it. Thus, he must first teach us the workings of the special lamp itself before we can even attempt to traverse the room.*

But what masterpiece would call for all that? Strangely enough, it is none other than one of the most commonly read classical Jewish works, Pirkei Avot ("The Ethics of the Fathers"), that well-known array of seemingly straightforward, homey pieces of advice for living an honest life that our Sages laid out for us, millennia ago.

Rambam's point is that Pirkei Avot is far more than what it seems. In fact, it is a work that explores the makeup of human character and the self in general, and it allows us a glimpse into the hearts and spirits of the pious and prophets along the way.

As we'll see, though, it isn't clear from the outset just who can be considered pious. In fact, the ideas we might have of what piety is all about are going to be challenged. What makes a person a prophet will also be confronted. Because while we might have our impressions, we really don't know, and we either under- or overestimate the prophet's "otherworldliness."

We'll notice, too, that Rambam mentions two concepts here that are very foreign to the modern mind: "perfection" and "true good fortune." How can a person ever be "perfect"? Can one ever be partly perfect and otherwise imperfect? And what is "true good fortune"?

Finally, Rambam humbly refuses to take credit for what he will be saying, for one reason or another, and claims only to be a conduit of others' wisdom.

What we have here, then, is the promise of guidance through layer upon layer of revelation into the human heart, soul, and mind, and a look beyond the ordinary into self-perfection, piety, and prophecy.

1. We already explained in our introduction to this work why its compiler placed this tractate in this order [of the Mishnah], and mentioned as well how beneficial it is.* And we also promised several times in this work [i.e., in the commentary to the Mishnah] to discuss this tractate's [i.e., *Pirkei Avot's*] beneficial points at some length.[2]

א. כְּבָר בֵּאַרְנוּ בְּהַקְדָּמַת חִבּוּר זֶה מַהוּ הַטַּעַם שֶׁהֵבִיא אֶת הַמְחַבֵּר הַזֶּה לִקְבּוֹעַ מַסֶּכְתָּא זוֹ בְּסֵדֶר הַזֶּה, וְגַם הִזְכַּרְנוּ אֶת גּוֹדֶל הַתּוֹעֶלֶת שֶׁיֵּשׁ בְּמַסֶּכְתָּא זוֹ, וּכְבָר הִבְטַחְנוּ כַּמָּה פְּעָמִים בְּמַה שֶׁקָּדַם בְּחִבּוּר זֶה שֶׁנְּדַבֵּר בְּמַסֶּכְתָּא זוֹ בְּעִנְיָנִים מוֹעִילִים, וְשֶׁאָנוּ נַאֲרִיךְ בּוֹ מְעַט.

כִּי אַף עַל פִּי שֶׁהִיא פְּשׁוּטָה וְקַלָּה

For, despite the fact that it seems straightforward and easy enough

We already explained...how beneficial it is — This is a confusing statement, so we'll take it bit by bit.

Rambam starts off by referring to his introduction to "this work." The work he's referring to isn't *Shemoneh Perakim*, the present work. After all, this statement itself begins his introduction to *Shemoneh Perakim*.

What "this work" refers to is Rambam's voluminous commentary to the Mishnah, which *Shemoneh Perakim* is a very small part of. "Our *introduction* to this work" refers to the overall in-

troduction Rambam wrote to that commentary.

"Its compiler," that is to say, the Mishnah's compiler, was the great and holy Rabbi Yehudah HaNasi. "This tractate" refers to *Pirkei Avot* ("The Ethics of the Fathers"); and "this order" refers to *Seder Nezikin*, one of the six "orders" or divisions of the Mishnah that includes *Pirkei Avot*.

In short, in the course of Rambam's comments to the Mishnah, he said he would eventually offer comments to

to understand and do, *Pirkei Avot* is still not easy for everyone to abide by. Furthermore, not everything in it can be understood without an adequate explanation. Yet it fosters great perfection* and true good fortune,* and therefore I decided to expand on the subject [more than I had originally envisioned].[3,4]

לְהַבִּינָה לְפִי הַפְּשַׁט הֲרֵי אֵין עֲשִׂיַּת כָּל הַכָּלוּל בָּה קַל לְכָל בְּנֵי אָדָם, וְגַם לֹא כָּל עִנְיָנֶיהָ מוּבָנִים בְּלִי פֵּירוּשׁ מַסְפִּיק, וְנוֹסָף לְכַךְ שֶׁהִיא מְבִיאָה לִידֵי שְׁלֵמוּת גְּדוֹלָה וְאוֹשֶׁר אֲמִתִּי, וּלְפִיכָךְ רָאִיתִי לְהַרְחִיב בָּה אֶת הַדִּבּוּר.

Pirkei Avot, which he did (and which will be found later on in this work) — but he subsequently decided to preface that commentary with these eight introductory chapters.[1]

great perfection — "Perfection" (*sheleimut*) is a misunderstood term. Many mistakenly take it to mean the ability to be all things to all people, to do everything flawlessly, and to never make a mistake. But that is not what Rambam is referring to.

A good analogy to "perfection" as he uses it here would be the feeling we sometimes have that a certain piece of music, work of art, book, or idea is perfect, simply because all of its parts seem to "gel" rather than overpower each other; because they seem to make their statement (i.e., do what they have to do) and then stop; and because they seem to capture the very essence of the thing they're trying to express. They aren't actually "perfect," since they do lack many things. A "perfect" symphony, for example, isn't expected to include other dimensions of perfection such as weather conditions, flavor, aroma, comfort, health, wisdom, or insight into the human condition. It's simply perfect for what it is.

That is the sort of perfection we're capable of achieving. That is, while

we're not expected to contain, provide for, or do everything, we are capable of being wholly balanced human beings, full amalgams of our spiritual, intellectual, and physical selves, who fulfill our purpose in life and express our potential. This will all become clear in the course of this work.

true good fortune — Most of us have rather pedestrian visions of good fortune, while others have rather exorbitant ones. The righteous, though, have a whole other sense of it.

Having lived their lives in pursuit of spiritual excellence and having achieved a measure of it, their visions of good fortune involve fully realizing that excellence. They long to sit at the feet of the wise and knowing, to be exposed to out-of-the-way secret ideas and truths the rest of us don't even know exist. And they most especially long to commune with God Almighty forever.

In fact, it could be said that we are each the products of our own dreams and realizations. The dreams we have of good fortune and the realizations we've come to about what it would take to achieve it define what we do, who our friends are, whom we marry, how we expend our energies, and so much more.

Some of us actually achieve the

2. The Sages, peace be upon them, said that "whoever wants to be pious should fulfill the words of *Pirkei Avot*" (*Bava Kama* 30a), and amongst us there is no greater level than piety other than prophecy.* In fact, it [piety] is what leads to [prophecy],* as our Sages said, "Piety leads to divine inspiration" (*Avodah Zarah* 20b).[5] Hence, it is clear from their words that living by the ethical directives of this tractate leads one to prophecy.[6] I will explain [below] the validity of this phenomenon, since it comprises a great portion of good character traits.*

ב. וּכְבָר אָמְרוּ, עֲלֵיהֶם הַשָּׁלוֹם (בבא קמא ל.), "הַאי מַאן דְּבָעֵי לְמֶהֱוֵי חֲסִידָא לְקַיֵּים מִילֵי דְּאָבוֹת." וְאֵין אֶצְלֵנוּ מַעֲלָה לְמַעֲלָה מִן הַחֲסִידוּת זוּלַת הַנְּבוּאָה וְהִיא הַמְּבִיאָה אֵלֶיהָ, כְּמוֹ שֶׁאָמְרוּ (עבודה זרה כ:), "חֲסִידוּת מְבִיאָה לִידֵי רוּחַ הַקֹּדֶשׁ." הִנֵּה נִתְבָּאֵר מִדִּבְרֵיהֶם שֶׁהַהִתְנַהֲגוּת בְּמוּסְרֵי מַסֶּכְתָּא זוֹ מְבִיאָה לִידֵי נְבוּאָה, וְהִנְנִי מְבָאֵר אֲמִתַּת דָּבָר זֶה, לְפִי שֶׁהִיא כּוֹלֶלֶת חֵלֶק גָּדוֹל מִן הַמִּדּוֹת.

וְרָאִיתִי לְהַקְדִּים לִפְנֵי שֶׁאַתְחִיל לְפָרֵשׁ הֲלָכָה הֲלָכָה פְּרָקִים מוֹעִילִים, שֶׁיּוּשַׂג לָאָדָם בָּהֶם הַקְדָּמוֹת, וְגַם יִהְיוּ לוֹ כְּמַפְתֵּחַ לְמַה שֶּׁנֶּאֱמַר לְקַמָּן בְּפֵירוּשׁ.

Thus, before explaining each halachah [i.e., each of *Pirkei Avot*'s statements], I thought I would first offer a few helpful chapters [i.e., *Shemoneh Perakim*] as an introduction, which will then act as a key to what will be said below [in my comments to *Pirkei Avot*].[7]

---

good fortune we seek all through our lives and live long enough to enjoy it. Others reach a point in their maturity when something deep in their hearts realizes that their dreams have been a sham and that it's too late to go back.

Rambam's point seems to be that we would all do well to discover the true ideal — a sense of what *real* good fortune is — before it's too late, and to pursue it. That true ideal can best be achieved by basing our lives upon the wise teachings that comprise *Pirkei Avot*.

no greater level than piety other than prophecy — That is to say, since piety is so elevated a spiritual rank that it just precedes prophecy, which

is the very highest level, and since living by the words of *Pirkei Avot* will bring one to piety, it's even more important to give a fuller and deeper explanation of *Pirkei Avot* than may have been originally planned.

leads to prophecy — And that's to say that not only does piety precede prophecy, it actually affords one with the greatest opportunity for it.

a great portion of good character traits — This one sentence serves as the preamble for the rest of the work. For what it says is that since living by the words of *Pirkei Avot* leads to piety, and piety leads to prophecy, and since so much of that is rooted

3. It is important to know, though, that I did not originate the ideas expressed or the explanations offered either in these chapters or in my commentary [to *Pirkei Avot*], but they are collected from the words of the Sages in Midrashim, the Talmud, and in their other works, as well as from the words of earlier and later philosophers [Jewish and non-Jewish],[8] and from the works of many others. Accept the truth from whoever utters it.[9]

Once in a while, though, I will quote verbatim from a well-known work [without indicating that it is a quote]. There is nothing wrong with this, since I am not taking credit for what someone else already said, and because I hereby acknowledge [what I will be doing].

I also will not say, "So-and-so said this" or "So-and-so said that" because that would be unnecessarily wordy.[10] Furthermore, it might make a reader who does not accept the author concerned think that what he said is harmful or has an untoward meaning that he is unaware of. Therefore I decided to leave out the author's name, for my aim is to help the reader and explain what is hidden away in this tractate.*

ג. וְדַע כִּי הַדְּבָרִים שֶׁאוֹמַר בַּפְּרָקִים הַלָּלוּ וּבַמֶּה שֶׁיָּבֹא מִן הַפֵּירוּשׁ אֵינָם עִנְיָנִים שֶׁחִדַּשְׁתִּים אֲנִי מִלִּבִּי, וְלֹא פֵּרוּשִׁים שֶׁאֲנִי הִמְצֵאתִים, אֶלָּא הֵם עִנְיָנִים מְלוּקָטִים מִדִּבְרֵי חֲכָמִים בְּמִדְרָשׁוֹת וּבַתַּלְמוּד וְזוּלָתוֹ מֵחִבּוּרֵיהֶם, וְגַם מִדִּבְרֵי הַפִילוֹסוֹפִים הָרִאשׁוֹנִים וְהָאַחֲרוֹנִים, וּמֵחִבּוּרֵי הַרְבֵּה מִבְּנֵי אָדָם, וְקַבֵּל הָאֱמֶת מִמִּי שֶׁאֲמָרָהּ.

וְאֶפְשָׁר שֶׁאָבִיא לִפְעָמִים עִנְיָן שָׁלֵם שֶׁהוּא לְשׁוֹן אֵיזֶה סֵפֶר מְפוּרְסָם, אֵין בְּכָל זֶה רוֹעַ, וְאֵינִי טוֹעֵן לְעַצְמִי מַה שֶּׁאֲמָרוּהוּ מִי שֶׁקְּדָמוּנִי, וְהִנְנִי מוֹדֶה בְּכָךְ.

וְאַף עַל פִּי שֶׁלֹא אַזְכִּיר אָמַר פְּלוֹנִי אָמַר פְּלוֹנִי, לְפִי שֶׁזֹּאת אֲרִיכוּת שֶׁאֵין בָּהּ תּוֹעֶלֶת. וְאוּלַי אֶגְרֹם שֶׁיִּכָּנֵס בְּלֵב מִי שֶׁאֵינוֹ מְקוּבָּל עָלָיו שֵׁם אוֹתוֹ אָדָם שֶׁאוֹתוֹ הַדָּבָר נִפְסָד וְיֵשׁ בּוֹ כַּוָּונָה רָעָה שֶׁאֵינָהּ יְדוּעָה לוֹ, וּלְפִיכָךְ נִרְאֶה לִי לְהַשְׁמִיט שֵׁם הָאוֹמֵר, כִּי מַטָרָתִי שֶׁתּוּשַׂג הַתּוֹעֶלֶת לַקּוֹרֵא וּלְבָאֵר לוֹ הָעִנְיָנִים הַכְּמוּסִים בְּמַסֶּכְתָּא זוֹ.

in character, there is therefore a need to expound upon character, piety, and prophecy. Rambam thus sets out to do that in *Shemoneh Perakim*. See our pivotal discussion of this in section 5 of chapter 4 below as well.

hidden away in this tractate — There are some people that others wouldn't accept the proverbial time of day from. Were a murderer, for example, to declare murder wrong, others would be likely to question his motives. If a politician whose positions they disagreed with said something they agreed with, they'd question their own

I will now begin by offering the chapters I thought it important to start off with, in keeping with my aim. There will be eight in all.

וְהִנְנִי עַתָּה מַתְחִיל בְּהַזְכָּרַת הַפְּרָקִים אֲשֶׁר רָאִיתִי לְהַקְדִּימָם כָּאן בְּהֶתְאֵם לְמַטָּרָתִי, וְהֵם שְׁמֹנָה פְּרָקִים.

SYNOPSIS

1. *As he said he would, Rambam set out to comment on Pirkei Avot. But since Pirkei Avot isn't easy to understand, despite appearances, and since not everyone can abide by what it offers, and since it touches upon such important, profound issues, Rambam decided to provide us with these eight chapters as an overall introduction to Pirkei Avot.*

2. *Our Sages assured us that anyone who lives by the words of Pirkei Avot will achieve piety. Since piety is a spiritual rank that is determined by our character, and since it is just below prophecy and leads directly to it, Rambam set out to explain all that here, too.*

3. *Rambam doesn't claim to have originated any of the ideas here. He acknowledges that they derive from the words of our Sages, from philosophers, and from others whom he often quotes verbatim, without citations, in order to explain the many things that are hidden away in Pirkei Avot.*

beliefs. That sad reality undoes a lot of truth and raises countless questions. Rambam therefore decided to forgo the formality and nicety of citing his sources in order to rise above this phenomenon, and offered his readers raw statements of truth.

There's another point to be made at this junction, as well. We seem to have an indication here that *Shemoneh Perakim* was written for the layperson rather than for scholars, since a layperson couldn't adduce sources cited, while a scholar could. We'll find, though, that this work is actually addressed to both.[11]

1

בנפש האדם וכחותיה
THE HUMAN NEFESH AND ITS CAPACITIES

I F WE ARE EVER GOING TO *better ourselves, we need to know just who we are, and what we're made of.*

Rambam's point in this chapter is that, ultimately, we're each comprised of a single indivisible self called "the nefesh" — that multihued core of our being that expedites nearly everything we do and are. And since self-improvement depends upon nefesh-improvement, and that in turn depends upon an understanding of the makeup of the nefesh and its component parts (i.e., who we are and what we're made of), we'll be examining all that here.

We'll thus discover that there are five components to the nefesh: our digestive systems, our senses, our imaginations, our emotions, and our intellects. While we can certainly consciously steer some of them in any direction, the others carry on by design alone and are beyond our control. This theme will prove to be crucial to our understanding of free will specifically and the human condition in general, as we will see.

The last point Rambam makes here is that reason is the "form" (the crucial, distinctive dimension) of our nefesh, while its other components are merely its "matter," and that we must actuate our reason if we are ever to achieve our potential. While Rambam doesn't delve into that here, he does elsewhere.

1. It is important to know that the human *nefesh* is one [in number], but it has many different functions.*

Some of these functions themselves have been called *nefashot*, which is why some, such as the physicians [of antiquity], have thought that a person has several *nefashot*.

א. דַּע כִּי נֶפֶשׁ הָאָדָם אַחַת וְיֵשׁ לָה פְּעוּלוֹת הַרְבֵּה שׁוֹנוֹת.

יֵשׁ שֶׁנִּקְרָאוֹת מִקְצַת אוֹתָן הַפְּעוּלוֹת נְפָשׁוֹת, וּלְפִיכָךְ יֵשׁ שֶׁחָשְׁבוּ בְּכָךְ שֶׁיֵּשׁ לְאָדָם נְפָשׁוֹת רַבּוֹת כְּמוֹ שֶׁחוֹשְׁבִים הָרוֹפְאִים, עַד שֶׁפָּתַח גָּדוֹל הָרוֹפְאִים שֶׁהַנְּפָשׁוֹת שָׁלֹשׁ: טִבְעִית, וְחִיּוּנִית, וְנַפְשִׁית.

The greatest of them all* claimed that there were three *nefashot*: the natural, the dynamic, and the spiritual.*

---

has many different functions — When Rambam says here that "the human *nefesh* is one [in number], but it has many different functions," he is touching upon a momentous issue that we will now address — the issue of "Who am I?"

In fact, we're each a melange of organically wedded but dissimilar aspects of ourselves that are often at odds. There are times when the body reigns, and we identify our beings with rank physicality. Other times our emotions reign, and we are swept away by one feeling or another. Yet at other times the intellect reigns, and we are either very crafty, perhaps, or sagacious, and centered in our minds.

All in all, though, Rambam's point is that we are each a single person with a number of different capacities. The self — the *nefesh* — is the conductor behind the miscellany of instruments that comprise our beings, and it somehow defines and infuses that orchestra with its will and intentions. In point of fact, many compare God's role in the universe to the *nefesh*'s own role in the life of the human being.

A question that will come up lat-er, though, is exactly which parts of our self do we control, and which not? Or, in other words, what are we responsible for in our being, and what is God responsible for? This will be discussed later on, when we consider free will and personal responsibility (see chapters 2 and 8).[1]

the greatest of them all — Hippocrates (circa 460–370 B.C.E.), considered the father of medicine.

the natural, the dynamic, and the spiritual — That is to say, the physicians of antiquity believed that we are comprised of three separate selves: the lowest self, which is identified with nativistic, primitive needs; the more creative, animate, dynamic self which is identified with action and change; and the higher, nonmaterial self which is identified with the transcendent.

They consequently saw each of us as three-roomed storehouses of inner conflict and contradiction, with nothing uniting those rooms other than their shared accommodations. In contrast, Jewish philsophy sees each individual as a "unified field."[2]

Some of these same functions are also called "capacities" or "parts," which is why the term "parts of the *nefesh*" is often used, for instance, by many philosophers. [Nevertheless,] though they speak of "parts," they do not mean that the *nefesh* can be divided into parts the way the body can. They are merely accounting for the different functions of the *nefesh*, which are all, nonetheless, integral parts of the one *nefesh*.[3]

2. As you know, improving a person's character amounts to healing his *nefesh* and its capacities.* Thus, just as a doctor treating the human body would first have to be familiar with the human body he is treating, as a whole and in part, as well as with what things would make it ill and avoid them and what things would heal it and utilize them [which will be discussed in this chapter and the

וְיֵשׁ שֶׁהֵם נִקְרָאִים כֹּחוֹת וַחֲלָקִים, עַד שֶׁאוֹמְרִים חֶלְקֵי הַנֶּפֶשׁ, וְשֵׁמוֹת אֵלּוּ מִשְׁתַּמְּשִׁים בָּהֶם הַרְבֵּה הַפִילוֹסוֹפִים. וְאֵין כַּוָּנָתָם בְּאָמְרָם חֲלָקִים שֶׁהִיא מִתְחַלֶּקֶת כְּהִתְחַלְּקוּת הַגּוּפוֹת, אֶלָּא הֵם מוֹנִים פְּעֻלּוֹתֶיהָ הַשּׁוֹנוֹת שֶׁהֵם לְגַבֵּי כְּלָלוּת הַנֶּפֶשׁ כַּחֲלָקִים לְגַבֵּי הַכְּלָלוּת הַמְחֻבֶּרֶת מֵאוֹתָם הַחֲלָקִים.

ב. וְאַתָּה יוֹדֵעַ שֶׁתִּקּוּן הַמִּדּוֹת אֵינוֹ אֶלָּא רְפוּאַת הַנֶּפֶשׁ וְכֹחוֹתֶיהָ, וּכְשֵׁם שֶׁהָרוֹפֵא הַמְרַפֵּא אֶת הַגּוּפוֹת צָרִיךְ שֶׁיֵּדַע תְּחִלָּה אֶת הַגּוּף שֶׁהוּא מְרַפֵּא אוֹתוֹ בִּכְלָלוֹ, וְחֶלְקֵי אוֹתוֹ הַגּוּף מַה הֵם, כְּלוֹמַר גּוּף הָאָדָם, וְצָרִיךְ לָדַעַת מַה הֵם הַדְּבָרִים הַגּוֹרְמִים לוֹ מַחֲלָה וְיִרְחַק מֵהֶם, וּמַה הֵם דְּבָרִים הַמַּבְרִיאִים אוֹתוֹ וְיִשְׁתַּמֵּשׁ בָּהֶם, כַּךְ

---

healing his *nefesh* and its capacities — Apparently the idea that self-improvement is connected to character improvement was axiomatic in Rambam's time, since he says, "As you know, improving a person's character amounts to healing his *nefesh*."

The modern age, however, seems to have untied that bond, taking self-improvement to be rooted in material improvement, professional improvement, improvement in interpersonal skills, and improvement of one's knowledge base, instead. We thus seem not to see self-improvement as character development so much as *circumstance*-development.

Accordingly, we often allow ourselves to admire and emulate immoral, ill-mannered, selfish, base people, simply because they're wealthy, powerful, popular, or knowledgeable. We permit ourselves to be lesser people than we'd objectively want ourselves to be, in order to achieve circumstantial development.

It would do us all well to step back for a moment and identify which form of improvement we are seeking, and to garner the strength necessary to strive for *true* self-improvement.[4,5]

next], similarly, anyone treating a *nefesh* in the hopes of refining someone's character would first have to be familiar with the scope and capacities of the *nefesh*,* as well as what would make it "ill"* and what would then heal it.*

Therefore, I will now [in order to make our analysis easier] state that the *nefesh* is comprised of five "parts": the digestive system, the senses, the imagination, the emotions, and the intellect.*

הַמְּרַפֵּא אֶת הַנֶּפֶשׁ וְרוֹצֶה לְטַהֵר אֶת הַמִּדּוֹת, צָרִיךְ שֶׁיֵּדַע אֶת הַנֶּפֶשׁ בְּכָל הֶקֵּפָהּ וַחֲלָקֶיהָ וּמַה גּוֹרֵם לְמַחֲלָתָהּ וּמַה הוּא הַמַּבְרִיאָהּ.

וְלָכֵן אֲנִי אוֹמֵר שֶׁחֶלְקֵי הַנֶּפֶשׁ חֲמִשָּׁה: הַזָּן, וְהַמַּרְגִּישׁ, וְהַמְדַמֶּה, וְהַמִּתְעוֹרֵר, וְהַהוֹגֶה.

---

the scope and capacities of the *nefesh* — To be discussed in chapter 3.

what would make it "ill" — To be discussed in chapter 4.

what would then heal it — Two points: first, the expression "improving a person's character" is related to *tikkun* in Hebrew, and "improving" seems to be the best working definition in this context, whereas in others, it would be translated otherwise.

Rambam uses a medical model here to explain his idea, and takes *tikkun* to mean healing. Thus, he sees personal flaws as instances of illness. He also makes the point that we would need to know the *nefesh* as well as a physician needs to know the body if we are ever to "heal" or improve it — which is to say that we need to know *ourselves* if we are ever to heal or improve our own character.

But *tikkun* can also be understood as the act of rectifying something — setting it right or recalibrating it. That is to say, it could be seen as the act of taking something in hand that is "off," looking it over closely, seeing exactly where it's off, looking for the dial or switch that would have to be adjusted to make the needed change, and carefully adjusting it to just the right point and no more, then trying the thing again after it has been adjusted.

In a sense, this is what is required of us if we're ever to improve our beings. We have to know just what's off — and just what dial to twist or turn if we're ever to repair our character. But how in the world do we do that? By first studying ourselves (i.e., our *nefesh*) in full, then applying that knowledge to the task at hand, as we will see in chapter 4 most especially.

the digestive system, the senses, the imagination, the emotions, and the intellect — This paragraph calls for some explanation because the terms Rambam uses aren't the ones we would use in modernity for the same processes.

First off, Rambam's term for what we refer to here as the "digestive system" is the "nutritive component." It actually includes growth and reproduction, which the ancients lumped together with digestion. We translated the "sentient component," as he put it,

3. We already mentioned earlier in this chapter that we will be limiting our discussion to the human *nefesh* [as we implied by the title of this chapter]. For the energy by which a human is nourished is not the same as that by which a donkey or horse is nourished, since humans are nourished by the human digestive system, while donkeys are nourished by the donkey digestive system, and vultures are nourished by the vulture digestive system. Nonetheless, the term "digestion" is used for each, even though the actions are not identical.*

We also use analogous terms to refer to humans' and other creatures' senses, even though a human being's senses are not like a horse's, [just like] no one species' senses are like any other's. For every species which has a *nefesh* has one unique to itself, with functions that are necessarily different from any other's. [Nonetheless,] some people equate the two functions and think they are identical, but this is not so.*

ג. וּכְבָר הִקְדַּמְנוּ בְּפֶרֶק זֶה שֶׁדְּבָרֵינוּ אֵינָם אֶלָּא בְּנֶפֶשׁ הָאָדָם. לְפִי שֶׁהַהֲזָנָה דֶּרֶךְ מָשָׁל שֶׁל הָאָדָם אֵינָהּ הַהֲזָנָה שֶׁל הַחֲמוֹר וְהַסּוּס, כִּי הָאָדָם נִיזּוֹן בְּחֵלֶק הַזָּן שֶׁבַּנֶּפֶשׁ הָאֱנוֹשִׁית, וְהַחֲמוֹר נִיזּוֹן בְּחֵלֶק הַזָּן שֶׁבַּנֶּפֶשׁ הַחֲמוֹרִית, וְהַדֶּקֶל נִיזּוֹן בְּחֵלֶק הַזָּן שֶׁבַּנֶּפֶשׁ שֶׁיֵּשׁ לוֹ, וְאוֹמְרִים אָמְנָם עַל כָּל אוֹתָם הַפְּרָטִים נִיזּוֹן בְּשִׁתּוּף הַשֵּׁם בִּלְבָד, לֹא שֶׁהָעִנְיָן עַצְמוֹ אֶחָד.

וְכֵן אוֹמְרִים עַל הָאָדָם וּבַעֲלֵי הַחַיִּים מַרְגִּישׁ בְּשִׁתּוּף הַשֵּׁם בִּלְבָד, לֹא שֶׁהֶהֶרְגֵּשׁ אֲשֶׁר בָּאָדָם הוּא הַהֶרְגֵּשׁ אֲשֶׁר בַּסּוּס, וְלֹא הַהֶרְגֵּשׁ אֲשֶׁר בְּמִין זֶה הוּא אוֹתוֹ הַהֶרְגֵּשׁ עַצְמוֹ אֲשֶׁר בְּמִין הָאַחֵר, אֶלָּא כָּל מִין וּמִין מֵאוֹתָם שֶׁיֵּשׁ לָהֶם נֶפֶשׁ יֵשׁ לוֹ נֶפֶשׁ מְיֻחֶדֶת זוּלַת נֶפֶשׁ הָאַחֵר, וְחִיּוּבֵי הוּא שֶׁתִּהְיֶינָה לְנֶפֶשׁ זֶה פְּעוּלוֹת וּלְנֶפֶשׁ זֶה פְּעוּלוֹת, וְיֵשׁ שֶׁתִּדְמֶנָה פְּעוּלָה זוּ לִפְעוּלָה זוּ וְיַחְשְׁבוּ עַל יְדֵי שְׁתֵּי הַפְּעוּלוֹת שֶׁהֵם דָּבָר אֶחָד בְּעַצְמוֹ, וְאֵין הַדָּבָר כֵּן.

---

as "the senses"; we termed his so-called "imaginative component" "the imagination," but we could have called it the "intuitive mind" or the "subconscious mind," as well (but all will prove to be a problem, as we'll see); his "stimulative component" became "the emotions"; and his "intellectual component" became "the intellect."

the actions are not identical — We know, for example, that unlike

human beings, sheep, giraffes, deer, cows, and camels chew their cud and have a complex, usually four-chambered stomach. Yet we use the term "digestion" to describe both types of digestive processes.

but this is not so — There's a point to Rambam's underscoring the fact that he is talking about the human *nefesh* exclusively — as well as to his making analogies the center of

We could compare it to three dark places, the first of which was illuminated by sunlight, the second by moonlight, and the third by candlelight. Thus, all three were "illuminated," but the source and generator of light in the first was the sun, the second's was the moon, and the third's was a flame.[6] Similarly, what generates human senses is a human *nefesh*, what generates a donkey's is a donkey *nefesh*,

וְהַמָּשָׁל בָּזֶה, כְּגוֹן שְׁלֹשָׁה מְקוֹמוֹת חֲשׁוּכִים, הָאֶחָד זָרְחָה עָלָיו הַשֶּׁמֶשׁ וְהוּאַר, וְהַשֵּׁנִי עָלָה בּוֹ הַיָּרֵחַ וְהוּאַר, וְהַשְּׁלִישִׁי הֻדְלַק בּוֹ נֵר וְהוּאַר. הֲרֵי כָּל אֶחָד מֵהֶם נִמְצָא בּוֹ הָאוֹר, אֶלָּא שֶׁסִּבַּת הָאוֹר הַזֶּה וּפוֹעֲלוֹ, הַשֶּׁמֶשׁ; וּפוֹעֵל הַשֵּׁנִי הַיָּרֵחַ; וּפוֹעֵל הַשְּׁלִישִׁי הָאֵשׁ. כַּךְ פּוֹעֵל רֶגֶשׁ הָאָדָם הִיא נֶפֶשׁ הָאָדָם, וּפוֹעֵל רֶגֶשׁ הַחֲמוֹר הִיא נֶפֶשׁ הַחֲמוֹר, וּפוֹעֵל

discussion when he says, "even though they're actually only analogous…" and "we also use analogous terms…." It's rooted in the fact that we often confuse who we are, what we feel, and what we experience, with what other beings are, feel, and experience.

We sometimes see animals seeming to act like humans, and we extend the analogy to claim that we're "all made of the same cloth." We speak of the "selfless and unconditional" love pets seem to offer (and we are utterly shocked, even stunned, when they bite or snarl). We allude to the "secret life of plants" because they seem to respond to speech and gesture, and we stretch the analogy to declare that they "seem to have a mind of their own." We even speak of the "character" of stones, as if etched lines bespeak experience, thought, and expressiveness.

Rambam's point seems to be that it would do us well to know that what appears to be, or what is said to be, isn't always so. Despite the assumptions of certain writers, filmmakers, or illustrators, animals,

plants, and stones don't feel, experience life, or think the way we do. We're human, and they're not. And while we humans are comprised of much of the physical matter other beings are comprised of, we far transcend their essence and core. For we have immortal souls, we reason, and we're capable of personal choice, as Rambam will underscore later on.

The other point to be made is that Rambam has another ulterior motive in all this, which is much more esoteric. Not only are human capacities different from animals', but they're also different from God's. For in fact, Rambam goes to great pains elsewhere to explain the anthropomorphisms in the Torah that seem to indicate that God has physical traits, in order to disaffirm that assumption and to contrast Him with ourselves.

He's apparently also alluding to this concept here, and underscoring the fact that, while we may use analogous terms to speak of human and animal faculties, as well as Divine ones, each is fundamentally and crucially different, and we'd do well not to fall into the trap of comparing them.

and what generates a vulture's is a vulture *nefesh*. The only thing they* have in common is an analogous term.[7]

Understand this principle well, for it is wonderful and important. Many philosophers have stumbled over it and arrived at absurd outlooks and false beliefs.

I return now to our subject, the parts of the [human] *nefesh*.

4. The digestive system encompasses the processes of ingestion, retention, digestion, per se, excretion of waste, growth, procreation, and metabolism.* As to the makeup of these seven capacities, what they do, how they work, in which organs their actions are more evident and visible, which are ongoing, and which are transient — that is all relevant to the art of medicine and has no place here.[8]

The senses encompass the five well-known senses of sight, hearing, taste, smell, and touch. The sense of touch functions throughout the body, rather than in a specific organ like the other four senses.[9]

רֶגֶשׁ הַפֶּרֶס הִיא נֶפֶשׁ הַפֶּרֶס, וְאֵין לָהֶם עִנְיָן הַכּוֹלְלָם זוּלַת שִׁתּוּף הַשֵּׁם בִּלְבָד.

וְהָבֵן עִנְיָן זֶה כִּי הוּא נִפְלָא וְחָשׁוּב, נִכְשָׁלִים בּוֹ רַבִּים מִן הַמִּתְפַּלְסְפִים, וּבָאוּ מִתּוֹךְ כַּךְ לְהַשְׁקָפוֹת מוּזָרוֹת וְדֵעוֹת בִּלְתִּי נְכוֹנוֹת.

וְאָחֱזֹר לְעִנְיָנֵנוּ בְּחֶלְקֵי הַנֶּפֶשׁ.

ד. וְאֹמַר, הַחֵלֶק הַזָּן, מִמֶּנּוּ הַכֹּחַ הַמּוֹשֵׁךְ, וְהַמַּחֲזִיק, וְהַמְעַכֵּל, וְהַפּוֹלֵט אֶת הָעוֹדְפִים, וְהַמְגַדֵּל, וְהַמּוֹלִיד בְּדוֹמֶה, וְהַמַּבְדִּיל אֶת הַלֵּיחוֹת עַד שֶׁמַּפְרִישׁ אֶת הַצָּרִיךְ לַיזוֹן בּוֹ וְהַצָּרִיךְ לְהַפָּלֵט, וְהַדְּבָרִים עַל שִׁבְעָה הַכֹּחוֹת הָאֵלּוּ וּבַמֶּה פּוֹעֲלִים, וְהֵיאַךְ פּוֹעֲלִים, וּבְאֵיזֶה אֵיבָרִים פְּעֻלָּתָם יוֹתֵר נִגְלֵית וְנִכֶּרֶת, וּמַה מֵהֶם מָצוּי תָּמִיד, וּמַה מֵהֶם פּוֹעֵל בִּזְמַן מְסוּיָּים, הֲרֵי כָּל זֶה נָחוּץ לִמְלֶאכֶת הָרְפוּאָה, וְאֵין בּוֹ צוֹרֶךְ בְּמָקוֹם זֶה.

וְהַחֵלֶק הַמַּרְגִּישׁ מִמֶּנּוּ חֲמֵשֶׁת הַכֹּחוֹת הַמְפוּרְסָמוֹת אֵצֶל הֶהָמוֹן, הָרְאוּת, וְהַשֵּׁמַע, וְהַטַּעַם, וְהָרֵיחַ, וְהַמִּשּׁוּשׁ וְהוּא מָצוּי בְּכָל שֶׁטַח הַגּוּף וְאֵין לוֹ אֵבָר מְיוּחָד כְּמוֹ לְאַרְבַּעַת הַכֹּחוֹת.

---

they — I.e., these three instances of "senses."

metabolism — What we refer to as metabolism is worded as follows in the text: "[the process] of extruding what's needed for digestion from what should be eliminated."

It should also be pointed out that this so-called "digestive system" in-

cludes other vital organs such as the kidneys, liver, heart, and so on, since they all aid in the digestive system directly or indirectly, as do other things. The ancients lumped them all together under "digestion" because it is digestion that keeps us alive and thus maintains the species (which explains the inclusion of procreation).

The imagination encompasses the capacity to retain impressions of experiences when they have vanished from the senses involved, and to compound some and separate others. It is the capacity that enables a person to combine certain experiences he has had along with others he never had nor ever could grasp — for example, to imagine an iron ship sailing in the air,* or an individual whose head is in the heavens while his feet are on the ground, or an animal with a thousand eyes, as well as many other such impossible things that are bred when the imagination combines things and produces a phantasm.*

וְהַחֵלֶק הַמְדַמֶּה, הוּא הַכֹּחַ הַזּוֹכֵר רְשָׁמֵי הַמּוּחָשׁוֹת אַחַר הֵעֶלְמָם מִלִּפְנֵי הַחוּשִׁים שֶׁהִשִּׂיגוּם, וּמַרְכִּיבָם זֶה בָּזֶה וּמַבְדִּילָם זֶה מִזֶּה, וּלְפִיכָךְ מַרְכִּיב הַכֹּחַ הַזֶּה מִן הַדְּבָרִים שֶׁהִשִּׂיג דְּבָרִים שֶׁלֹּא הִשִּׂיגָם מֵעוֹלָם וְאִי אֶפְשָׁר לְהַשִּׂיגָם, כְּמוֹ שֶׁמְּדַמֶּה הָאָדָם אֳנִיַּת בַּרְזֶל רָצָה בָּאֲוִיר, אוֹ מִין אָדָם רֹאשׁוֹ בַּשָּׁמַיִם וְרַגְלָיו עַל הָאָרֶץ, וּבַעַל חַי בְּאֶלֶף עֵינַיִם לְמָשָׁל, וְהַרְבֵּה מִן הַנִּמְנָעוֹת הַלָּלוּ מַרְכִּיב הַכֹּחַ הַמְדַמֶּה וּמַמְצִיאָם בַּדִּמְיוֹן.

---

sailing in the air — Of course, Rambam is describing something quite ordinary in our age and not at all impossible, the airplane. From this, we could simply comment that while we in modernity are privileged to have reasoned out the laws of aerodynamics, Rambam's generation hadn't. Or maybe the existence of airplanes only underscores Rambam's point that we could go further and say that reason (analysis, research, experimentation, and so on) alone can be depended on, rather than mere imagination.

But there's yet another point to be made. As Rabbi Mordechai Rabinowitz explains in his comments to the encyclopedic *Rambam La'Am* (vol. 18, p. 159, note 17), Rambam may be alluding to actual *self*-propulsion here, which is not the same as the characteristics of airplanes. For while airplanes certainly lift off the ground and fly, they nonetheless lack the innate ability to fly that birds have, though they do an excellent job

of *seeming* to, and they accomplish the same end. Nonetheless, at best an airplane can be said to offer an effective illusion of self-propulsion, while in essence, it is an example of a brilliant sleight-of-hand.

It's analogous perhaps to power steering. It's not my own strength that has the wheel turn so easily — it's the power steering's mechanism that does so. Nonetheless, from a distance it seems as if it was my personal strength allowing for such ease of movement.

The point to be made, then, is that while *illusions* of the "impossible" can be quite brilliantly concocted, nothing truly impossible can ever be constructed, despite our imagining that it could. Yet we in modernity are quite satisfied with simulations of the impossible and accept it as the real thing.

produces a phantasm — In other words, our imagination "creates" by retaining impressions of experiences

(That is where the Mutakel-limun[12] made their great, absurd mistake upon which was built an erroneous basis about the difference between what is essential [i.e., what is necessarily so], what is possible [i.e., what may or may not be so], and what is impossible [i.e., what simply cannot be so].

וְכָאן טָעוּ כַּת הַמְדַבְּרִים הַטָעוּת הַמוּזָרָה הַגְּדוֹלָה אֲשֶׁר עָלֶיהָ בָּנוּ יְסוֹד הַטָעֲיוֹתֵיהֶם בַּחֲלוּקַת הַמְחוּיָב וְהָאֶפְשָׁרִי וְהַנִּמְנָע, שֶׁהֵם חָשְׁבוּ אוֹ דִמוּ לִבְנֵי אָדָם שֶׁכָּל הַמִתְדַמֶה אֶפְשָׁרִי, וְלֹא יָדְעוּ שֶׁהַכֹּחַ הַזֶה מַרְכִּיב עִנְיָנִים נִמְנְעֵי הַמְצִיאוּת, כְּמוֹ שֶׁהִזְכַּרְנוּ.

They themselves believed or convinced others to believe that whatever can be imagined is possible.[13] They did not realize that the imagination can concoct impossible things, as we have said.)

we've had or things we've come in contact with in the past, then comparing and contrasting them with other experiences or things, or with experiences or things we've read or heard about, and it then comes up with an original phenomenon out of the mix.

But the examples of it here ("an iron ship sailing in the air, an individual whose head is in the heavens while his feet are on the ground, an animal with a thousand eyes...") don't seem to lend themselves to a modern understanding of either creativity or imagination. After all, it doesn't take much to conceive of, for example, an iron ship defying gravity and sailing in midair when you consider the fact that huge and heavily weighted ships seem to defy gravity over water all the time. (In fact, based on that same principle, we can project that what must have inspired the first ships themselves was the sight of huge fallen logs coursing downriver after storms, or the sight of large people floating on the sea of their own volition.)

So rather than creativity, what we have here are examples of what we would call extension and extrapolation — a case of one instance of buoyancy begetting another, more daring instance of it, that can then beget even more daring instances of it.

As such, the imagination clearly doesn't "create" so much as recreate, expand upon, or supplement. God alone creates. Only He can generate something utterly original and without precedent, i.e., He alone "creates something out of nothingness."

Then again, if you'd ever seen an iron ship sailing far away, it might for a moment seem to be sailing in midair, which we'd indeed refer to as a phantasm, a figment of the imagination. Perhaps that is the kind of "creative" or "imaginary" phenomenon Rambam is talking about.

There is another point to be made, though. We in modernity are truly infatuated with imagination — not so much with that corner of it that allows for technological and productive advance, which is often beneficial (and frequently respected rather than loved), but with the phantasm

The emotions encompass the capacity to either crave something or despise it. They are the capacity that enables a person to seek something out or avoid it, to be sympathetic toward something or have reservations about it. They include anger and desire, fear and heroism, cruelty and compassion, love and hatred, and many other such incidentals of the *nefesh*.*

וְהַחֵלֶק הַמִּתְעוֹרֵר הוּא הַכֹּחַ שֶׁבּוֹ יִשְׁתּוֹקֵק הָאָדָם לְאֵיזֶה דָבָר אוֹ יִמְאָסֵהוּ. וּמִכְלַל הַפְּעוּלוֹת אֲשֶׁר תִּהְיֶינָה מִן הַכֹּחַ הַזֶּה הַדְּרִישָׁה וְהַבְּרִיחָה, וְהָאַהֲדָה לְדָבָר מְסֻיָּים אוֹ הַהִסְתַּיְּיגוּת מִמֶּנּוּ, הַכַּעַס וְהָרָצוֹן, הַפַּחַד וְהָעוֹז, הָאַכְזָרִיּוּת וְרַחֲמָנוּת, וְהָאַהֲבָה וְהַשִּׂנְאָה, וְהַרְבֵּה מֵאֵלּוּ הַמִּקְרִים הַנַּפְשִׁיִּים.

end of the creative spectrum. We are so addictively under the influence of television, movies, literature, and the like that we even define our values or base our dreams and aspirations upon others' fantasies about the "good life," as opposed to a life of goodness.

We seek guidance and inspiration from fictional characters, for example, and try to shimmy and stretch our beings — our very *nefesh* — to fit literary contours and to satisfy fictional expectations. We often defy reason in the process: witness the poor souls who grew up emulating morally flawed "heroes" and cynical "anti-heroes," and who lack a sense of their own personal greatness and faith as a consequence.

This is the absurd and phantasmic aspect of the imagination that undoubtedly disturbed Rambam and the ancients. This is the aspect of it that stands in direct contradistinction to human reason, which he and they so admired.

It's important to realize that the "imagination" can also refer to what we call the subconscious mind. For as Rambam points out later on, "the

imagination function[s] while a person is asleep" and "neither thought nor personal dersire apply" to it, i.e., you can't control it (2:1), which clearly refers to the subconscious mind in a dream state.[10, 11]

...and many other such incidentals of the *nefesh* — First off, what we translate as "the emotions" literally reads "the arousal capacity of the *nefesh*," and it is derived from the classical notion of the "appetitive capacity," i.e., our capacity to either have an appetite (a "taste") for something or not.

It is the capacity we all have to be drawn toward or repelled by something or another, and, in Rambam's words, "to be angry or satisfied, fearful or brave, cruel or compassionate, loving or hateful, and the like." We know it as our emotions.

Interestingly enough, the word "appetite" (as in "appetitive capacity") is associated with being drawn *toward* something (i.e., as we said, it's related to the term for having an "appetite" for something), while the word "emotion" is associated with moving *away* from something (it is

In fact, all the parts of the body serve as agents of these capacities [of the *nefesh*], i.e., the emotions], including the hands, with their ability to act; the feet, with their ability to walk; the eyes, with their ability to see; and the heart, with its ability to be either brave or fearful.* The same goes for all the other external and internal organs and their functions — they all serve as agents of the emotions.[14]

וּכְלֵי הַכֹּחוֹת הַלָּלוּ כָּל אֶבְרֵי הַגּוּף,
כְּגוֹן כֹּחַ הַיָּד לִפְעוֹלָה, וְכֹחַ הָרֶגֶל
לַהֲלוֹךְ, וְכֹחַ הָעַיִן לִרְאִיָּיה, וְכֹחַ הַלֵּב
לָעוּז אוֹ לְפַחַד, וְכַךְ שְׁאָר הָאֵבָרִים
הַפְּנִימִיִּים וְהַחִיצוֹנִיִּים הֵם וְכֹחוֹתֵיהֶם
אֵינָם אֶלָּא כֵּלִים לְכֹחַ זֶה הַמִּתְעוֹרֵר.

---

comprised of the prefix "e," meaning "away," and "motion"). So what we have are two perspectives of the same drive.

Rambam's use of the term "incidentals of the *nefesh*" alludes to the classical differentiation between "essences" and "incidentals" — in other words, between the thing itself and what's tangential to it. His point is that our tastes, moods, and dispositions are all incidental to our essential selves. For as has been pointed out elsewhere, there are people, places, and things themselves; and qualities about those people, places, and things that *incidentally happen to* characterize them without really defining them (see *Moreh Nevuchim* 1:52).

So, while a person might for example be tall and stout, his height and weight really don't touch upon his essential being. Those qualifiers help describe him, but they don't determine who he is. Rambam's point, as we said, is that our tastes and the like are incidental to us, rather than essential. What is essential, as Rambam will assert at the end of the chapter, is one's ability to reason, and the quality of his or her *nefesh*.

At the risk of stating the obvious, let me assert that we in Western modernity take certain incidentals to be essential qualities of a person. That becomes clear by observing how we describe ourselves — either by what we happen to do for a living, by where we live, or by the kinds of clothing we wear.

What also needs to be said is that by virtue of the fact that we define each other in rather mundane and tangential ways, we tend to perceive humankind as a whole as rather small and superficial.

There's another point to be made about our emotions. They're often the most teeming-with-life parts of ourselves, and seem to be the very center of our inner lives. While on one level that perspective is problematic, because it discounts the mind, on another level it is undoubtedly rooted in the fact that the great majority of our free will, which is so essential to our humanity, lies in our emotions. In fact, it can be said that our emotions serve as the main theater of free choice.

either bold or fearful — ...which is either a commendable or blameworthy trait, depending on circumstances (as Rambam will explain in the fourth chapter).

And the intellect encompasses the human capacity to reason,* speculate, acquire knowledge, and differentiate between good and bad actions.[15]

Some of its functions are practical, and others are speculative. Practical functions are either mechanical or conceptual. The speculative ones touch upon our awareness of the nature of the immutables[16] (which are called "the sciences"*).

Mechanical functions include the capacity to acquire skills like carpentry, agriculture, medicine, or navigation, and the speculative ones touch upon the capacity to think about doing something one would like to do when he wants to do it, whether it is feasible to do it or not, and if so how to do it.*

That is all we will say about the *nefesh.**

וְהַחֵלֶק הַהוֹגֶה הוּא הַכֹּחַ הַמְצוּי לְאָדָם אֲשֶׁר בּוֹ יַשְׂכִּיל, וּבוֹ תִּהְיֶה הַחֲשִׁיבָה, וּבוֹ הוּא קוֹנֶה אֶת הַמַּדָּעִים, וּבוֹ הוּא מַבְדִּיל בֵּין הָרַע וְהַטּוֹב מִן הַפְּעוּלוֹת.

וְהַפְּעוּלוֹת הַלָּלוּ מֵהֶם מַעֲשִׂי וּמֵהֶם עִיּוּנִי, וְהַמַּעֲשִׂי מִמֶּנּוּ מְלַאכְתִּי, וּמִמֶּנּוּ מַחֲשַׁבְתִּי. וְהָעִיּוּנִי הוּא אֲשֶׁר בּוֹ יֵדַע הָאָדָם אֶת הַנִּמְצָאִים שֶׁאֵינָן מִשְׁתַּנִּים מִכְּפִי שֶׁהֵן, וְאֵלֶּה הֵם הַנִּקְרָאִים מַדָּעִים סְתָם.

וְהַמְלַאכְתִּי הוּא הַכֹּחַ אֲשֶׁר בּוֹ אָנוּ לוֹמְדִים אֶת הַמְלָאכוֹת כְּגוֹן הַנַּגָּרוּת וַעֲבוֹדַת הָאֲדָמָה וְהָרְפוּאָה וְהַסַּפָּנוּת. וְהַמַּחֲשַׁבְתִּי הוּא אֲשֶׁר בּוֹ חוֹשֵׁב עַל הַדָּבָר שֶׁהוּא רוֹצֶה לַעֲשׂוֹתוֹ בִּזְמַן שֶׁיִּרְצֶה לַעֲשׂוֹתוֹ אִם אֶפְשָׁר לַעֲשׂוֹתוֹ אוֹ לָאו, וְאִם הָיָה אֶפְשָׁרִי אֵיךְ רָאוּי שֶׁיֵּעָשֶׂה.

זֶהוּ מַה שֶׁרָאוּי לְהַזְכִּיר כָּאן מֵעִנְיְנֵי הַנֶּפֶשׁ.

---

the human capacity to reason — See section 5 of this chapter.

"the sciences" — Or, "pure science." As is known, there is "pure science," whose results are not necessarily applicable to practical life but may eventually prove to be; and "applied science," which has a practical agenda and end.

how to do it — The "intellect" is thus our capacity to think pragmatically or to extrapolate, derive, and study the nature of things and act on that knowledge. It thus transcends instinct, which is passive. It embodies

the uniquely human capacity to take one's destiny into one's own hands by acting on one's own and making moral and spiritual life choices. But there is one human capacity that is yet greater than the intellect — reason. Rambam will discuss it shortly.

the *nefesh* — …itself. From chapter 2 onward, *Shemoneh Perakim* will mostly speak about where in the *nefesh* free will reigns; how free our will is, in fact; what we are to do, now that we know we have free will; and the farthest reaches and greatest expressions of free will.

5. It is important to know, though, that this single *nefesh*, whose capacities and parts we have described above, is a sort of "matter," and reason is its "form."*

If the *nefesh* never achieves its form [i.e., it never reaches its potential], then its aptitude to achieve it would have been for naught, and its existence is worthless.*

ה. וְדַע שֶׁזּוּ הַנֶּפֶשׁ הָאַחַת אֲשֶׁר קָדַם תֵּיאוּר כֹּחוֹתֶיהָ אוֹ חֲלָקֶיהָ הִיא כַּחוֹמֶר, וְהַשֵּׂכֶל, לָהּ צוּרָה. וְאִם לֹא תוּשַׂג לָהּ הַצוּרָה הֲרֵי תִּהְיֶה מְצִיאוּת הַהֲכָנָה אֲשֶׁר בָּהּ לְקַבָּלַת אוֹתָהּ הַצוּרָה לְבַטָּלָה, וּכְאִלּוּ מְצִיאוּתָהּ לָרִיק וְהוּא אוֹמְרוֹ (משלי

---

reason is its "form" — Although Rambam states at the very end of this section that "this is not the place for a discussion about form and matter, or about the different degrees of reason and how to acquire them," we nonetheless need to define these terms, and to expand somewhat on the ideas expressed here, since they're so unfamiliar to most of us.

"Matter" is the material substance from which everything is made. "Form" is what gives definition (or spirit) to that particular matter. So, for example, before it can be said to "take on life," a painting is basically a splash of colors on a canvas. What makes it a "real" painting is the *form* that blob of paint takes, which then defines it and functions as its spirit. Likewise, a person is at bottom a splash of flesh and bones who only becomes a "real" person by virtue of his or her "form" or defining spirit.

According to Rambam himself, "reason" is the intellectual capacity to "break things down into their parts," i.e., to analyze, systematize, differentiate, and correlate components; and to "speculate about them abstractly and to attempt to determine their essences and what motivated their coming into being," i.e., to isolate a thing's essence from its

contents and surmise things about its roots and sources. It also entails the ability to "generalize and universalize things, and to separate the essential from the circumstantial," i.e., to think abstractly and nonconcretely about a thing and to refer to it in general rather than specific terms (see *Moreh Nevuchim* 1:73).

With this in mind, we now understand Rambam's statement here to the effect that the "*nefesh*...is a sort of 'matter,' and reason is its 'form' " to mean that the defining spirit and life of all the "stuff" that comprises our self is our ability to reason.

its existence is worthless — This sentence seems ambiguous. On one hand, it seems to be saying that a *nefesh* that never reaches its potential would itself then prove to be worthless, while on the other, it seems to be saying that its aptitude to reach its potential would have been worthless.

In fact, Rambam seems to be saying both. His point seems to be that any individual who doesn't reach his or her potential on his or her own would prove to be "worthless" (i.e., tragically ineffectual) in the end. And over and above that, his or her God-given aptitude to reach it would ap-

Thus it is said, "A *nefesh* without knowledge is not good"* (Proverbs 19:2), which means to say that a *nefesh* that has not achieved its ideal form — i.e., a *nefesh* "without knowledge" — is "not good."* [17, 18]

However, this is not the place for discussion about form and matter, or about the different degrees of reason and how to acquire them. Furthermore, it is not necessary for what we want to say about character,[19] but it is more appropriate to the *Sefer HaNevuah,** which we have mentioned. Thus, I shall end this chapter here and go on to the next.[20]

י"ט ב'), "גַּם בְּלֹא דַעַת נֶפֶשׁ לֹא טוֹב,"
כְּלוֹמַר, שֶׁמְּצִיאוּת נֶפֶשׁ שֶׁלֹּא הוּשְׂגָה
לָהּ צוּרָה אֶלָּא הִיא נֶפֶשׁ בְּלֹא דַעַת
לֹא טוֹב.

אֲבָל הַדִּבּוּר עַל הַצּוּרָה וְהַחוֹמֶר
וְהַשְׂכָלִים כַּמָּה הֵם וְהֵיאַךְ נִקְנִים
אֵין זֶה מְקוֹמוֹ. וְאֵין לָזֶה צוֹרֶךְ בְּמַה
שֶּׁאָנוּ רוֹצִים לְדַבֵּר עַל הַמִּדּוֹת, וְהוּא
מַתְאִים בְּסֵפֶר הַנְּבוּאָה שֶׁהִזְכַּרְנוּ.
וְכָאן אֲסַיֵּים פֶּרֶק זֶה וְאַתְחִיל אַחֵר.

---

parently have been "for naught," and this would also have demeaned God in the process!

This is a terribly haunting statement. For not only would we not "count," if you will, in such an instance — God's will for us itself would seem not to "count" either! There would seem to be no greater calamity, no greater instance of cosmic pandemonium than that. Yet who among us seems en route to reaching his or her potential?

We take heart, though, in the realization that all of us do indeed fulfill our soul's mission in this life. But that is a more passive activity than reaching our potential; for while the latter is in our hands, the former is in God's. However, this subject is far beyond the scope of our discussion here.

is not good — The verse is usually translated to read, "It is not good for a *nefesh* to be without knowledge."

Sefer HaNevuah — This book, *The Book of Prophecy*, was supposed to serve as an exposition of the words of the prophets but was never completed. Rambam did, however, weave much of what he had prepared for it into his *Moreh Nevuchim*.

Synopsis

1. *Though the human nefesh has several functions and capacities, it is nonetheless a single entity.*

2. *Since improving character traits amounts to healing the nefesh, it is important to understand the nefesh the way a doctor understands the body. We will thus begin by discussing its five capacities: the digestive system, the senses, the imagination, the emotions, and the intellect.*

3. *Though the human and animal nefesh seem to share various functions because identical terms are used to describe both, they are actually widely different. Our discussion is limited to the human nefesh.*

4. *The human digestive system encompasses ingestion, retention, digestion per se, excretion of waste, growth, procreation, and metabolism; the senses encompass seeing, hearing, tasting, smelling and touching; the imagination encompasses the capacity to retain impressions of experiences and to compare and contrast them, as well as to combine things within one's experience with things beyond it, and to concoct impossible mental combinations of things; the emotions encompass the capacity to crave something or reject it, as well as to actually express personal and emotional proclivities through the different parts of the body; and the intellect encompasses the capacity to reason, speculate, acquire knowledge, and differentiate between good and bad forms of behavior within the realm of the practical and the speculative.*

5. *One's nefesh is a sort of "matter" whose "form" is his ability to reason. If one's nefesh never achieves its form, then its potential to do that would have been for naught. But that and other such themes is beyond our discussion of character, so we won't delve into them.*

2

במריי כחות הנפש ובידיעת החלק אשר
בו או לו ימצאו המעלות והמגרעות

THE CAPACITY OF THE *NEFESH*
TO DISOBEY AND WHERE ITS
VIRTUES AND FLAWS ARE FOUND

W E'RE ENJOINED BY GOD *to consciously and intentionally do His bidding as laid out by the mitzvot, and to perfect our characters and intellects in the process. We're to be rewarded for our obedience, and to suffer the consequences of our disobedience. Yet some contend that like our physiology, our characters are predetermined and "fixed in stone" at birth; while others go so far as to say that our very lives and actions are predetermined — subject to "fate" or "luck." They contend that we have no conscious control over any of it, and thus could not be expected to do God's bidding or be subject to reward or punishment either.*

In this chapter Rambam explains which parts of our beings (i.e., our nefesh) we indeed have dominion over and which we don't. For in fact, a part of us is beyond our conscious control and is actually subject to forces beyond us — our inborn natures, parts of our body, and external circumstances, while the rest of us is indeed subject to free will. This chapter will lay out the physiological details of all this, while chapter 8 below will discuss the philosophical ramifications of it.

In fact, we learn that we have conscious control over our emotions, senses, and intellects, and that we have no conscious control over our imaginations (in the sense we'll explain) or our digestive systems. As such, mitzvah observance and self-perfection is only relevant to our emotions, senses, and intellects.

1. It is important to know that the acts of disobedience and obedience mentioned in the Torah actually apply to only two parts of one's *nefesh*: his senses and his emotions.* Hence, sins and mitzvot are relevant to them alone.*

א. דַּע כִּי הַמֶּרִי וְהַמִּשְׁמַעַת הַתּוֹרָנִיִּים אֵינָם נִמְצָאִים אֶלָּא בִּשְׁנֵי חֲלָקִים מֵחֶלְקֵי הַנֶּפֶשׁ, וְהֵם הַחֵלֶק הַמַּרְגִּישׁ וְהַחֵלֶק הַמִּתְעוֹרֵר בִּלְבַד, וּבִשְׁנֵי הַחֲלָקִים הָאֵלּוּ תִּהְיֶינָה כָּל הָעֲבֵירוֹת וְהַמִּצְווֹת.

his senses and his emotions — It's at this juncture that Rambam is easing us into the issue of free will and personal responsibility. All sorts of thorny questions arise in this realm, like, "Am I free to do whatever I want to do?" "How can I be held responsible for what I'm forced to do by nature?" "Doesn't God control the universe, including my actions?" "Do only humans have the wherewithal to make conscious decisions?" and more. We will delve into much of that at length in chapter 8 below.

His point here is to map out just where we have conscious control and can thus express our will freely, and where we don't. For as he said in 1:2 above, "Anyone treating a *nefesh* in the hopes of refining his character would first have to be familiar with the scope and capacities of the *nefesh*." Hence, we're taught here that part of the *nefesh*'s scope entails free will, which is expressed in only some of the *nefesh*'s capacities — in our senses and emotions (as well as our intellect to a degree, as we'll soon see).[1,2]

...to them alone — As we indicated in chapter 1's first note, it could be said that we're each essentially an orchestra of many instruments led by a single conductor, i.e., the self. But our analogy breaks down at a certain point, because there are some "instruments" that seem to function on their own without direction, and others that will only play when directed. That is to say, there are parts of our beings that seem to have a mind or will of their own and to thus defy direction, for example, our autonomic nervous system. In contrast, other parts do accommodate conscious direction.

So it seems clear that on the one hand, the conductor that is our self simply cannot be held responsible for the performance of those stubbornly independent, self-sufficient parts; while on the other, he's utterly responsible for those parts that answer to his every beck and call.

In a sense then, the question is, which parts of myself am I accountable for, and which are God's re-

Indeed, the digestive system and the imagination* are not subject to obedience and disobedience [i.e., to free will], since neither thought nor personal desire apply to either one, and because one cannot prevent either one of them from working by thinking or limit their functions with a specific action. After all, both of these capacities — i.e., the digestive system and the imagination — function while a person is asleep, unlike any of the other capacities.*

אֲבָל הַחֵלֶק הַזָּן וְהַמְדַמֶּה אֵין מִשְׁמַעַת בָּהֶם וְלֹא מֶרִי, וְכֵיוָן שֶׁאֵין לַחֲשִׁיבָה וּלְרָצוֹן בָּהֶם פְּעוּלָה כְּלַל, וְאֵין הָאָדָם יָכוֹל עַל פִּי מַחֲשַׁבְתּוֹ לְהַשְׁבִּית אֶת פְּעוּלָתָם אוֹ לְהַגְבִּילָם בִּפְעוּלָה מְסוּיֶּימֶת. הֲלֹא תִרְאֶה שֶׁשְׁנֵי הַחֲלָקִים הַלָּלוּ כְּלוֹמַר הַזָּן וְהַמְדַמֶּה פּוֹעֲלִים בִּזְמַן הַשֵּׁינָה מַה שֶׁאֵין כֵּן בִּשְׁאָר כֹּחוֹת הַנֶּפֶשׁ.

sponsibility (since He "programmed" them, and thus determined from the first that they'd be out of my conscious control)? Or, where does my power lie as a human being, and where am I powerless?

To extend our analogy of an orchestra and conductor, the orchestra that we ourselves are seems to play an oddly creative series of pieces that features both live musicians and prerecorded ones at the same time. The conductor must do his best to ensure the success of the piece being played at any moment, and would thus need to take into account the makeup and contributions of the musicians playing right then and there, as well as the prerecorded ones.

Done well, that would be a masterful performance — a perfect blend of the immediate and fixed. And if somehow or another a prerecorded artist's performance proved to be less than expected, but the live performance proved sterling, the piece as a whole would be judged "near-perfect" with allowances made for what, after all, was out of the conductor's control. However, if an aspect of the *live* performance some-

how failed, the piece would be judged a dismal failure, despite the successful prerecorded performance (or because of it).

Our power, then, could be said to lie in our ability to do the best we can with what's beyond our control (the "prerecorded" component), and to conduct the live orchestra, which is subject to our control, as masterfully as possible.

Hence, we'll learn here that the only parts of our being over which we have conscious control are our emotions and senses (and our intellects to some degree), while we have no conscious control over our imaginations or digestive systems. This is why mitzvah observance specifically, and self-perfection in general, is only relevant to our emotions, senses, and intellects.

imagination — The "imagination" in this context refers to the subconscious mind (see end of our note on p. 32 ["produces a phantasm"]).

other capacities — Some might argue against Rambam's statement that we cannot affect our digestive

There is some confusion, though, when it comes to the intellect. Nonetheless, I hold that obedience and disobedience [i.e., free will] apply to this capacity, too, when it comes to adopting sound or unsound ideas.* Still, the intellect cannot do anything that can be said to be either a mitzvah or a sin per se, which is why I said above that sins and mitzvot apply to the [other] two capacities alone.*

אֲבָל הַחֵלֶק הַהוֹגֶה הֲרֵי יֵשׁ בּוֹ
מְבוּכָה, אֲבָל אֲנִי אוֹמֵר שֶׁאֶפְשָׁר
שֶׁיִּמָּצֵא גַּם בָּזֶה הַכֹּחַ הַמִּשְׁמַעַת
וְהַמֶּרִי בְּהַאֲמָנַת מַחֲשָׁבָה נִפְסֶדֶת אוֹ
בְּהַאֲמָנַת מַחֲשָׁבָה אֲמִתִּית, אֲבָל אֵין
בּוֹ מַעֲשֶׂה שֶׁאֶפְשָׁר לְהָנִיחַ עָלָיו סְתָם
שֵׁם מִצְוָה אוֹ עֲבֵירָה, וּלְפִיכָךְ אָמַרְתִּי
לְעֵיל כִּי בְּאוֹתָם שְׁנֵי הַחֲלָקִים יִמָּצְאוּ
הָעֲבֵירוֹת וְהַמִּצְוֹת.

---

systems or imaginations through thought and personal will. After all, they'd point out, we can consciously direct and alter our imaginations, or change our diet and thus affect our digestion.

But as Rambam argues later on, the part of our mind that we *do* have conscious control over is our intellect. As such, we can reason to ourselves that it would be good to imagine this or that rather than what first occurs to us; or to eat this way rather than that. But those would be outright conscious, willed acts initiated by our intellects rather than our imaginations or digestive systems, which we indeed have no direct or conscious control over.

Nonetheless, to clarify Rambam's words themselves at this point in the text, we'd explain him to mean that since the digestive system and imagination work despite us, in our sleep, they're obviously out of our control, and thus out of the realm of free will, and so we needn't answer for what they do. (They're prerecorded performers, to use our analogy in the note above.)[3]

sound or unsound ideas — That is to say, we've been granted the capacity and freedom to choose our ideas. It follows, then, that while we cannot be held responsible for our subconscious thoughts (see our note above ["imagination"]), we are held responsible for our conscious decisions.

The serious student of spiritual growth can draw succor from this, for it indicates that while he or she is liable to have unholy subconscious thoughts, that is par for the course, and he or she isn't expected *not* to. Where our responsibility lies is in our rejection or acceptance of those subconscious thoughts, our dwelling upon them, and our either acting on them or not. For, in essence, what matters is one's adoption of "sound" or "unsound" ideas and viewpoints.

the [other] two capacities alone — I.e., the senses and emotions.

It seems that the central issue here is whether thoughts "occur" to us passively, or we actually bring them on by dint of will. Rambam apparently contends that ideas do oc-

2. Now, there are two sorts of personal virtues: character virtues and intellectual virtues; and parallel to them are two exactly opposite sorts of flaws.

Intellectual virtues touch upon one's intellect, and they encompass wisdom (i.e., knowing the remote and immediate causes of things after first recognizing the existence of the thing that one is investigating);* reason, which includes the inborn ability to think (i.e., common sense), as well as any degree of reason one has developed within himself[6] (though this is

ב. אֲבָל הַמַּעֲלוֹת הֵם שְׁנֵי סוּגִים,
מַעֲלוֹת מִדּוֹתִיּוֹת וּמַעֲלוֹת הֶגְיוֹנִיּוֹת,
וּכְנֶגְדָּן שְׁנֵי סוּגֵי הַמִּגְרָעוֹת.

הַמַּעֲלוֹת הַהֶגְיוֹנִיּוֹת הֵן נִמְצָאוֹת
לַחֵלֶק הַהוֹגֶה, מֵהֶם הַחָכְמָה, וְהִיא
יְדִיעַת הַסִּבּוֹת הָרְחוֹקוֹת וְהַקְּרוֹבוֹת
אַחֲרֵי יְדִיעַת מְצִיאוּת הַדָּבָר אֲשֶׁר
חוֹקְרִים אֶת סִבּוֹתָיו. וְהַשֵּׂכֶל, מִמֶּנּוּ
הַשֵּׂכֶל הָעִיּוּנִי וְהוּא הַמָּצוּי לָנוּ בַּטֶּבַע,
כְּלוֹמַר, מוּשְׂכָּלִים רִאשׁוֹנִיִּים. וּמִמֶּנּוּ
הַשֵּׂכֶל הַנִּקְנֶה, וְאֵין כָּאן מְקוֹמוֹ.

cur to us, but that the option of adopting an idea as a fact and acting accordingly or of rejecting it and refusing to act on it is in our own hands.

This touches on a theme Rambam introduces in chapter 6. He speaks in section 1 there about the sort of person who "struggles with his longings and withstands the promptings of his personal bents, desires, and disposition."

He offers a number of arguments there about that sort of individual, going beyond our concerns here. But what is relevant to the point at hand is this. Our "longings...personal bents, [and] desires" and even our personality (which is nothing less than the whole of our longings, bents and desires, and then some) are all based on ideas that occur to us in an instant and which we oftentimes give no thought to — but which prod us into action, nonetheless.

It seems the point to be made is that we'd need to learn how to "strug-

gle with [our] longings," too, to come to realize — *capture* — those fleeting thoughts and their consequent proddings, if we're ever to improve ourselves. We would then need to either consciously adopt them or reject them, for that is where our free will lies.[4]

wisdom (i.e., knowing the...causes of things...that one is investigating) — Rambam seems to define wisdom differently than we would. While we would take wisdom to be a body of knowledge that has been honed and seasoned by the age, experience, and depth of being of the person possessing it, he seems to see it as being the culmination of the following process of analysis:

The individual is somehow puzzled by a phenomenon (either physical or spiritual) that has been suggested to him, and he sets out to determine if it is actually valid or not. He surmises that it is, and then sets out to determine just what brought

not the place to expand on that); as well as clarity of mind and adroitness of understanding (i.e., one's ability to grasp things instantaneously or almost so). The defects of this capacity are the opposites of these [qualities] or parallel to them.*

3. But character virtues apply only to the emotions, which the senses merely serve.* There are many

וּמִמֶּנּוּ זַכּוּת וְטוּב הַהֲבָנָה, וְהוּא טוֹב הַתְּפִיסָה לְכָל דָּבָר בִּמְהִירוּת בְּלִי זְמַן, אוֹ בִּזְמַן מוּעָט מְאֹד, וּמִגְרְעוֹת הַכֹּחַ הַזֶּה הֵפֶךְ אֵלּוּ אוֹ כְּנֶגְדָּן.

ג. אֲבָל הַמַּעֲלוֹת הַמִּדוֹתִיּוֹת הֵן נִמְצָאוֹת לַחֵלֶק הַמְעוֹרֵר בִּלְבָד. וְחֵלֶק הַמַּרְגִּישׁ הוּא בְּעִנְיָן זֶה מְשָׁרֵת בִּלְבַד לַחֵלֶק הַמִּתְעוֹרֵר. וּמַעֲלוֹת הַחֵלֶק

this phenomenon about. But things have many antecedents, some of which are immediate, close at hand, and obvious; and others of which are remote, and far removed either in time, place, or circumstance, and thus far more arcane. Rambam's wise person would delve into all this.

While we'd take all this as indicative of being inquisitive and erudite, we wouldn't take it as a mark of wisdom, per se. But we could legitimately assume that Rambam also factored in the aforementioned "age, experience, and depth of being" of the person described as wise. As such, the only difference between our definition of wisdom and his is that ours doesn't factor in the subject of "the body of knowledge," while Rambam contends (at the beginning of chapter 5) that the object of one's knowledge should always be to "comprehend God Almighty as much as a human being can."

So we might, for example, consider certain historians, economists, or criminologists as wise. After all, they too delve into the remote and immediate causes of things. But Rambam apparently wouldn't characterize them thus, simply because

they don't delve into the knowledge of God.[5]

...or parallel to them — In short, a virtuous mind dwells on physical and metaphysical causes and effects, it evolves, and it is inherently clear, pure, and quick. In contrast, a flawed mind dwells on incidentals and happenstance, it stagnates, and it is muddled and slow.

It would thus do us all well to consider just what our mind fixes itself onto; how fresh, fertile, and green our thoughts are; and how quick and electric our grasp is.[7]

which the senses merely serve — As we pointed out in our note on p. 41 ("to them alone"), our power lies in our ability to do the best we can with what is beyond our control and to conduct the live orchestra, which is subject to our control, as well as we can.

We've been informed above that the only parts of our being that we have conscious control over are our emotions and senses (and our intellects to some degree), and that we have no conscious control over our imaginations or digestive systems.

qualities connected with this capacity [i.e., connected with how we respond to our emotions], including temperance, generosity, justice, patience, humility, goodwill, courage, sensitivity, and others [many of these traits and others will be discussed in chapter 4 in detail].[9] Character flaws are characterized by the minimizing or exaggerating of any one of them.*

הַזֶּה מְרוּבִּים מְאֹד, כְּגוֹן הַפְּרִישׁוּת וְהַנְּדִיבוּת וְהַצֶּדֶק וְהַמְּתִינוּת וְהָעֲנָוָה וְעֵיִן טוֹבָה וְהָאוֹמֶץ וְהַמּוֹרֶךְ וְזוּלָתָם, וּמִגְּרְעוֹת הַחֵלֶק הַזֶּה הוּא הַמִּעוּט בָּאֵלֶּה אוֹ הַהַגְזָמָה בָּהֶם.

אֲבָל הַחֵלֶק הַזָּן וְהַמְדַמֶּה לֹא יֵיאָמֵר בּוֹ מַעֲלָה וְלֹא מִגְרַעַת, אֶלָּא אוֹמְרִים בּוֹ שֶׁהוּא מִתְנַהֵל כָּרָאוּי אוֹ שֶׁלֹּא כָּרָאוּי, כְּמוֹ שֶׁאוֹמְרִים, פְּלוֹנִי עִכּוּלוֹ טוֹב אוֹ בָּטֵל עִכּוּלוֹ אוֹ נִתְקַלְקֵל, אוֹ נִתְקַלְקֵל דִּמְיוֹנוֹ

But neither the digestive system nor the imagination have anything to do with such virtues or flaws. All we can say is that they either function well or not, as in "So-and-so digests well," "he cannot digest at all," or "he doesn't digest well"; or "So-and-so's imagination functions

---

We're told here, though, that our senses (which, again, we do have control over) *serve* our emotions. Yet we're told in 1:4 above that *all* the parts of the body serve our emotions. So why are our senses set apart here from our bodily organs when it comes to free will and personal control?

The answer seems to lie in one fact. While we certainly have conscious control over *some* of our body parts, and no control over others (i.e., we can, for example, control our arms and decide to use them for good or bad ends, yet we cannot consciously control our duodenums), and we likewise have conscious control over some of our senses and no control over others (i.e., we can consciously set out to taste something, touch it, etc., yet we often hear things we'd rather not), there's nonetheless a big difference between the two: I can consciously *change my emotions* — i.e., my mood — by means

of my senses. I can taste, listen to, observe, whiff, or touch things that will make me happy and good-hearted, for example; or taste, listen to, etc., other things that will make me short-tempered and irritable. The conscious movements of my limbs and the like, on the other hand, are less likely to change my mood and emotions. As such, the senses more *directly* and significantly serve my emotions than anything else. And I'd do well to learn to use my senses to better myself and to serve God.

The latter theme will be introduced and discussed in chapter 5 below.[8]

...of any one of them — See 4:1 below, where Rambam favors personal traits that "lie midway between two extremes, both of which are bad — one because it goes too far, and the other because it does not go far enough."

normally" or "his imagination doesn't function normally." None of this applies to character virtues or flaws.[10,11] This, then, is what we set out to include in this chapter.

אוֹ שֶׁהוּא מִתְנַהֵל כָּרָאוּי. וְאֵין בְּכָל זֶה לֹא מַעֲלָה וְלֹא מִגְרַעַת. וְזֶהוּ מַה שֶּׁרָצִינוּ לִכְלוֹל בְּפֶרֶק זֶה.

SYNOPSIS

1. *The sins and mitzvot enunciated in the Torah only apply to our senses and emotions, not to our digestive system or imagination. They apply to our intellect when it comes to convictions, but not when it comes to behavior.*

2. *There are two sorts of personal virtues and flaws: intellectual-based ones and character-based ones. Intellectual virtues (which are obviously relevant to our intellect) include wisdom, reason, and purity of mind; intellectual flaws are their opposite.*

3. *Character virtues or flaws are relevant to our emotions, which our senses merely serve. Such virtues include abstinence, generosity, justice, patience, humility, goodwill, courage, sensitivity, and others. Character flaws entail the minimizing or exaggerating of any one of them. But neither our digestive system nor our imagination have any role in issues of character.*

3

בתחלואי הנפש

DISEASES OF THE NEFESH

A LITTLE REVIEW IS IN ORDER.
Rambam said in the first chapter that "improving a person's character" — which is the aim of this work — "amounts to healing his nefesh and its capacities." He also said there that anyone thus treating a nefesh would first have to be familiar with its "scope and capacities." He then set out to acquaint us with the nefesh's capacities in the first chapter, and its "scope," i.e., the role each capacity plays in free will and self-determination, in the second chapter.

What this chapter does, then, is bring us back to the notion of "healing" or treating the nefesh, which the next chapter then expands upon.

Rambam also said in chapter 1 that anyone treating a nefesh would have to be familiar with what "determines that it is 'ill'" as well. In other words, he'd have to know just how we define a healthy or unhealthy nefesh. And Rambam focuses on that in this chapter, too.

Turning a corner, though, Rambam then offers advice for us all, rather than for the physicians and philosophers he'd been addressing until now. He first contends that we would all do well to be aware of our character virtues and flaws. Then he advises anyone proving to suffer from an ill nefesh to consult with the sort of sage-practitioner (i.e., nefesh physician) who would administer the sort of treatment offered in chapter 4.

1. The ancients pointed out that a *nefesh* can be [inherently] healthy or ill, just as the body can be. By definition, a healthy *nefesh* and its parts are predisposed to doing good, benevolent, and pleasant things. An ill *nefesh* and its parts are predisposed to doing bad, harmful, and disgraceful things.* But [we won't concern ourselves here with] the health or illness of the body, which is something that the art of medicine delves into.*

Now, when people are ill and their senses are off-kilter, they imagine sweet things to be bitter and bitter things to be sweet. They regard pleasant things as unpleasant, and they crave and enjoy things that healthy people would never enjoy, that may even harm them. They might eat minerals,* char-

א. אָמְרוּ הַקַּדְמוֹנִים שֶׁיֵּשׁ לַנֶּפֶשׁ בְּרִיאוּת וְחֹלִי כְּמוֹ שֶׁיֵּשׁ לַגּוּף בְּרִיאוּת וְחֹלִי, וּבְרִיאוּת הַנֶּפֶשׁ הִיא שֶׁיִּהְיוּ תְּכוּנוֹתֶיהָ וּתְכוּנוֹת חֲלָקֶיהָ תְּכוּנָה שֶׁתְּהֵא עוֹשָׂה בָהּ לְעוֹלָם הַטּוֹבוֹת וְהַחֲסָדִים וְהַמַּעֲשִׂים הַנָּאִים. וְחָלְיָהּ הוּא שֶׁיִּהְיוּ תְּכוּנוֹתֶיהָ וּתְכוּנוֹת חֲלָקֶיהָ תְּכוּנָה שֶׁתַּעֲשֶׂה בָהּ לְעוֹלָם אֶת הָרָעוֹת וְהַנְּזָקִים וְהַמַּעֲשִׂים הַמְגֻנִּים. אֲבָל בְּרִיאוּת הַגּוּף וְחָלְיוֹ הֲרֵי מְלֶאכֶת הָרְפוּאָה חוֹקֶרֶת עַל כַּךְ.

וּכְשֵׁם שֶׁבַּעֲלֵי חוֹלֵי הַגּוּפוֹת נִדְמֶה מֵחֲמַת קִלְקוּל הַרְגָּשָׁתָם בְּדָבָר הַמָּתוֹק שֶׁהוּא מַר וּבְדָבָר שֶׁהוּא מַר שֶׁהוּא מָתוֹק, וּמִתְאָרִים לְעַצְמָם דָּבָר הַנָּאוֹת כְּבִלְתִּי נָאוֹת, וְתִתְחַזֵּק תַּאֲוָתָם וְתִגְדַּל הֲנָאָתָם בִּדְבָרִים שֶׁאֵין בָּהֶם הֲנָאָה כְּלָל אֵצֶל הַבְּרִיאִים, וְלֹא עוֹד אֶלָּא שֶׁיֵּשׁ בָּהֶם נֶזֶק כְּגוֹן

---

doing bad, harmful, and disgraceful things — Rambam is speaking about inborn dispositions here, rather than about learned or acquired ones. For in fact, *Shemoneh Perakim* will be demonstrating how to cure ourselves of our chronic rather than acute *nefesh* diseases. Acute emotional flareups are undoubtedly due to either underlying congenital imbalances that have to be uprooted in the ways he'll illustrate in this chapter, or they are due to false convictions arrived at later on in life, which can be corrected by embracing the sorts of truisms offered later.[1]

...medicine delves into — There is something about all this that touches

the heart deeply and seems intuitively correct and just. After all, don't the best among us do good, benevolent, and pleasant things; and don't the worst in fact do the opposite? What's odd, though, is Rambam's use of the word "healthy" or "ill" in this context rather than "good" and "bad," as we would have expected. Why, in other words, didn't he say that "a good *nefesh* and its parts" — a good person — "is predisposed to doing good, benevolent, and pleasant things, while a bad *nefesh* and its parts" — a bad person — "is predisposed to doing bad, harmful, and disgraceful things"?

But that's apparently his point. Good and bad deeds are in fact bycoal, soil, very pungent or sour foods, or other such things that healthy people would find revolting and never want.

Likewise, those whose *nefesh* is ill — i.e., bad people with bad character traits — imagine bad things to be good, and good things to be bad, and always pursue goals that are actually harmful which they imagine to be good, simply because their *nefesh* is ill.*

2. Just as ill people who are unschooled in medicine would go to a doctor when they realized they were ill, and the doctor would then tell them what to do, warn them not to eat things they

אֲכִילַת הַנֶּתֶר וְהַפֶּחָם וְהֶעָפָר וּדְבָרִים הָעֲפוּצִים מְאֹד וְהַחֲמוּצִים מְאֹד וְכַיּוֹצֵא בְאֵלּוּ מִן הַדְּבָרִים אֲשֶׁר לֹא יִתְאַוּוּ לָהֶם הַבְּרִיאִים אֶלָּא מוֹאֲסִים אוֹתָם.

כַּךְ חוֹלֵי הַנֶּפֶשׁ כְּלוֹמַר הָרְשָׁעִים וּבַעֲלֵי הַמִּגְרָעוֹת נִדְמֶה לָהֶם בִּדְבָרִים אֲשֶׁר הֵם רָעִים שֶׁהֵם טוֹבִים, וּבְאוֹתָם אֲשֶׁר הֵם טוֹבִים שֶׁהֵם רָעִים, וְהָרָשָׁע שׁוֹאֵף תָּמִיד אֶת הַמַּטָּרוֹת שֶׁהֵם לְפִי הָאֱמֶת רָעוֹת, וּמְדַמֶּה מֵחֲמַת מַחֲלַת נַפְשׁוֹ שֶׁהֵן טוֹבוֹת.

ב. וּכְשֵׁם שֶׁהַחוֹלִים יוֹדְעִים מַחֲלָתָם וְאֵינָם בְּקִיאִים בִּמְלֶאכֶת הָרְפוּאָה שׁוֹאֲלִים לְרוֹפְאִים וְאֵלֶּה מוֹדִיעִים אוֹתָם מַה שֶּׁרָאוּי לָהֶם לַעֲשׂוֹת,

---

products of well or ill people. They are (moral and spiritual) symptoms of a person's state of being. He'll indicate later on, though, that there are in fact antidotes to illnesses of the being.[2]

minerals — Rambam specifies "potassium nitrate."

...their *nefesh* is ill — The idea of using taste preferences to determine well-being has gone by the wayside in our day and age. Except for a few practitioners considered off the medical mainstream, contemporary Western medical professionals and laypeople simply ascribe "odd tastes" to caprice and eccentricity.

The idea of using moral preferences and personal ambitions as determinants of a person's overall well-being also seems to have gone by the wayside. We're likely to avoid making comments about a person's choices in that realm (except in extreme cases), simply because we consider such things a person's "own business," and not subject to judgment.

Still, the idea of eccentricities of tastes as well as of behavior should give us pause. Aren't people found guilty of legal or moral offenses likely to have odd tastes in entertainment, for example, or in whom they admire? Cannot we *all* be taken to be the product of our tastes, predilections, thoughts, and goals?

If nothing else, we would do well to mull over our own quirks and habits, and consider them in the light of the sort of person we'd like to be.[3]

imagine to be sweet, and have them take loathsome, bitter things to heal them, after which they could once again differentiate between what is [truly] good-tasting and what is loathsome — likewise those whose *nefesh* is ill should go to the sages who can heal the *nefesh*,* who would then warn them against doing the sorts of bad things they thought were good, and then treat their character by using the methods which cure the traits of the *nefesh*, which we will describe in the next chapter.*

וּמַזְהִירִים אוֹתָם מִמַּה שֶׁהָיוּ מְדַמִּין עָרֵב, וְיַכְרִיחוּם לָקַחַת דְּבָרִים הַנִּגְעָלִים הַמָּרִים הַמַּבְרִיאִים אֶת גּוּפוֹתֵיהֶם וְאָז יַחְזְרוּ לִבְחוֹר אֶת הַטּוֹב וְלִגְעוֹל אֶת הַנִּגְעָל, כַּךְ חוֹלֵי הַנֶּפֶשׁ רָאוּי לָהֶם לִשְׁאוֹל אֶת הַחֲכָמִים שֶׁהֵם רוֹפְאֵי הַנְּפָשׁוֹת, וְאֵלּוּ יַזְהִירוּם מֵאוֹתָן הָרָעוֹת שֶׁהֵם חוֹשְׁבִים אוֹתָן טוֹבוֹת, וִירַפְּאוּם בִּפְעוּלָה אֲשֶׁר בָּהּ מְרַפְּאִין מִדּוֹת הַנֶּפֶשׁ שֶׁנְּבָאֲרֵם בַּפֶּרֶק שֶׁאַחַר זֶה.

But if people don't sense that their *nefesh* is ill and imagine that it is [or, that they are] well, or if they sense it is ill but they will not submit to treatment — they will suffer the same fate of any patient who continues pursuing pleasure

אֲבָל חוֹלֵי הַנֶּפֶשׁ שֶׁאֵינָם מַרְגִּישִׁים אֶת מַחֲלָתָם וּמְדַמִּין אוֹתָהּ בְּרִיאוּת, אוֹ שֶׁמַּרְגִּישִׁים וְאֵינָם מִתְרַפְּאִים, הֲרֵי סוֹפָם יִהְיֶה מַה שֶּׁדֶּרֶךְ לִהְיוֹת סוֹף

---

the sages who can heal the *nefesh* — We're hard pressed to arrive at an English term for such a practitioner. The term *metaphysician* comes to mind, but it simply isn't accurate, because a metaphysician would delve into spiritual matters alone. Considering the fact that we've indicated above[2] that Rambam is using the term *nefesh* here to refer to our emotions, for the most part, we considered using the term "psychiatrist," since psychiatrists are trained in both psychology and physiology. But today psychiatrists tend to offer pharmacological solutions to personal imbalances. We are tempted to use the popular term "holistic physician," but it might carry negative connotations for some. So we've settled on the word "sage."

In point of fact, Rambam is refer-ring to someone like himself, for he was a physician, metaphysician, psychologist, and sage.

...in the next chapter — Notice Rambam doesn't say that we should seek out a sage when we realize our *nefesh* is ill the way he pointed out that we tend to visit a doctor when we realize we're ill. Apparently this is because most of us don't realize when our character is off-kilter, and we tend to go about blithely accepting everything we do at face value. His implication is that going to a sage when we are off-kilter should be as logical and natural for us as going to a doctor when we're physically out of sorts.

The issue will be addressed, though, in the next paragraph and thereafter.

and does not submit to treatment would: they will surely perish [prematurely].[4]

3. But as for those who sense they are ill [i.e., that their *nefesh* is ill] and yet continue pursuing pleasure, the Book of Truth* describes them as saying, "I will go about with a stubborn heart, to add drunkenness to thirst" (Deuteronomy 29:18). For while they may mean to quench their thirst, they actually only make themselves thirstier yet.[5]

But as for those who don't sense [that their *nefesh* is ill], King Solomon often depicted them, and said [of them], "The fool's ways are blameless in his own eyes; but one who takes counsel is a sage" (Proverbs 12:15), referring to one who listens to a sage who tells him which path is truly correct, rather than what he thinks is correct. He also said, "There is a path that seems straightforward to a person that [actually] ends in the ways of death" (ibid. 14:12).

And he said of those who are so *nefesh*-ill that they cannot differentiate between what would harm them and what would help them, "The way of wrongdoers is like darkness; they never know why they may stumble" (ibid. 4:19).

I will describe the art [i.e., the methodology] of healing the *nefesh* in the fourth chapter.

הַחוֹלֶה אִם הָלַךְ אַחַר תַּאֲווֹתָיו וְאֵינוֹ מִתְרַפֵּא שֶׁהוּא יֹאבַד בְּלִי סָפֵק.

ג. אֲבָל הַמַּרְגִּישִׁים וְהוֹלְכִים אַחַר תַּאֲווֹתֵיהֶם, עֲלֵיהֶם אָמַר סֵפֶר הָאֱמֶת בְּתָאֲרוֹ אֶת דִּבְרֵיהֶם (דברים כ"ט י"ח), "כִּי בִשְׁרִירוּת לִבִּי אֵלֵךְ לְמַעַן סְפוֹת הָרָוָה אֶת הַצְּמֵאָה," כְּלוֹמַר שֶׁהוּא מִתְכַּוֵּן לִרְווֹת צְמָאוֹנוֹ וְהוּא מוֹסִיף עַצְמוֹ צִמָּאוֹן.

אֲבָל אוֹתָם שֶׁאֵינָם מַרְגִּישִׁים הֲרֵי תֵּיאֲרָם שְׁלֹמֹה הַרְבֵּה, אָמַר (משלי י"ב ט"ו), "דֶּרֶךְ אֱוִיל יָשָׁר בְּעֵינָיו וְשׁוֹמֵעַ לְעֵצָה חָכָם," כְּלוֹמַר הַמְקַבֵּל אֶת עֲצַת הֶחָכָם שֶׁמּוֹדִיעוֹ הַדֶּרֶךְ שֶׁהוּא יָשָׁר בֶּאֱמֶת לֹא אוֹתוֹ שֶׁהוּא חוֹשֵׁב אוֹתוֹ יָשָׁר. וְאָמַר (שם י"ד י"ב), "יֵשׁ דֶּרֶךְ יָשָׁר לִפְנֵי אִישׁ וְאַחֲרִיתָהּ דַּרְכֵי מָוֶת."

וְאָמַר בְּאוֹתָם חוֹלֵי הַנֶּפֶשׁ שֶׁהֵם אֵינָם יוֹדְעִים מַה יַּזִּיק לָהֶם וְלֹא מַה יוֹעִיל לָהֶם (שם ד' י"ט), "דֶּרֶךְ רְשָׁעִים כָּאֲפֵלָה לֹא יָדְעוּ בַּמֶּה יִכָּשֵׁלוּ."

אֲבָל מְלֶאכֶת רְפוּאַת הַנְּפָשׁוֹת הִיא כְּמוֹ שֶׁאֲתָאֵר בַּפֶּרֶק הַזֶּה הָרְבִיעִי.

Synopsis

1. A healthy *nefesh* always does good, benevolent, and pleasant things, while an unhealthy one always does bad, harmful, and disgraceful things. Now, just as someone whose senses are off-kilter would confuse bitter with sweet and pleasant with unpleasant, and may even crave harmful things, someone whose *nefesh* is off-kilter would likewise confuse bad actions with good ones, and would pursue harmful goals.

2. Just as an ill person would go to a doctor who would then tell him what to do, what to avoid, and what to take to be well, one whose *nefesh* is ill should likewise go to a "doctor" of the *nefesh*, who would tell him what to do and what not to do to be well. Nonetheless, if one's *nefesh* is ill without his knowing, or if one knows it is ill but refuses to submit to treatment, then, like the patient who continues to do whatever he pleases rather than submit to treatment, he, too, will surely perish.

3. Those who do realize their *nefesh* is ill but don't submit to treatment will go about pursuing pleasure to no avail. They would be wise to seek counsel from a sage, rather than fumble about in the darkness.

4

ברפואת מחלות הנפש

TREATING DISEASES OF THE NEFESH

THIS CHAPTER FOLLOWS FAST *on the heels of the previous one, which first offered us insight into the makeup of an ill nefesh, and then promised us a treatment protocol for it here.*

In the course of Rambam's presentation of that protocol, a couple of things become clear: that piety isn't what it might seem to be, and that there is a specific Jewish type of piety which is far more balanced than other, non-Jewish forms of "piety."

Before he touches upon that, though, Rambam suggests here the types of balanced traits we should indeed strive for. They include temperance (rather than either indulgence or asceticism), generosity (rather than stinginess or extravagance), courage (rather than daring or cowardice), happiness (rather than brashness or dullness), humility (rather than arrogance or self-abasement), earnestness (rather than boastfulness or meekness), contentment (rather than indulgence or sloth), composure (rather than short-temperedness or apathy), shamefacedness (rather than audacity and bashfulness), and the like.

But in their erroneous belief that piety demands character extremes, as people of other faiths mistakenly contend, many Jews of high ideals and with great spiritual aspirations come to err. They believe that people who act daringly, who exhibit indifference in the face of things that others are taken by, or who always seem content and temperate — or, on the other hand, who are extrava-

gant and boastful — are admirable and "truly" pious.

But they are wrong. True Jewish piety entails much, much more. As Rambam portrays it, it is determined by one's intellectual pursuits besides his personal qualities, as well as a pursuit of truth. It's also marked by a reasonable, even-handed pious quest for closeness to God by means of the very human qualities He Himself has implanted within us. (It is also comprised of yet another trait which will be enunciated in the next chapter.)

As Rambam noted elsewhere, "Should you think that envy, lust, honor, and similar things are bad traits that remove a man from the world, and that one should thus remove himself from them, and you go to the opposite extreme and not eat meat, drink wine, marry, live in a fine house, or dress in decent clothes, and dress in sackcloth and hard wool and the like instead, as gentile priests do — that would alse be the wrong way" (Hilchot Dei'ot 3:1).

Some well-intentioned Jewish aspirants noted that some truly pious Jewish souls would indeed go to extremes sometimes. So they followed the gentiles' example in the mistaken belief that that was how one in fact becomes pious. But the occasional extreme acts of the truly pious were exceptions to the rule, and were only engaged in to safeguard their moral well-being and to avoid the risk of a sort of spiritual contamination from unholy surroundings.

Rambam's point, once again, is that we're meant to live reasonable lives and to thus avoid extremes as we serve God in this world.

He does indeed fulfill his promise here to "offer the art of healing the nefesh." In short, it comes down to reversing your behavior from one extreme to the other when it goes awry, steering it around till it anchors itself in equilibrium, and then repeating the corrected, balanced deed over and over again until it becomes second nature.

His final point is that, at bottom, we're to always judge our own actions and strive for balance in them. For if we do, we'll be people of high caliber, we'll draw close to God and satisfy His wishes, and we will thus serve Him in the best of ways.

1. Good deeds are those which lie midway between two extremes, both of which are bad — one because it goes too far, and the other because it does not go far enough.*	א. הַמַּעֲשִׂים אֲשֶׁר הֵם טוֹב הֵם הַמַּעֲשִׂים הַמְאוּזָּנִים הַמְמוּצָעִים בֵּין שְׁנֵי קְצָווֹת שֶׁשְּׁנֵיהֶם רָע, הָאֶחָד הַגְּזָמָה וְהַשֵּׁנִי מִיעוּט. וְהַמַּעֲלוֹת הֵן

Virtuous qualities are those inborn or learned traits midway between

---

far enough — Rambam said at the beginning of chapter 3 above that

"healthy *nefashot*...are predisposed to doing good, benevolent, and pleasant

two bad qualities, one of which is excessive, and the other of which is inadequate.* It is in fact these qualities which foster the former kinds of deeds.*

2. An example [of a quality that would lead to good deeds] is temperance,* a trait that lies midway between indulgence and asceticism.* [Since] it is good to be temperate* [it follows that]

תְּכוּנוֹת נַפְשִׁיוֹת וְהֶרְגֵּלִים מְמוּצָעִים בֵּין שְׁתֵּי תְכוּנוֹת רָעוֹת, שֶׁהָאַחַת יֶתֶּר וְהַשְּׁנִיָּה חָסוּר, וּמֵהֶתְכוּנָה הַזּוּ יָבוֹאוּ אוֹתָם הַמַּעֲשִׂים.

ב. הַמָּשָׁל בָּזֶה הַפְּרִישׁוּת, הִיא מִדָּה מְמוּצַעַת בֵּין הַתַּאַוְתָנוּת וּבֵין הֶעְדֵּר הַרְגָּשַׁת הַהֲנָאָה, הֲרֵי הַפְּרִישׁוּת הִיא מִן הַמַּעֲשִׂים הַטּוֹבִים. וּתְכוּנַת הַנֶּפֶשׁ הַמְּבִיאָה לִידֵי הַפְּרִישׁוּת, הִיא מִן הַמַּעֲלוֹת הַמִּדּוֹתִיּוֹת, וְהִנֵּה

the personal quality that leads to it is a virtuous one, for both indul-

things" by definition. He thus spells out here just what good deeds are (and by extension, what benevolent and pleasant deeds are).

Good deeds are the sorts of things that someone who is less than perfect, and whose elements sometimes clash, does to reach his goal. Bad deeds are the sorts of things that someone who is likewise less than perfect and whose elements also clash does when he goes too far or not far enough to reach his goal.[1]

which is inadequate — Our "qualities" are good or bad character traits that we're either born with or adopt, that run the gamut from one extreme to the other. While most of us express character extremes from time to time (when we're hard pressed, for example), virtuous qualities go to neither extreme and always lie somewhere midrange. In fact, we often refer to virtuous, principled people as "even tempered," "level-headed," "cool-headed," "balanced," etc.[2]

...the former kinds of deeds — That is to say, persons with dispositions

that are neither excessive nor inadequate go neither too far in their actions, nor not far enough. Simply put: virtuous people do good things.

Though he accentuates deeds here, Rambam will be citing "traits" more than deeds per se, as we'll soon see.

temperance — Or, "abstinence" (*perishut* in Hebrew). We prefer "temperance" in this context, because it better addresses the contrasts Rambam is talking about.

asceticism — Lit., utter indifference to physical pleasure.

Actually, we in modernity see "temperance" as fairly extreme and quaint; "asceticism" as neurotic and utterly extreme; "occasional indulgence" as out-and-out healthy, normal, and very human; and "utter indulgence" as an extreme — though perhaps an enviable one. Hence, occasional indulgence is *our* skewed ideal.

it is good to be temperate — Lit., since temperance is among the good deeds.

gence, which is one extreme,* and asceticism, which is the other,* are utterly wrong. And the two qualities that would lead to them — both the one that produces indulgence (which is an excess), and the other that produces asceticism (which is an inadequacy) — are flaws.*

The same goes for generosity,* which lies midway between stinginess and extravagance;[3] courage, which lies midway between daring and cowardice; happiness, which lies midway between brashness and dullness;[4] humility, which lies midway between arrogance and self-abasement; earnestness, which lies midway between boastfulness and meekness; contentment,[5] which lies midway between indulgence and sloth; composure which lies midway between short-temperedness and apathy; shamefacedness, which lies midway between audacity and bashfulness; and the rest.[6,7]

(We need not offer exact terms for what we are referring to, as long as we can be understood.)

הַהַאֲוָתָנוּת הוּא הַקָּצֶה הָרִאשׁוֹן, וְהֶעְדֵּר הָרֶגֶשׁ הַהֲנָאָה לְגַמְרֵי הוּא הַקָּצֶה הָאַחֲרוֹן, וּשְׁתֵּיהֶם רַע בְּהֶחְלֵט. וּשְׁתֵּי הַתְּכוּנוֹת הַנַּפְשִׁיּוֹת שֶׁמֵּהֶן בָּאָה הַהַאֲוָתָנוּת, וְהִיא הַתְּכוּנָה הַיְתֵירָה, וְהֶעְדֵּר הָרֶגֶשׁ, וְהִיא הַתְּכוּנָה הַחֲסֵרָה, הֲרֵי הֵם יַחַד שְׁתֵּי מִגְרָעוֹת מִמִּגְרְעוֹת הַמִּדּוֹת.

וְכֵן הַנְּדִיבוּת מְמוּצַעַת בֵּין הַכִּילוּת וְהַפַּזְרָנוּת. וְהָאוֹמֶץ מְמוּצָע בֵּין חֵרוּף הַנֶּפֶשׁ וְהַמּוֹרֶךְ. וְהַבְּדִיחוּת מְמוּצַעַת בֵּין הַחֻצְפָּה וְהַטִּמְטוּם. וְהָעֲנָוָה מְמוּצַעַת בֵּין הַגַּאֲוָה וְשִׁפְלוּת הָרוּחַ, וְהָרְצִינוּת מְמוּצַעַת בֵּין הַהִתְהַדְּרוּת וְהַשִּׁפְלוּת, וְעַיִן טוֹבָה מְמוּצַעַת בֵּין הַהַאֲוָתָנוּת וְהָעַצְלוּת, וְהַמְתִינוּת מְמוּצַעַת בֵּין הָרִגְזָנוּת וְהַקְּרִירוּת. וְהַבַּיְשָׁנוּת מְמוּצַעַת בֵּין הָעַזּוּת וְהַהִכָּלְמוּת. וְכֵן הַשְּׁאָר.

וְאֵינֶנּוּ צְרִיכוֹת לְשֵׁמוֹת מוּנָחִים לָהֶם דַּוְקָא אִם הָעִנְיָנִים מוּסְבָּרִים וּמוּבָנִים.

---

one extreme — Lit., the former extreme, excessiveness.

the other — Lit., the latter extreme, inadequacy.

are flaws — In other words, a virtuous disposition would encourage temperance, rather than indulgence or asceticism.

generosity — At the end of this paragraph Rambam adds that "we

need not offer exact terms for what we are referring to, as long as we can be understood," apparently because the terms he's about to use often lose something in translation, and after all, he was using Arabic terms that had been translated from Greek ones (which were then translated into the Hebrew terms we're referring to and translating into English). The point is that while the terms may not be exact the idea should be clear: the ideal is to pursue balanced traits.

3. Now, people often err in these matters and think that going to one extreme [or the other] is good and a virtue [i.e., rooted in a virtue]. Some, for example, consider excessive behavior to be good, and take daring to be a virtue, and thus call daring people "brave." When they see someone acting with extreme rashness and exposing himself to danger, purposefully endangering his life (and then by chance escaping unhurt), they praise him and refer to him as "brave."* Or they might consider [instances of] the other extreme to be good, and thus refer to an apathetic person as tolerant; a lazy one as content; and someone who is an ascetic simply because of his lethargic nature as temperate.[8] Along the same lines they consider [instances of] extravagance[9] and boastfulness to be praiseworthy.

But all this is wrong. What is truly praiseworthy is balance, and that is what a person should strive for and direct all his actions towards.[10]

ג. וְרַבּוֹת טוֹעִים בְּנֵי אָדָם בִּפְעוּלוֹת הַלָּלוּ וְחוֹשְׁבִים אֶת אֶחָד הַקְּצָווֹת טוֹב וּמַעֲלָה מִמַּעֲלוֹת הַנֶּפֶשׁ, יֵשׁ שֶׁחוֹשְׁבִים אֶת הַקָּצֶה הָאֶחָד טוֹב, כְּמוֹ שֶׁחוֹשְׁבִים חֵרוּף הַנֶּפֶשׁ מַעֲלָה, וְקוֹרִין הַמְחָרְפִים נַפְשָׁם אַמִּיצִים, וְכַאֲשֶׁר רוֹאִים מִי שֶׁהוּא בְּתַכְלִית חֵירוּף הַנֶּפֶשׁ וְהַהִתְמַסְּרוּת לַסַּכָּנוֹת וּמוֹסֵר עַצְמוֹ לַסַּכָּנָה בְּכַוָּנָה, וְאֶפְשָׁר שֶׁיִּנָּצֵל בְּמִקְרֶה, מְשַׁבְּחִים אוֹתוֹ בְּכָךְ וְאוֹמְרִים זֶה אַמִּיץ. וְיֵשׁ שֶׁחוֹשְׁבִים אֶת הַקָּצֶה הָאַחֲרוֹן וְאוֹמְרִים עַל קְרִיר הַנֶּפֶשׁ — מָתוּן, וְעַל הָעַצְלָן — טוֹב עַיִן, וְעַל נֶעְדַּר הַהֶרְגֵּשׁ בַּהֲנָאוֹת מֶחֱמַת רַדְמוּת טִבְעוֹ — פָּרוּשׁ. וְעַל דֶּרֶךְ הַטָּעֻיּוֹת הַלָּלוּ חוֹשְׁבִים אֶת הַפַּזְרָנוּת וְהַהִתְהַדְּרוּת מִן הַמַּעֲשִׂים הַמְשׁוּבָּחִים.

כָּל זֶה טָעוּת, אֶלָּא מְשׁוּבָּח בֶּאֱמֶת הַמְּצוּעַ, וְאֵלָיו צָרִיךְ הָאָדָם לְהִתְכַּוֵּון, וִיכַוֵּון כָּל מַעֲשָׂיו תָּמִיד כְּלַפֵּי הַמְּצוּעַ הַזֶּה.

וְדַע, שֶׁאֵלּוּ הַמַּעֲלוֹת וְהַמִּגְרָעוֹת הַמִּדּוֹתִיּוֹת אֵינָם נִקְנִים וּמִתְחַזְּקִים בַּנֶּפֶשׁ אֶלָּא בַּמֶּה שֶׁאָדָם חוֹזֵר עַל אוֹתָן הַפְּעוּלוֹת הַבָּאוֹת מֵאוֹתָהּ הַמִּדָּה פְּעָמִים רַבּוֹת בִּזְמָן מְמוּשָׁךְ,

Still and all, it is important to realize that one only acquires virtues and flaws and they only come to affix themselves to the *nefesh* when we repeat the deeds [or, modes of behavior] associated with them over and over again for a long period of time, and on a regular basis.[11]

"brave" — That is to say, some people mistakenly judge extremes of behavior rooted in wrongful, unbalanced dispositions as good and virtuous.

Hence, when we do good things [over and over again, for an extended period of time], we acquire virtues; and when we do bad things [over and over again, for an extended period of time], we acquire flaws.*

4. Now, no one is born with an inherently virtuous or flawed character, as we will explain in the eighth chapter. In fact, we are clearly [born with certain good and bad qualities, as well as] acclimated from childhood onward to behave the way our family and friends* do.[12] That behavior could either be balanced, or it could be extreme* in the sorts of ways we have depicted (which would then indicate an unhealthy *nefesh*). It is therefore important for an individual to engage in the kinds of things done to treat a physical ailment [in order to balance and thus heal his *nefesh*].

For when the body goes off-kilter [or, off-balance], we first determine the direction it is heading in, and deliberately reverse its course until it returns to equilibrium [or, to balance]. Once it does, we stop reversing its course and allow it to do whatever will keep it

וְכַאֲשֶׁר נִתְרַגֵּל בָּהֶם, הֲרֵי אִם הָיוּ אוֹתָן הַמַּעֲשִׂים טוֹבִים הֲרֵי נִקְנֵית לָנוּ מַעֲלָה, וְאִם הָיוּ רָעִים הֲרֵי נִקְנֵית לָנוּ מִגְרַעַת.

ד. וּלְפִי שֶׁהָאָדָם בְּטִבְעוֹ מִתְּחִלָּתוֹ אֵינוּ לֹא בַּעַל מַעֲלָה וְלֹא בַּעַל מִגְרַעַת, כְּמוֹ שֶׁנְּבָאֵר בְּפֶרֶק הַשְּׁמִינִי, וְהוּא מִתְרַגֵּל בְּלִי סָפֵק מִקַּטְנוּתוֹ לְמַעֲשִׂים בְּהֶתְאֵם לְמִנְהַג מִשְׁפַּחְתּוֹ וְאַנְשֵׁי עִירוֹ, וְיֵשׁ שֶׁאוֹתָם הַמַּעֲשִׂים בֵּינוֹנִיִּים, וְיֵשׁ שֶׁהֵם בַּקָּצֶה הָרִאשׁוֹן אוֹ בָּאַחֲרוֹן, כְּמוֹ שֶׁבֵּיאַרְנוּ, וְנִמְצָא שֶׁזֶּה כְּבָר חָלְתָה נַפְשׁוֹ, וְרָאוּי שֶׁיִּתְנַהֵג כְּדֶרֶךְ שֶׁמִּתְנַהֲגִים בִּרְפוּאַת הַגּוּפוֹת.

כְּשֵׁם שֶׁהַגּוּף אִם נָטָה מֵאִזּוּנוֹ רָאִינוּ לְאֵיזֶה צַד נָטָה וְיָצָא וְנַעֲשָׂה נֶגְדּוֹ הֶפְכּוֹ עַד שֶׁיַּחֲזוֹר לְאִזּוּנוֹ, וְכַאֲשֶׁר יְאוּזָּן נִסְתַּלֵּק מֵאוֹתוֹ הַהֵפֶךְ, וְנַחֲזוֹר

---

acquire flaws — We're obviously not talking about inborn qualities here, but acquired ones (despite our discussion in the previous chapter).

In essence, Rambam's point is that while we're each certainly predisposed to certain character traits, we're all nonetheless capable of change, growth, and self-transcendence. What is called for is the implanting and affixing of the new character traits about to be discussed into our beings.

friends — Lit., fellow townspeople.

it could be extreme — Lit., it is [an instance of] one or the other extreme.

in balance.* We should do the same when it comes to character traits.[13]

Suppose, for example, we were to encounter someone who is disposed toward allowing himself very little (which is a serious personal flaw),* who thus did bad things, as we have explained in this chapter [that is to say, he engaged in extreme self-denial]. If we wished to cure him of this illness, we would not order him to [merely] act generously [toward himself; i.e., to start allowing himself some amenities], for that would be like treating someone overcome by heat with something [merely] lukewarm, which would not be able to cure him of his illness. Instead, we would order him to prac-

לְהִתְמִיד בְּמָה שֶׁיַּעֲמִידֶנּוּ עַל אִזּוּנוֹ, כָּךְ נַעֲשֶׂה גַם בְּמִדּוֹת.

וְהַמָּשָׁל בָּזֶה, אִם רָאִינוּ אָדָם שֶׁכְּבָר נִקְנוּ לוֹ תְכוּנוֹת נַפְשִׁיּוֹת בְּנַפְשׁוֹ שֶׁהוּא מְצַמְצֵם מְאֹד עַל עַצְמוֹ שֶׁזּוּ מִגְרַעַת מִמְּגְרְעוֹת הַנֶּפֶשׁ, וְהַמַּעֲשֶׂה הַזֶּה שֶׁהוּא עוֹשֶׂה מִן הַמַּעֲשִׂים הָרָעִים כְּמוֹ שֶׁבֵּיאַרְנוּ בְּפֶרֶק זֶה, אִם רָצִינוּ לְרַפֵּא אֶת הַחוֹלֶה הַזֶּה לֹא נְצַוֵּהוּ לְהִתְנַהֵג בִּנְדִיבוּת, לְפִי שֶׁזֶּה כְּמוֹ שֶׁמְּרַפֵּא אֶת מִי שֶׁגָּבְרָה בּוֹ הַחֲמִימוּת בְּדָבָר הַמְּאוּזָּן שֶׁאֵין זֶה מְרַפְּאוֹ מֵחָלְיוֹ, אֶלָּא רָאוּי לְצַוּוֹת לָזֶה שֶׁיִּנְהַג בְּפַזְּרָנוּת פַּעַם אַחַר פַּעַם, וְיַחֲזוֹר כַּמָּה פְעָמִים בְּמַעֲשֵׂה הַפַּזְּרָנוּת עַד שֶׁתָּסוּר מִנַּפְשׁוֹ הַתְּכוּנָה שֶׁהֱבִיאַתּוּ לִכִילוּת עַד שֶׁכִּמְעַט תּוּשַׂג לוֹ תְּכוּנַת הַפַּזְּרָנוּת אוֹ יְהֵא קָרוֹב לָהּ, וְאָז נְסַלְּקֶנּוּ מִפְּעוּלוֹת הַפַּזְּרָנוּת וּנְצַוֵּהוּ לְהִתְמִיד בְּמַעֲשֵׂה הַנְּדִיבוּת וְיִתְנַהֵג כָּךְ תָּמִיד שֶׁלֹּא יַפְלִיג וְלֹא יֶחְסַר.

tice being extravagant [toward himself; i.e., to start allowing himself to be profligate] again and again, many times over, until he would have expunged his quality of stinginess [i.e., self-denial] and had become well-nigh extravagant [or, profligate — for a time], or nearly so. We would then discourage him from being extravagant [toward himself; i.e., from being profligate] and tell him to be [merely] generous [toward himself; i.e., by only allowing himself some amenities] — no more, and no less — all the time [from them on].[14]

---

keep it in balance — To use common enough examples, if a diabetic took too much insulin and became faint as a consequence, a practitioner might suggest that the patient eat or drink something sweet so as to achieve balance, then stop, in much the same way as spoken of here. And if a practitioner were to determine

that a patient overcompensates for one weak muscle by using the opposing one too much, and the opposing muscle then becomes sore, the practitioner would strive for balance between them as well.

a serious personal flaw — We'll discuss the significance of referring

And were we to encounter someone extravagant [i.e., someone who demands many amenities for himself], we would have to enjoin him to act stingily [i.e., to deny himself amenities] again and again. Yet we wouldn't have him act stingily [i.e., in a self-abnegating way] as often as we would have the other person act extravagantly* [i.e., profligately].

5. This point [i.e., the aforementioned procedure] is the protocol to follow and the secret of healing [a *nefesh*]. Since a person would more easily and more likely go from extravagance to generosity than from stinginess to generosity, and he would more easily and likely go from asceticism to [mere] temperance than from indulgence

וְכֵן אִם רְאִינוּהוּ פַּזְרָן הֲרֵי נְצַוֵּהוּ
לִנְהוֹג בְּדֶרֶךְ הַכִּילוּת כַּמָּה פְּעָמִים,
אֲבָל לֹא נְצַוֵּהוּ לַחֲזוֹר עַל מַעֲשֵׂה
הַכִּילוּת פְּעָמִים רַבּוֹת כְּמוֹ שֶׁצִּוִּינוּהוּ
בְּמַעֲשֵׂה הַפַּזְרָנוּת.

ה. וּנְקוּדָה זוֹ הִיא חֹק הָרִיפּוּי וְסוֹדוֹ,
לְפִי שֶׁחֲזָרַת הָאָדָם מִן הַפִּזְרָנוּת אֶל
הַנְּדִיבוּת יוֹתֵר קַל וְקָרוֹב מִשֶּׁיַּחֲזוֹר מִן
הַכִּילוּת אֶל הַנְּדִיבוּת. וְכֵן חֲזָרַת נֶעְדַּר
הָרֶגֶשׁ הַהֲנָאוֹת אֶל הַפְּרִישׁוּת יוֹתֵר קַל
וְקָרוֹב מֵחֲזָרַת הַמִּתְאַוֶּתָן אֶל הַפְּרִישׁוּת,
וּלְפִיכָךְ נְצַוֶּה לְהִתְאַוֶּתָן לַחֲזוֹר עַל פְּעוּלוֹת
הָעֶדֶר הַהֲנָאָה יוֹתֵר מִמַּה שֶׁנְּצַוֶּה לְנֶעְדָּר
הָרֶגֶשׁ לַחֲזוֹר עַל פְּעוּלוֹת הַתְאַוָתָנוּת.
וּנְחַיֵּיב אֶת רַךְ הַלֵּבָב לִנְהוֹג בְּחֵרוּף
נֶפֶשׁ יוֹתֵר מִמַּה שֶׁנְּצַוֶּה אֶת הַמְחָרֵף
נַפְשׁוֹ לִנְהוֹג בְּמוֹרֶךְ, וְנַרְגִּיל אֶת הַשָּׁפָל
בְּהִתְגַּדְּרוּת יוֹתֵר מִמַּה שֶׁנַּרְגִּיל אֶת
הַמִּתְגַּדֵּר בְּשִׁפְלוּת.

וְזֶהוּ חֹק רְפוּאַת הַמִּדּוֹת. זָכְרֵהוּ.

to [mere] temperance, we would thus tell a self-indulgent person to engage in asceticism longer than we would tell an ascetic person to engage in self-indulgence. We would oblige a cowardly person to practice daring longer than we would oblige a daring person to practice cowardice. And we would train a meek person to exhibit boastfulness longer than we would train a boastful person to exhibit meekness.

Again, this is the protocol to follow for healing character. Remember it.*

to this flaw as an especially serious one in section 5 below.

act extravagantly — We'll soon discuss the curious fact that Rambam focuses on generosity and stinginess in terms of self-denial and self-profligacy, as well as why he suggests that we would not have to enjoin

someone who is profligate to deny himself things quite as much as we would have to enjoin someone who already denies himself things to be profligate.

Remember it — This is apparently a very important section of the chapter — especially coming on the heels of the previous section which it expands upon. Rambam clearly signals as much by bracketing it with, "This...is the protocol to follow and the secret of healing" at its beginning, and "This is the protocol to follow for healing character. Remember it," at its end.

Indeed, it will prove to be a pivotal section of the entire book, since it serves to portray just what piety is, and what it isn't. But a superficial reading wouldn't show how important it is, so we'd do well to consider carefully what Rambam is actually saying.

Let's first recall the strategy he laid out in the previous section.

We'd treat someone with an extreme disposition by taking him to the opposite extreme, and by having him act that way again and again for a while. Then we'd bring him back to the center.

Rambam points out here, though, that certain extremes would not have to remain at their opposite extreme for quite as long as others. Why? Because of the "protocol and secret of healing" discussed here. So let's examine this protocol and try to determine just why.

He indicated above that "were we to encounter someone extravagant, we would have to enjoin him to act *stingily* again and again. Yet we would not have him act stingily as often as we would have...[someone who had exhibited stinginess] act extravagantly." As he explains here, the reason for this is because "a person would more easily...go from extravagance to generosity, than from stinginess to generosity."

On the surface of it, that seems quite logical. After all, a person *would* more likely go from being ex-

travagant to being merely generous than he would from being stingy to generous, since less is demanded of him in the first instance.

But this is where we have to be careful, and to remember just how Rambam is defining his terms. Recall that he's referring to extravagance, generosity, and stinginess toward *oneself* — not toward others. For as we indicated above, Rambam's "extravagance" refers to being profligate toward *oneself*, his "generosity" refers to allowing *oneself* amenities, and his "stinginess" refers to *self*-abnegation.

So when Rambam says here that "a person would more easily...go from extravagance to generosity than from stinginess to generosity," he's actually saying that a person would find it easier going from *being profligate toward himself* to *only allowing himself some amenities*, then he would go from being *self-abnegating* to *only allowing oneself some amenities*.

But that seems absurd, since it implies that we'd more easily *deny* ourselves things than allow them to ourselves, which is the very opposite of what we accepted as logical above! There's only one solution. Here, Rambam isn't referring to those of us who would indeed rather have more than less and wouldn't deny ourselves things if we could help it. *He's referring to individuals striving for piety.* And he's defining true, Jewish piety in the process.

For indeed, people hoping to achieve piety *would* more easily go from "extravagance" — from being profligate toward themselves, to mere "generosity" — to only allowing themselves some amenities; from "stinginess" — from denying themselves amenities — to "generosity"

6. As a consequence [i.e., in light of the facts presented above, as we will explain], the pious [i.e., the truly pious — those who are pious by Jewish, Torah-based standards] would not allow their dispositions to remain [merely] balanced. Instead, they would lean somewhat toward excess or inadequacy, in order to safeguard themselves [against sin as well as against imbalance].

ו. וּבִגְלַל עִנְיָן זֶה לֹא הָיוּ הַחֲסִידִים מַעֲמִידִין תְּכוּנוֹת נַפְשָׁם בִּתְכוּנוֹת הַמְמוּצָעוֹת בְּשָׁוֶה, אֶלָּא הָיוּ נוֹטִים נְטִיָּה מְעַטָּה כְּלַפֵּי הַיִּתּוּר אוֹ הַחִסוּר דֶּרֶךְ סְיָיג.

כְּלוֹמַר, שֶׁהֵם נוֹטִים דֶּרֶךְ מָשָׁל מִן הַפְּרִישׁוּת כְּלַפֵּי הָעֹדֶר הָהֶרְגֵּשׁ בְּהַנָּאוֹת מְעַט, וּמִן הָאוֹמֶץ כְּלַפֵּי חֵרוּף הַנֶּפֶשׁ מְעַט, וּמִן הָרְצִינוּת כְּלַפֵּי

So, for example, they would tend to be somewhat more ascetic than temperate,* somewhat more daring than courageous,* somewhat

---

— to allowing themselves amenities! For these people are striving for a higher, more spirit-based life than most, and they're willing to do with less material things in the process.

There are a number of things that Rambam has to make clear to people striving toward piety. For just as there are undesirable extremes of character, there are likewise undesirable extremes of piety. There's too little piety (i.e., as exemplified by indulgence), and too much piety (i.e., as exemplified by austerity and abstemiousness). His point is that true, *Jewish* piety is balanced between the two (with rare exception, as we'll see). Those who follow extreme, non-Jewish, abstemious forms of "piety" — whom he's speaking about most specifically (see section 9 below) — are wrong.

After all (as he says there), our Sages "derided people who were for all intents and purposes *imprisoning* themselves with their self-imposed oaths [of abstention] by saying...'Has the Torah not already forbidden enough that you have to forbid yet

other things?' "

Similarly, Rambam's other "prescriptions" for *nefesh* treatment in this section follow suit, and only stand to reason with the above in mind.[15]

more ascetic than temperate — That is, since a person would "more likely go from asceticism to temperance than from indulgence to temperance," the pious would lean somewhat toward asceticism rather than lapse into indulgence. But they wouldn't lapse into utter asceticism either, which is also Rambam's point. The operative term here, and in the examples to follow, is "somewhat."

more daring than courageous — Since some daring is called for. But as Rambam pointed out in section 3 above, "people often err in these matters and think that going to one extreme is good and...praise [someone who would do something extremely daring] as brave.... But all this is wrong."

more earnest than boastful,* somewhat more humble than meek,[16] and the like. Our Sages alluded to this when they spoke of "[going] beyond the letter of the law [i.e., going beyond the mean]" (*Berachot* 7a).

Once in a while, though, some pious individuals would tend toward an extreme, such as fasting [for greater periods of time than the tradition requires of us], staying awake all night [to pray, study, or meditate]; doing without meat and wine; separating from women [i.e., limit relations with their wives]; wearing coarse wool and sackcloth; dwelling on mountainsides; or withdrawing to the desert. But the only reason they did any of those things was to heal themselves,* as we have explained, or because everyone around them was becoming corrupt and they perceived that they would also become corrupt by staying in contact with them and witnessing their actions; or they suspected that befriending those individuals would corrupt their own characters.* So they left and went to the desert,

הַהִתְהַדְּרוּת מְעַט. וּמֵהָעֲנָוָה כְּלַפֵּי שִׁפְלוּת הָרוּחַ מְעַט, וְכֵן בְּכָל הַשְּׁאָר, וְעִנְיָן זֶה הוּא הָרֶמֶז בְּאָמְרָם (ברכות ז.), "לִפְנִים מִשּׁוּרַת הַדִּין."

אֲבָל מַה שֶׁעָשׂוּ מִקְצַת אֲנָשִׁים הַחֲסִידִים בְּמִקְצַת הַזְּמַנִּים אֲשֶׁר נָטוּ כְּלַפֵּי הַקָּצֶה הָאֶחָד, כְּגוֹן הַצּוֹם, וּנְדוּד שֵׁינָה בַּלַּיְלָה, וְהֲנָחַת אֲכִילַת בָּשָׂר וּשְׁתִיַּת יַיִן, וְהַרְחָקַת הַנָּשִׁים, וּלְבִישַׁת הַצֶּמֶר וְהַשַּׂק, וּמְגוּרֵי הֶהָרִים, וְהַהִתְבּוֹדְדוּת בַּמִּדְבָּרוֹת, לֹא עָשׂוּ שׁוּם דָּבָר מִזֶּה אֶלָּא עַל דֶּרֶךְ הָרְפוּי, כְּמוֹ שֶׁבֵּיאַרְנוּ, וְגַם מֵחֲמַת קִלְקוּל אַנְשֵׁי עִירָם, כַּאֲשֶׁר רָאוּ שֶׁגַּם הֵם יִתְקַלְקְלוּ בְּפִגִּישָׁתָם אִתָּם וּבִרְאִיַּית מַעֲשֵׂיהֶם, וְשֶׁיֵּשׁ חֲשָׁשׁ שֶׁחֶבְרָתָם תִּגְרוֹם לָהֶם קִלְקוּל מִדּוֹתֵיהֶם,

---

more earnest than boastful — ...and to thus incline somewhat toward humbleness, but not too much so.

The most widely known Hebrew version of *Shemoneh Perakim* (Ibn Tibbon's) says at this point that the pious would tend to be "somewhat more tenderhearted than [merely] kindhearted," which reads better than what is offered here (in Rabbi Y. Kapach's translation from the Arabic). It is inherently logical and doesn't interfere with the difference between humility and meekness,

soon to come up.

was to heal themselves — Lit., for health's sake — for the health of their *nefesh*, and for their moral well-being.

...their own characters — That is to say, the wise know that they are affected by their environment both manifestly and subliminally, and that this is true, regardless of whether they're close to others in that environment or not.

where there were no bad people to be found.[17, 18] As the prophet [Jeremiah], peace be upon him, put it, "Oh, to be in the wilderness [or a voyager's inn; to thus abandon my people and leave them. For they are all adulterers, an assembly of renegades]" (Jeremiah 9:1).

7. Now, when some fools who had no idea why the pious were acting this way saw them do these things, they thought that was a good way to act, and they did likewise, in the belief that they would thus become like them. They afflicted their bodies in all kinds of ways [in pursuit of asceticism] and believed they would thus achieve personal virtues and were doing good, since [(they believed)] that was how a person draws close to God — as if God is the enemy of the body, and wants to destroy and annihilate it!*

לְפִיכָךְ יָצְאוּ מִבֵּינֵיהֶם לְמִדְבָּרוֹת מָקוֹם שֶׁאֵין שָׁם אָדָם רָע, כְּדֶרֶךְ שֶׁאָמַר הַנָּבִיא עָלָיו הַשָּׁלוֹם (ירמיה ט' א'), "מִי יִתְּנֵנִי בַמִּדְבָּר."

ז. וְכַאֲשֶׁר רָאוּ הַסְּכָלִים אֶת הַחֲסִידִים הָאֵלּוּ שֶׁעָשׂוּ פְּעוּלוֹת אֵלּוּ וְלֹא יָדְעוּ אֶת כַּוָּנָתָם, חָשְׁבוּ שֶׁהֵם טוֹב וְנָהֲגוּ בָּהֶם בְּחָשְׁבָם שֶׁיִּהְיוּ כְּמוֹתָם, וְהָיוּ מְעַנִּים אֶת גּוּפָם בְּכָל מִינֵי עִנּוּיִם, וְחוֹשְׁבִים שֶׁכְּבָר הִשִּׂיגוּ מַעֲלָה וְעָשׂוּ טוֹב, וְשֶׁבְּכָךְ יִתְקָרְבוּ לִפְנֵי ה', כְּאִלּוּ ה' אוֹיְבוֹ שֶׁל גּוּף וְרוֹצֶה לְאַבְּדוֹ וּלְהַשְׁמִידוֹ.

וְאֵינָם יוֹדְעִים שֶׁאוֹתָם הַמַּעֲשִׂים רָע, וְשֶׁבָּהֶם תּוּשַׂג מִגְרַעַת מִמַּגְרְעוֹת הַנֶּפֶשׁ.

וַהֲרֵי הֵם דּוֹמִים לְמִי שֶׁאֵין לוֹ יְדִיעָה בִּמְלֶאכֶת הָרְפוּאָה שֶׁרָאָה שֶׁהָרוֹפְאִים הַמֻּמְחִים הִשְׁקוּ לַחוֹלִים מְסֻכָּנִים "שחם אלחנט'ל'" "ואלמחממודה" "ואלצבר" וְכַיּוֹצֵא בָּהֶם וּמְנָעוּם מִן הַמְּזוֹנוֹת, וְעַל יְדֵי כַּךְ הִבְרִיאוּ מִמַּחֲלָתָם וְנִיצוֹלוּ מִן הַסַּכָּנָה

They never realized that those were in fact bad things to do, and that they would acquire flaws that way [instead].

They would be like some fool who knew nothing about medicine, who saw expert practitioners giving cathartics* to dangerously ill patients and not allowing them to eat, and through this they were healed and their lives were quite dramatically saved. The sort of fool we are referring to would say to himself, "If those things can heal a sick

---

annihilate it — Rambam's point is that the body is holy, too — when used for good ends. Denying the body its needs is as ill-advised as overindulging it, since both are

extremes and hence, bad.

giving cathartics — Rambam cites the Arabic terms for cathartics here.

person, they would certainly keep a healthy person well and even make him healthier!" And he would start to take them regularly and to do the sorts of things those ill people were doing — but would become ill instead!

As such, anyone who was healthy* who nonetheless took such "remedies" [i.e., such extreme measures] would undoubtedly become ill, much the same way.

8. The perfect Torah which perfects us (as he who knew [i.e., King David] attested to when he said, "God's Torah is perfect, it makes the fool wise and restores the *nefesh*" [Psalms 19:8]) never charged us to do any of this. Rather, it wants us to live normally [or, according to the dictates of human nature] and to follow a balanced path: to eat and drink what is permissible in balanced measure;[19] to cohabit in ways permitted in balanced measure; to develop the world in a just and honest way, rather than live in caves or on mountaintops; not to wear sackcloth or coarse wool; and to thus never strain, deplete, or afflict our bodies.[20]

It also cautions us about what comes to us by tradition thusly: "It is said of the Nazirite* that 'the *kohen* will...atone for him, for having sinned against the *nefesh*'* (Numbers 6:11). Our Sages asked, "Against

הַצָּלָה גְדוֹלָה, אָמַר אוֹתוֹ הַסָּכָל אִם הָיוּ הַדְּבָרִים הָאֵלּוּ מְרַפְּאִים אֶת הַחוֹלֶה, כָּל שֶׁכֵּן וְקַל וָחוֹמֶר שֶׁיַּעֲמִידוּ אֶת הַבָּרִיא בִּבְרִיאוּתוֹ אוֹ שֶׁיּוֹסִיפוּ לוֹ בְּרִיאוּת, וְהִתְחִיל לְהִשְׁתַּמֵּשׁ בָּהֶם תָּמִיד וְהִתְנַהֵג בְּהַנְהָגַת הַחוֹלִים, הֲרֵי הוּא יֶחֱלֶה בְּלִי סָפֵק.

כַּךְ אֵלּוּ, הֵם חוֹלֵי הַנֶּפֶשׁ בְּלִי סָפֵק בְּהִשְׁתַּמְּשָׁם בִּרְפוּאוֹת בִּהְיוֹתָם בְּרִיאִים.

ח. וְזוֹ הַתּוֹרָה הַתְּמִימָה הַשְּׁלֵמָה הַמְשַׁלֶּמֶת אוֹתָנוּ, כְּמוֹ שֶׁהֵעִיד עָלֶיהָ יוֹדְעָהּ (תהלים י"ט ח'), "תּוֹרַת ה' תְּמִימָה מַחְכִּימַת פֶּתִי, מְשִׁיבַת נָפֶשׁ," לֹא צִוְּתָה בְּשׁוּם דָּבָר מִזֶּה, אֶלָּא רָצְתָה שֶׁיְּהֵא הָאָדָם טִבְעִי הוֹלֵךְ בְּדֶרֶךְ הַמְמוּצָעִית, יֹאכַל מַה שֶּׁמּוּתָּר לוֹ לֶאֱכוֹל בְּמִצּוּעַ, וְיִשְׁתֶּה מַה שֶּׁמּוּתָּר לוֹ לִשְׁתּוֹת בְּמִצּוּעַ, וְיִבְעוֹל מַה שֶּׁמּוּתָּר לוֹ לִבְעוֹל בְּמִצּוּעַ, וְיִבְנֶה אֶת הָאָרֶץ בְּצֶדֶק וּמִשְׁפָּט, וְלֹא שֶׁיָּגוּר בִּמְעָרוֹת וּבֶהָרִים, וְלֹא שֶׁיִּלְבַּשׁ אֶת הַשַּׂק וְהַצֶּמֶר, וְלֹא שֶׁיּוּגִיעַ אֶת גּוּפוֹ, וִיעַיְּיפוֹ וִיעַנֵּהוּ.

וְהִזְהִיר עַל זֶה בַּמֶּה שֶׁבָּא לָנוּ בַּקַּבָּלָה אָמַר בְּנָזִיר (במדבר ו' י"א),

which *nefesh* did he sin? His own, by abstaining from wine. We can thus argue that if someone who [merely] denied himself wine needs atonement — how much more so then does someone who denies himself things* in general" (*Taanit* 11a).

We also see from their own words that our prophets and our Sages conducted themselves in a balanced way, and safeguarded their *nefesh* and body as the Torah obliged them to.*

In fact, through His prophet's words, God Himself responded to someone who asked whether or not he should continue fasting annually [as an extra measure of piety] on a particular day of the year. That person asked Zachariah, "Should I weep in the fifth month, should I become a Nazirite, as I did for so

"וְכִפֶּר עָלָיו מֵאֲשֶׁר חָטָא עַל הַנָּפֶשׁ," וְאָמְרוּ (תענית י"א.), "וְכִי עַל אֵיזֶה נֶפֶשׁ חָטָא זֶה, אֶלָּא שֶׁמָּנַע עַצְמוֹ מִן הַיַּיִן, וַהֲלֹא דְבָרִים קַל וָחוֹמֶר, מַה זֶּה שֶׁצִּיעֵר עַצְמוֹ מִן הַיַּיִן צָרִיךְ כַּפָּרָה — הַמְצַעֵר עַצְמוֹ מִכָּל דָּבָר וְדָבָר עַל אַחַת כַּמָּה וְכַמָּה."

וְגַם בְּדִבְרֵי נְבִיאֵינוּ וְחַכְמֵי תוֹרָתֵינוּ מָצָאנוּ, שֶׁהֵם תָּמִיד מִתְנַהֲגִים בְּמִצּוּעַ וְשׁוֹמְרִים נַפְשָׁם וְגוּפָם כְּמוֹ שֶׁחִיְּיבָה אוֹתָם הַתּוֹרָה.

וְהֵשִׁיב ה' יִתְעַלֶּה עַל יְדֵי נְבִיאוֹ לְמִי שֶׁשָּׁאַל עַל תַּעֲנִית יוֹם אֶחָד בַּשָּׁנָה הַאִם יַתְמִיד עַל כַּךְ אוֹ לֹא, וְהוּא

himself to practice a limited degree of asceticism (usually for a relatively short period of time), in order to draw close to God. He avoids wine and all grape products; he doesn't shave or cut his hair; and he avoids coming in contact with the dead. At the conclusion of his Nazirite status, he brings an offering, along with its appropriate accessories (see Numbers 6:1–21, where the Nazirite is discussed).

sinned against the *nefesh* — The usual understanding is that the Nazirite sinned by coming in contact with a dead person (referred to here as a "*nefesh*," a dead individual). But the Sages (soon to be cited) understood it to mean that the Nazirite sinned against his own *nefesh* by depriving himself of things and thus being too extreme.

denies himself things — I.e., things that are otherwise permissible.

as the Torah obliged them to — The following question could be raised: If in fact the prophets and Sages conducted themselves in a balanced way as we're supposed to, and observed the same Torah we observe, then what differentiates them from us?

The answer lies in the fact that they observed the mitzvot more meticulously and painstakingly than we do; they delved more deeply and assiduously into the process of rectifying their character and honing their minds than we do; and they only went to extremes when that was called for, unlike ourselves.

many years?" (Zachariah 7:3). [God] responded, "When you fasted and mourned in the fifth and seventh months for these seventy years, did you actually fast for My sake? And when you eat and drink now, do you not eat and drink for your own sake?"* (ibid. 7:5–6).

He then commanded him to pursue balance and character virtues rather than to fast. As he said, "Thus says the Lord of Hosts: Render true judgment, and let each man show kindness and compassion to his brother; [and the widow you shall not oppress]" (ibid., 9–10), which was

אָמְרָם לִזְכַרְיָה (זכריה ז' ג'), "הַאֶבְכֶּה בַּחֹדֶשׁ הַחֲמִישִׁי הִנָּזֵר כַּאֲשֶׁר עָשִׂיתִי זֶה כַּמֶּה שָׁנִים," וַהֲשִׁיבָם (שם ז' ה'), "כִּי צַמְתֶּם וְסָפוֹד בַּחֲמִישִׁי וּבַשְּׁבִיעִי וְזֶה שִׁבְעִים שָׁנָה הֲצוֹם צַמְתֻּנִי אָנִי וְכִי תֹאכְלוּ וְכִי תִשְׁתּוּ הֲלֹא אַתֶּם הָאֹכְלִים וְאַתֶּם הַשֹּׁתִים."

וְצִוָּה אוֹתָם בְּמִצּוּעַ וּבְמַעֲלוֹת בִּלְבַד לֹא בְצוֹם, וְהוּא אָמְרוּ לָהֶם (שם ז' ט'), "כֹּה אָמַר ה' צְבָקוֹת לֵאמֹר מִשְׁפַּט אֱמֶת שְׁפֹטוּ וְחֶסֶד וְרַחֲמִים עֲשׂוּ אִישׁ אֶת אָחִיו וְכוּ'." וְאָמַר אַחַר כַּךְ (שם ח' י"ט), "כֹּה אָמַר ה' צְבָקוֹת צוֹם הָרְבִיעִי וְצוֹם הַחֲמִישִׁי וְצוֹם הַשְּׁבִיעִי וְצוֹם הָעֲשִׂירִי יִהְיוּ לְבֵית יְהוּדָה לְשָׂשׂוֹן וּלְשִׂמְחָה וּלְמוֹעֲדִים טוֹבִים וְהָאֱמֶת וְהַשָּׁלוֹם אֱהָבוּ."

then followed by, "Thus says the Lord of Hosts: The fasts of the fourth, the fifth, the seventh, and the tenth months* will turn to joy and gladness and to goodly festivals for the house of Judah; and you shall love truth and peace" (ibid. 8:19).

Know that "truth" refers here to the intellectual virtues, because

---

for your own sake — In other words, someone asked God, through His prophet Zachariah, whether he should continue going to an extreme that was once appropriate — even once it was no longer appropriate — for the sake of piety. In response, he was asked whether his intentions were even sincere when the original degree of abstinence was called for. The prophet says that he would do better to concentrate on being truly and appropriately pious at this point in time, rather than going to extremes.[21]

...the tenth month — The fast of the

fourth month refers to the one observed on the seventeenth of Tammuz, which harkens back to the invasion of Jerusalem; the fast of the fifth month refers to the one observed on the ninth of Av, which harkens back to the destruction of the Holy Temple; the fast of the seventh month refers to the one observed on the third of Tishrei, which harkens back to the murder of Gedaliah; and the fast of the tenth month refers to the one observed on the tenth of Tevet, which harkens back to the rise of the king of Babylon over Jerusalem (see *Rashi*, Zachariah 8:19).

they encompass immutable truths (as we indicated in the second chapter);* and that "peace" refers here to character virtues, which bring about peace in the world.*

I will now return to the subject at hand.

וְדַע שֶׁ"הָ"אֱמֶת" הֵן הַמַּעֲלוֹת הַהֶגְיוֹנִיוֹת לְפִי שֶׁהֵם אֲמִתִּיוֹת לֹא יִשְׁתַּנּוּ, כְּמוֹ שֶׁהִזְכַּרְנוּ בְּפֶרֶק הַשֵּׁנִי, וְ"הַשָּׁלוֹם" הַמַּעֲלוֹת הַמִּדּוֹתִיּוֹת שֶׁבָּהֶם יִהְיֶה הַשָּׁלוֹם בָּעוֹלָם.

וְאֶחֱזוֹר לְעִנְיָנִי.

---

in the second chapter — See 2:2.

which bring about peace in the world — "Peace" implies a state of coexistence and unanimity between one-time opponents. I might make "peace," for example, between "sweet" and "sour" by creating a "sweet and sour" soup — a soup noted for being both sweet and sour at the same time. As such, peace comes about when opposites are used in combination to arrive at a new phenomenon that blends the two in unexpected ways, and allows for the coexistence of both.

Though it is usually not spoken of in such terms, following the path of balance advocated by Rambam can also be seen as acting in a way that makes peace between two antithetical behaviors — that takes the best of both, and synthesizes them into an ethical and temperamental combination of the two.

Let's examine the virtues Rambam cites next to their extremes, and see just what we mean. The virtue "temperance" is contrasted with indulgence and asceticism. What temperance actually is, is the allowance for some indulgence side by side with some asceticism. For after all, not only do we want to indulge our

cravings from time to time, but as Rambam seems to indicate, there's something in the human heart that also "craves" asceticism, as an expression of deep religious devotion. Being temperate, I have the best of both worlds. I can indulge to a degree and be ascetic to a degree.

The same is true of the other traits as well. I can be "courageous" and thus daring yet cowardly to degrees at the same time; "happy" and thus be both brash and dull; "humble" and both arrogant and meek; etc.

We find some proof for this in Rambam's terminology above. He says at the beginning of section 4 that if "we were to encounter someone who is disposed toward allowing himself very little...we would not order him to [merely] act generously [if we were to treat him for this illness]. *For that would be like treating someone overcome by heat with something [merely] lukewarm, [which simply would not work].*"

The word we translated as "lukewarm" above actually reads "balanced," as it does throughout this chapter. The way it is used here, though, suggested the use of "lukewarm." Our point is that, in fact, "lukewarm" is a workable illustration of Rambam's concept of bal-

9. If those members of our faith who try to imitate [the ascetic, spiritual practices of] other nations — who I am specifically referring to here* — were to say that they only afflict their bodies and deny themselves pleasure altogether in order to train themselves* to lean somewhat toward an extreme as one must do (as we have explained in this chapter), they would be wrong, as we shall explain.

The Torah only prohibited what it prohibited and commanded what it commanded for this reason: that we [learn to] avoid extremes and [to] follow the correct path.*

ט. וְאִם יֹאמְרוּ אֵלּוּ מִבְּנֵי אוּמָתֵינוּ אֲשֶׁר נִתְדַּמּוּ לָעַמִּים, שֶׁדְּבָרַי כָּאן אֵינָם אֶלָּא בָהֶם, שֶׁאֵינָם עוֹשִׂים מַה שֶׁהֵם עוֹשִׂים מֵעִנּוּיֵי גוּפוֹתֵיהֶם וּבְטוּל תַּעֲנוּגוֹתֵיהֶם, אֶלָּא עַל דֶּרֶךְ הַהַכְשָׁרָה לִכֹוחוֹת הַגּוּף, כְּדֵי שֶׁיִּהְיוּ נוֹטִים כְּלַפֵּי הַצַּד הָאֶחָד מְעַט, עַל הַדֶּרֶךְ שֶׁבֵּאַרְנוּ בְּפֶרֶק זֶה, שֶׁרָאוּי שֶׁיְּהֵא הָאָדָם כָּךְ, הֲרֵי זֶה טָעוּת מִצִּדָּם, כְּמוֹ שֶׁנְּבָאֵר.

וְהוּא, שֶׁהַתּוֹרָה לֹא אָסְרָה מַה שֶׁאָסְרָה, צִוְּתָה מַה שֶׁצִּוְּתָה, כִּי אִם מִסִּבָּה זוֹ, כְּלוֹמַר, כְּדֵי שֶׁנִּתְרַחֵק מִן הַצַּד הָאֶחָד יוֹתֵר עַל דֶּרֶךְ הַהַכְשָׁרָה.

כִּי אָסוּר כָּל הַמַּאֲכָלוֹת הָאֲסוּרוֹת, וְאִסּוּר הַבִּיאוֹת הָאֲסוּרוֹת, וְהָאַזְהָרָה עַל הַקְּדֵשָׁה, וְחִיּוּב כְּתֻבָּה וְקִדּוּשִׁין,

It thus forbade us certain foods, prohibited various acts of cohabitation, warned us against prostitutes,* obliged us to write a marriage contract [which assures the sanctity of the marriage and betokens mutual commitment] and to betroth someone [rather than to sponta-

---

ance. For lukewarm is both somewhat warm and somewhat cold, and hence a synthesis of the two, just as generosity, for example, is a synthesis of stinginess and extravagance.

That having been said, it seems logical to propose that going from one trait to its opposite and then back again can also be seen as experiencing both, and coming to realize the wisdom of a synthesis of the two.

who I am specifically referring to here — See our note on p. 61 above ("Remember it") for the significance of this statement.

to train themselves — Lit., in order to train their bodies' capacities.

...and to follow the correct path — We discussed Rambam's overviews on the role and intentions of Torah in our second supplementary note to chapter 2.

against prostitutes — This refers to Deuteronomy 23:18's warnings that there "never be prostitutes among the daughters of Israel, nor among the sons of Israel," prohibiting the practice of prostituting oneself to pagan priests, as well as to prostitution in general.

neously give in to one's impulses] who is nevertheless not available to us [conjugally] all the time and is actually forbidden to us during menstruation and after childbirth (as well as under those conditions which the Sages instituted in order to limit cohabitation, including their warning against engaging in it in the daytime, as we explained in *Sanhedrin* 7:4*). But God only commanded us in all this in order to draw us far away from indulgence and to have us go beyond the mean, toward asceticism, in order to strengthen within us the trait of temperance.*

וְעִם כָּל זֶה אֵינָהּ מוּתֶּרֶת תָּמִיד, אֶלָּא אֲסוּרָה בִּזְמַנֵּי הַנִּדָּה וְהַלֵּדָה, וְלֹא עוֹד אֶלָּא שֶׁעָשׂוּ זְקֵנֵינוּ הַגְבָּלוֹת כְּדֵי לְמַעֵט בְּתַשְׁמִישׁ וְהִזְהִירוּ מִזֶּה בַּיּוֹם כְּמוֹ שֶׁבֵּאַרְנוּ בְּסַנְהֶדְרִין (פרק ז' משנה ד'). שֶׁכָּל זֶה לֹא צִוָּה ה' עָלֵינוּ אֶלָּא כְּדֵי שֶׁנִּתְרַחֵק מִגְּבוּל הַתַּאֲוָתָנוּת הָרְחָקָה גְּדוֹלָה, וְנֵצֵא מִן הַמְמֻצָע כְּלַפֵּי הֶעְדֵּר הַהֶרְגֵּשׁ בְּתַאֲוַת מְעַט, כְּדֵי שֶׁתִּתְחַזֵּק בְּנַפְשֵׁנוּ תְּכוּנַת הַפְּרִישׁוּת.

Indeed, everything in the Torah having to do with the giving of tithes,*

וְכֵן כָּל מַה שֶׁבָּא בַתּוֹרָה, מִנְתִּינַת הַמַּעְשְׂרוֹת, וְהַלֶּקֶט, וְהַשִּׁכְחָה, וְהַפֵּאָה,

---

as we explained in *Sanhedrin* 7:4 — This is a reference to Rambam's comments to the Mishnah in *Sanhedrin*.

...the trait of temperance — That is to say, the Torah restricted our eating habits in order to temper our appetite for food and drink, which is often such a temptation. Similarly, it restricted our sexual proclivities to the point where not only can we not indulge freely in intercourse with anyone we'd care to — but instead we are to commit ourselves to someone through a legal contract, and then not even to indulge with him or her at any time we would care to. All in order to temper that greatest of human appetites.[22]

the giving of tithes — As he will put it at the end of this paragraph, Rambam now cites several mitzvot that seem to require us to be

extravagant in our charity and good works. As he'll point out, though, they're actually "meant to draw us far away from stinginess and toward extravagance, in order to foster generosity." We'll cite the verses relevant to those mitzvot now, and highlight their seeming extravagance. It is said of tithing (our first example):

"You will surely tithe all the produce of your seed that the field brings forth every year.... *Do not forsake the Levite within your gates; you must not forsake him, for he has no portion nor inheritance with you. At the end of three years bring forth the tithe of your produce in that year and lay it up inside your gates. And the Levite who has no part nor inheritance with you, the stranger, the orphan, and the widow within your gates will come to eat and be satisfied,* so that God, your Lord, may bless all the work of your hand" (Deuteronomy 14:22–29).

The verse also says, "When you

the gleaning of the harvest,* forgotten sheaves,* the corner of the
field,* the fallen grapes,* and the
gleaning of the vineyard;* as well as the rules of the Sabbatical year*
and the Jubilee year,* and offering enough charity to meet the needs

וְהַפֶּרֶט, וְעוֹלְלוֹת, וְדִין הַשְׁמַטָה
וְהַיוֹבֵל, וְהַצְּדָקָה דֵי מַחְסוֹרוֹ, כָּל זֶה

---

have finished tithing all the tithes of
your produce of the third year...*and
have given it to the Levite, the stranger, the orphan, and the widow, so that
they may then eat within your gates
and be filled*, you are then to say before God your Lord, 'I have taken
the hallowed things out of my house,
and have given them to the Levite,
the stranger, the orphan, and the
widow, according to all Your mitzvot
that You have commanded me'"
(ibid. 26:12–13).

the gleaning of the harvest — As it
is written, "And when you reap your
land's harvest, *do not...gather the
gleanings of your harvest*" (Leviticus
19:9).
 And, "When you reap the harvest
of your land, do not gather any
gleaning of your harvest. *Leave them
to the poor and to the stranger*" (ibid.
23:22).

forgotten sheaves — As it is written,
"When you cut the harvest in your
field and have forgotten a sheaf in
the field, *do not go back to fetch it; it
should be for the stranger, the orphan,
and the widow*....When you beat your
olive tree, *do not go over the boughs
again; it should be for the stranger, the
orphan, and the widow. When you
gather the grapes of your vineyard,
do not glean it again; it should be for
the stranger, the orphan, and the
widow*" (Deuteronomy 24:19–21).

the corner of the field — As it is
written, "When you reap your land's
harvest, *do not reap to the very
corners of your field*" (Leviticus 19:9).
 And, "When you reap your land's
harvest, *do not completely go up to
the corners of your field when you
reap...leave them to the poor and the
stranger*" (ibid. 23:22).

the fallen grapes — As it is written,
"Do not...gather every grape of your
vineyard; *leave them for the poor and
stranger*" (Leviticus 19:10).

the gleaning of the vineyard — As it
is written, "Do not glean your
vineyard...*leave them for the poor and
stranger*" (Leviticus 19:10).

the Sabbatical year — As it is
written, "At the end of every seven
years...*every creditor who lends
something to his neighbor should
release it*; he should not demand it of
his neighbor or brother"
(Deuteronomy 15:1–2).

the Jubilee year — As it is written,
"Count seven Sabbaths of years for
yourself, seven times seven years....
Sanctify the fiftieth year, and
proclaim liberty throughout the
land to all its inhabitants.... It will
be a Jubilee year to you. *Return every
man to his possession, and every man
to his family*. Do not sow nor reap
anything that grows in the course of

of the individual* comes very close to extravagance. But they are meant to draw us far away from stinginess and toward extravagance, in order to strengthen within us the trait of generosity.*

In fact, if you were to reflect upon most of the mitzvot you would discover that they are meant to discipline our personal capacities in just such a way.*

קָרוֹב לְפַזְרָנוּת כְּדֵי שֶׁנִּתְרַחֵק מִגְּבוּל הַכִּילוּת מֶרְחָק גָּדוֹל וְנִתְקָרֵב לִגְבוּל הַפַּזְרָנוּת כְּדֵי שֶׁתִּתְחַזֵּק בָּנוּ מִדַּת הַנְּדִיבוּת.

וְעַל דֶּרֶךְ זוֹ הִתְבּוֹנֵן בְּרוֹב הַמִּצְוֹת תִּמְצָא שֶׁכֻּלָּם מַכְשִׁירִים כּוֹחוֹת הַנֶּפֶשׁ.

it, nor gather the grapes of your vine.... You shall eat the produce of the field. In the Jubilee year return every man to his possession. And if you sell something to your neighbor, or buy something from him, do not defraud one another. *Buy from your neighbor according to the number of years after the Jubilee, and he should sell the fruits to you according to the number of years. Increase its price according to the number of years [despite the loss], and if the years are few, lower its price; for he is to sell you the fruit according to the number of the years. Do not defraud one another....* If your brother becomes poor and has sold away some of his possession, and his kin comes to redeem it, he should [be allowed to] redeem what his brother sold.... If your brother has become poor...then relieve him; though he may be a stranger or a sojourner, in order for him to live with you. *Take no interest from him.... Do not give him your money for interest nor loan him your food for profit....* If your brother who dwells with you becomes poor and is sold to you [as an indentured servant], *do not compel him to serve as a slave.* He should be like a hired servant and a sojourner to you. He

should serve you up to the Jubilee year...and then depart from you, both he and his children with him, and return to his family and to the possession of his fathers..." (Leviticus 25:8–41).

to meet the needs of the individual — This refers to contributing to people who had once been self-sufficient and then became poor, and doing so to the degree where they are able to live in the manner they had been used to living before (see *Ketubot* 67b).

...the trait of generosity — That is to say, the Torah enjoined us to not only offer charity once in a while, but to actually lessen and possibly compromise our own income and to purposefully sacrifice some of our own needs for others, in order to temper our innate selfishness and self-centeredness.[23]

...in just such a way — Just a couple of paragraphs back, Rambam said that all the Torah asks of us is that we "learn to avoid extremes." And yet here, he says that it asks us to "discipline our personal capacities," which isn't the same thing at all.

For example, the Torah forbade vengeance and avenging a murder with the declarations, "Do not take revenge or bear a grudge" (Leviticus 19:18), "[If you see the donkey of someone who hates you lying beneath its burden, refrain yourself from leaving it to him; rather] help him lift it" (Exodus 23:5), "[Do not watch your brother's donkey or ox fall down on the roadside and then hide from them; rather, help him lift them up again" (Deuteronomy 22:4), all in order to temper short-temperedness and anger.*[25]

It is likewise written, "[Do not watch your brother's ox or sheep go astray and hide yourself from them; rather, return them to your brother" (ibid. 22:1), in order to discourage stinginess;* and "Rise up before the aged and honor the old" (Leviticus 19:32), "Honor your father and mother" (Exodus 20:12), and "Do not deviate from the sentence [the judges] will declare to you" (Deuteronomy 17:11), in order to discourage the trait of audacity and encourage the trait of shame.

However, it then steers us away from the other extreme, timidity, by saying, "[Do not hate your brother in your heart;] but surely reproach your neighbor [when that is called for, nonetheless] and do

כְּגוֹן מַה שֶּׁאָסְרָה אֶת הַנְקָמָה וּגְאֻלַּת הַדָּם בְּאָמְרוֹ (ויקרא י"ט י"ח), "לֹא תִקּוֹם וְלֹא תִטּוֹר," (שמות כ"ג ה') "עָזֹב תַּעֲזֹב," (דברים כ"ב ד') "הָקֵם תָּקִים," כְּדֵי שֶׁיֶּחֱלַשׁ כֹּחַ הָרֹגֶז וְהַכַּעַס.

וְכֵן (שם כ"ב א') "הָשֵׁב תְּשִׁיבֵם," כְּדֵי שֶׁתָּסוּר תְּכוּנַת הַצַּיְקָנוּת, וְכֵן (ויקרא י"ט ל"ב) "מִפְּנֵי שֵׂיבָה תָקוּם וְהָדַרְתָּ פְּנֵי זָקֵן," (שמות כ' י"ב) "כַּבֵּד אֶת אָבִיךָ וְאֶת אִמֶּךָ," (דברים י"ז י"א) "לֹא תָסוּר מִן הַדָּבָר אֲשֶׁר יַגִּידוּ לְךָ," כְּדֵי שֶׁתָּסוּר תְּכוּנַת הָעַזּוּת וְתַשֵּׂג תְּכוּנַת הַבּוּשָׁה.

וְכֵן, הִרְחִיק גַּם מִן הַקָּצֶה הָאַחֲרוֹן, כְּלוֹמַר, הַהַכְלָמוּת, וְאָמַר (ויקרא י"ט י"ז), "הוֹכֵחַ תּוֹכִיחַ אֶת עֲמִיתֶךָ

His point seems to be that the only way we'll ever train ourselves to keep away from extremes is by disciplining our personal capacities. For as he pointed out above in section 1, it is our inner makeup that determines our actions, and leads them either toward moderation or toward excess.[24]

to temper short-temperedness and anger — Since anger derives from and fuels the urge to take revenge.

to discourage stinginess — Since a stingy, self-serving person wouldn't be willing to spend the amount of time it would take to return someone else's stray sheep.

not bear a sin because of him" (Leviticus 19:17), and "[Do not favor anyone in judgment; hear out the small as well as the great,] do not fear anyone [for judgment is God's]" (Deuteronomy 1:17), to also discourage us from timidity and keep us on a balanced path.[26]

So when some utter fool comes along [in quest of piety] and wants to expand upon that by disallowing [himself] even more food and drink than usual, by prohibiting marriage [i.e., by prohibiting himself to marry] aside from the prescribed sexual restrictions, and by handing over all of his money to the poor or to the Temple over and above the Torah's demands for Temple donations, charity, and valuation* — he is actually doing wrong and, without knowing it, he has gone to one of the other extremes, and has utterly forsaken balance.

וְלֹא תִשָּׂא עָלָיו חֵטְא," (דברים י"ז א') "לֹא תָגוּרוּ מִפְּנֵי אִישׁ," כְּדֵי שֶׁתָּסוּר גַּם הַהַכְלָמוּת וְנִשָּׁאֵר בַּדֶּרֶךְ הַמְמֻצַּעַת.

וְאִם בָּא הָאָדָם הַסָּכָל בְּלִי סָפֵק וְחָשַׁב לְהוֹסִיף עַל דְּבָרִים אֵלּוּ כְּגוֹן שֶׁיֶּאֱסֹר הָאוֹכֶל וְהַשְּׁתִיָּה יוֹתֵר מִמַּה שֶׁנֶּאֱסַר מִן הַמַּאֲכָלוֹת, וְיֶאֱסֹר הַנִּשּׂוּאִין יוֹתֵר עַל מַה שֶּׁנֶּאֱסַר מִן הַבִּיאוֹת, וְיִתֵּן כָּל מָמוֹנוֹ לַעֲנִיִּים אוֹ לְהֶקְדֵּשׁ יוֹתֵר עַל מַה שֶׁיֵּשׁ בַּתּוֹרָה מִן הַצְּדָקָה וְהַהֶקְדֵּשׁוֹת וְהָעֲרָכִין הֲרֵי זֶה עוֹשֶׂה מַעֲשֶׂה רָע וְהוּא אֵינוֹ יוֹדֵעַ שֶׁהוּא יִמָּצֵא בְּקָצֶה הָאֶחָד וְיֵצֵא מִן הַמִּצוּעַ לְגַמְרֵי.

וְיֵשׁ לַחֲכָמִים בָּעִנְיָן זֶה דְּבָרִים שֶׁלֹּא רָאִיתִי מֵעוֹלָם יוֹתֵר נִפְלָאִים מֵהֶם, וְהוּא בַּגְּמָרָא דִּבְנֵי מַעֲרָבָא בַּתִּשִׁיעִי דִנְדָרִים (הלכה א') דִּבְּרוּ בִּגְנוּת הַמְחַיְּבִין אֶת עַצְמָם שְׁבוּעוֹת וּנְדָרִים עַד שֶׁנִּשְׁאָרִים כְּמוֹ אֲסִירִים, וְשָׁם אָמְרוּ לְשׁוֹן זֶה, "אָמַר רַב אִידִי בְּשֵׁם רַבִּי יִצְחָק, לֹא דַיֶּךָ בְּמַה שֶׁאָסְרָה לְךָ תּוֹרָה אֶלָּא שֶׁאַתָּה אוֹסֵר

In fact, our Sages said the most wondrous thing I have ever seen about this very matter in the ninth chapter of *Nedarim* in the Jerusalem Talmud. They derided people who were for all intents and purposes imprisoning themselves with their self-imposed oaths [to forbid themselves even more things than the Torah itself forbids] by saying, "Rabbi Idi said in the name of Rabbi Yitzchak, 'Has the Torah not already forbidden enough that you have to forbid yet other things?'" (Je-

---

valuation — An amount of money, based upon the contributor's own "market value," that he would vow to contribute to the Holy Temple.

rusalem Talmud, *Nedarim* 9:1). And that is exactly what we have been referring to when it comes to being balanced rather than excessive or insufficient.

10. Thus, it is clear from what we have said in this chapter* that it is proper to favor balanced actions and to only resort to an extreme in order to heal oneself or to counterbalance another, opposite extreme.

[Be] like the medical expert who, if he saw in himself even a small symptom he would not ignore it or allow the illness to take hold to the point where he would need the strongest medicines available, or if he knew that one of his organs is weak, he would watch over it constantly and avoid things that would harm it and favor things that would either help treat it or prevent it from getting weaker yet.

It is likewise important for the healthy individual* to constantly

עָלֶיךָ דְּבָרִים אֲחֵרִים," וְזֶהוּ הָעִנְיָן שֶׁהִזְכַּרְנוּהוּ בְּדִיּוּק בְּלִי תּוֹסֶפֶת וְלֹא חִסָּרוֹן.

י. הִנֵּה נִתְבָּאֵר מִכָּל מַה שֶּׁאָמַרְנוּ בְּפֶרֶק זֶה, שֶׁכְּלְפֵּי הַמַּעֲשִׂים הַמְמֻצָּעִים רָאוּי לְהִתְכַּוֵּן, וְשֶׁאֵין רָאוּי לָצֵאת מֵהֶם לְשׁוּם קָצֶה מִשְׁתֵּי הַקְּצָווֹת, אֶלָּא עַל דֶּרֶךְ הָרְפוּי וְהַהַקְבָּלָה בַּדָּבָר הַנֶּגְדִּי.

כְּמוֹ שֶׁהָאָדָם הַבָּקִי בִּמְלֶאכֶת הָרְפוּאָה, אִם רָאָה שֶׁמִּזְגוֹ נִשְׁתַּנָּה שִׁנּוּי מוּעָט לֹא יִתְעַלֵּם מִכָּךְ וְלֹא יַנִּיחַ אֶת הַמַּחֲלָה לְהִתְחַזֵּק בּוֹ עַד שֶׁיִּצְטָרֵךְ לְרִפּוּי חָזָק בְּתַכְלִית. וְכֵן אִם יֵדַע שֶׁאֵיזֶה אֵבֶר מֵאֶבְרֵי גוּפוֹ חָלוּשׁ, שׁוֹמֵר עָלָיו תָּמִיד וּמִתְרַחֵק מִדְּבָרִים הַמַּזִּיקִים לוֹ, וּמְבַקֵּשׁ מַה שֶׁיּוֹעִיל לוֹ כְּדֵי שֶׁיַּבְרִיא אוֹתוֹ הָאֵבֶר אוֹ כְּדֵי שֶׁלֹּא יוֹסִיף חֻלְשָׁה.

כַּךְ הָאָדָם הַשָּׁלֵם רָאוּי לוֹ לְבַקֵּר מִדּוֹתָיו תָּמִיד, וְיִשְׁקוֹל מַעֲשָׂיו, וְיִבְחוֹן תְּכוּנוֹת נַפְשׁוֹ יוֹם יוֹם, וְכָל זְמַן שֶׁיִּרְאֶה נַפְשׁוֹ נוֹטֶה כְּלַפֵּי קָצֶה מִן הַקְּצָווֹת, יָחִישׁ אֶת הָרְפוּי, וְאַל יַנִּיחַ לַתְּכוּנוֹת הָרָעוֹת לְהִתְחַזֵּק בַּחֲזְרוֹ עַל מַעֲשֶׂה רַע כַּמָּה פְעָמִים, כְּמוֹ שֶׁבֵּאַרְנוּ. וְכֵן

scrutinize his character, to weigh his actions, and to gauge his disposition every single day and to quickly treat himself as soon as he notices himself inclining toward one extreme or another, rather than allowing bad qualities to develop by repeating a wrongful deed again and again, as we explained. Also, one should be conscious of his per-

---

...in this chapter — See section 6 above.

the healthy individual — The original can also be worded as the "whole" or "perfect" individual. However, we've

chosen "healthy" here to maintain the analogy. Note, though, that the term "healthy" would refer here to one's moral or spiritual health, while in the instance just before this, it referred to one's physical health.

sonal flaws and always try to treat them, as we said earlier, since in any case everyone has his flaws.*

As the philosophers already put it: "It would be hard and hardly likely to find someone who by nature possesses all the virtuous character traits and intellectual traits." But the following [sorts of] things were said many times over in the books of the prophets: "Indeed, He does not trust His servants* [and accuses His angels of folly]" (Job 4:18); "What can prove mortal man righteous to God? How can any mortal born of woman be

יָשִׂים נֶגֶד עֵינָיו אֶת הַמִּדָּה הַגְּרוּעָה שֶׁבּוֹ, וְיִשְׁתַּדֵּל לְרַפְּאֹתָהּ תָּמִיד, כְּמוֹ שֶׁהִקְדַּמְנוּ, כֵּיוָן שֶׁעַל כָּל פָּנִים יֵשׁ לְכָל אָדָם מִגְּרָעוֹת.

לְפִי שֶׁכְּבָר אָמְרוּ הַפִּילוֹסוֹפִים, שֶׁקָּשֶׁה וְרָחוֹק שֶׁיִּמָּצֵא מִי שֶׁהוּא מֻטְבָּעוֹ מְעֻתָּד לְכָל הַמַּעֲלוֹת הַמִּדּוֹתִיּוֹת וְהַהֶגְיוֹנִיּוֹת. אֲבָל בְּסִפְרֵי הַנְּבִיאִים הֲרֵי דֻבַּר זֶה בָּהֶם הַרְבֵּה, אָמַר (אִיּוֹב ד' י"ח), "הֵן בַּעֲבָדָיו לֹא יַאֲמִין וְכוּ'," (שם כ"ה ד') "וּמַה יִּצְדַּק אֱנוֹשׁ עִם קֵל וּמַה יִּזְכֶּה יְלוּד אִשָּׁה," וּשְׁלֹמֹה אָמַר בְּהֶחְלֵט (קהלת ז' כ'), "כִּי אָדָם אֵין צַדִּיק בָּאָרֶץ אֲשֶׁר יַעֲשֶׂה טוֹב וְלֹא יֶחֱטָא."

pure?" (ibid. 25:4); and as Solomon said outright, "For there is no one so righteous upon this earth who does [only] good and does not sin"* (Ecclesiastes 7:20).

...since everyone has his flaws — In short, we'd do well to develop a deep and all-inclusive self-awareness. Most of us simply don't strive for that, though, largely because the truth hurts. For indeed the sort of introspection called for only proves how imperfect we are, and how wrong and petty we can be.

Yet we need to suffer the psychic ache and trauma of self-revelation if we're ever to reach our potential, much the way a patient would have to suffer the physical ache and trauma of surgery to be well.[27]

...He does not trust His servants — That is to say that if God finds that He cannot trust His own Heavenly servants and angels to be free of folly and personal error, how dare we

assume that we are faultless?

...does not sin — Also see the statement in section 4 above, that "no one is born with an inherently virtuous or flawed character," and the opening statement in chapter 8 which reads, "It is not possible for man to be born either inherently lofty or inherently flawed, just as it is impossible for him to be born instinctively adept at a trade."

In chapter 6 below we'll return to the difference between the views of the philosophers (i.e., Aristotle and his adherents) that while it is "hard and hardly likely to find someone who by nature possesses all the virtuous intellectual and character traits," it is nonetheless not impossible, and Rambam's view that it is in-

11. Nonetheless, as you know, God said to Moses, master of all earlier and later prophets, "Because you did not believe in Me [enough] to sanctify Me* [in the eyes of the people of Israel, you will not bring this congregation into the land that I have given them]" (Numbers 20:12); "[Aaron will be gathered to his people; he will not enter into the land which I have given to the people of Israel], because you [i.e., Moses and Aaron both] rebelled against My word [at the waters of Meribah]" (ibid. 20:24); and

יא. וְאַתָּה יוֹדֵעַ כִּי אֲדוֹן הָרִאשׁוֹנִים וְהָאַחֲרוֹנִים מֹשֶׁה רַבֵּינוּ, עָלָיו הַשָּׁלוֹם, כְּבָר אָמַר לוֹ ה' יִתְעַלֶּה (במדבר כ' י"ב), "יַעַן לֹא הֶאֱמַנְתֶּם בִּי לְהַקְדִּישֵׁנִי," (שם כ' כ"ד) "עַל אֲשֶׁר מְרִיתֶם אֶת פִּי," (דברים ל"ב נ"א) "עַל אֲשֶׁר לֹא קִדַּשְׁתֶּם."

כָּל זֶה וְחֵטְאוֹ, עָלָיו הַשָּׁלוֹם, הָיָה שֶׁנָּטָה כְּלַפֵּי אַחַת מִשְּׁתֵּי הַקְּצָווֹת מִמַּעֲלָה אַחַת מִן הַמַּעֲלוֹת הַמִּדּוֹתִיּוֹת, וְהִיא הַמְתִינוּת, כַּאֲשֶׁר נָטָה כְּלַפֵּי הַכַּעַס בְּאָמְרוֹ (במדבר כ' י'), "שִׁמְעוּ נָא הַמּוֹרִים," מִחָה ה' בּוֹ שֶׁאִישׁ כָּמוֹהוּ יִכְעַס בִּפְנֵי קְהַל יִשְׂרָאֵל בְּמָקוֹם שֶׁאֵין הַכַּעַס רָאוּי בּוֹ.

"[Because you sinned against Me before the people of Israel at the waters of Meribah-Kadesh, in the Zin Desert,] because you did not sanctify Me [in the midst of the people of Israel...you will not enter the land I am giving the people of Israel]" (Deuteronomy 32:51–52).

But what was his sin? He inclined toward an extreme of a particular personal virtue, composure, by expressing anger* and saying, "Listen now, you rebels! [Must we fetch you water from this rock?]" (Numbers 20:10). And God objected to the fact that a man like himself would express anger toward the congregation of Israel when it was inappropriate.

deed impossible to find such a person. The difference will prove to be significant.

Because you did not believe in Me... to sanctify Me — This section seems to depart from the flow of the chapter. Rambam even relates to that digression at the end, saying, "We have strayed from our intentions for this chapter, but...." Actually, the point of this section is to offer a

single, solitary exception to the statement made in the previous one, that "everyone has his flaws," since Moses will prove to have become flawless, despite appearances to the contrary. (See 7:4 below.)

expressing anger — That is to say, composure is the virtuous midway point between wrath and indifference. Moses expressed anger, which approaches (but doesn't reach) wrath.

For when someone of his caliber does something like this, he profanes God's Name. Because the people studied every move he made and everything he said, and learned from them, and hoped to merit true bliss both in this world and in the World to Come by [duplicating] them.* So how could he express anger, which is a bad thing to do, as we explained, and a product of a bad disposition?[28]

But God's remarks that Moses had "rebelled against [His] word" (Numbers 20:24) can only be explained thusly: Moses was not speaking to simple people or to people of low worth, but rather, to a people whose most humble of women were on par with [the prophet] Ezekiel the son of Buzzi, as our Sages pointed out.* They would examine everything he would say or do, and when they saw him grow angry, they said, "He certainly has no personal flaws. If he did not know that God was angry at us from asking for water and that we already angered Him, he [Moses] would not have expressed anger at us."

In fact, though, God *did not* express anger or wrath when He spoke to Moses about this incident. He merely said, "Take the staff [and gather the assembly together, both you and Aaron, your brother, and speak to the rock before their eyes. It will issue water, and you will

וּכְגוֹן זֶה, בְּיַחַס לְאוֹתוֹ הָאָדָם חִלּוּל ה', לְפִי שֶׁכָּל תְּנוּעוֹתָיו וּדְבָרָיו כּוּלָם לְמֵדִים מֵהֶם, וּבָהֶם מְקֻוִּים לִזְכּוֹת לְאוֹשֶׁר הָעוֹלָם הַזֶּה וְהַבָּא, וְהֵיאַךְ יָבוֹא מִמֶּנּוּ הַכַּעַס וְהוּא מִמַּעֲשֵׂה הָרָע, כְּמוֹ שֶׁבֵּאַרְנוּ, וְלֹא יָבֹא אֶלָּא מִתְּכוּנָה רָעָה מִתְּכוּנוֹת הַנֶּפֶשׁ.

אֲבָל אָמְרוּ בְּעִנְיָן זֶה, "מְרִיתֶם פִּי" הוּא כְּמוֹ שֶׁאֲבָאֵר, וְהוּא, שֶׁהוּא לֹא הָיָה מְדַבֵּר עִם הֲמוֹנִיִּים וְלֹא עִם מִי שֶׁאֵין לוֹ מַעֲלָה, אֶלָּא עִם אֲנָשִׁים אֲשֶׁר הַקְּטַנָּה שֶׁבִּנְשֵׁיהֶם כִּיחֶזְקֵאל בֶּן בּוּזִי, כְּמוֹ שֶׁהִזְכִּירוּ חֲכָמִים (מכילתא פרשת בשלח לפסוק "זֶה קֵלִי וְאַנְוֵהוּ"), וְכָל מַה שֶּׁיֹּאמַר אוֹ יַעֲשֶׂה בּוֹחֲנִים אוֹתוֹ, וְכַאֲשֶׁר רָאוּהוּ שֶׁכָּעַס, אָמְרוּ, שֶׁהוּא עָלָיו הַשָּׁלוֹם אֵינוֹ מֵאוֹתָם שֶׁיֵּשׁ לָהֶם מִגְרַעַת מִדּוֹתִית, וְלוּלֵא שֶׁיָּדַע שֶׁה' הִתְאַנַּף עָלֵינוּ בִּשְׁאֵלַת הַמַּיִם וְשֶׁאָנוּ כְּבָר הִכְעַסְנוּ לְפָנָיו יִתְעַלֶּה לֹא הָיָה כּוֹעֵס.

וְלֹא מָצָאנוּ לְה' יִתְעַלֶּה בְּדִבְּרוֹ עִמּוֹ בְּעִנְיָן זֶה כַּעַס וְלֹא רֹגֶז, אֶלָּא אָמַר לוֹ (במדבר כ' ח') "קַח אֶת הַמַּטֶּה וְכוּ'

---

by [duplicating] them — That is, they hoped to learn from his example.

...as our Sages pointed out — We're

taught that "a mere handmaid saw more at the [splitting of the Red] Sea than Ezekial the son of Buzzi the Kohen and all the other prophets ever saw" (*Mechilta, Beshalach*).

thus bring them water out of the rock,] and give the congregation and their animals something to drink" (Numbers 20:8).

We have strayed from our intentions for this chapter, but we have thus solved a major difficulty in the Torah which much has been said about, and in the context of which it has often been asked, "What sin did he commit, anyway?" Compare what we have said about this to what others have said, and let the truth have its way.

I will return now to my original point.

12. If a person would weigh his actions all the time and strive for balance, he will become a person of the very highest caliber.* He will thus draw close to God and satisfy His wishes, for this is the most perfect form of divine service.

As our Sages, of blessed memory, explained this matter, "Whoever calculates his ways will merit to see the salvation of the Holy One, blessed is He, as it is said, 'I will show God's salvation to him who sets (v'sam) his way aright' (Psalms 50:23). Rather than read v'sam ('who sets'), read v'sham ('who calculates')" (Sotah 5b); and shuma refers to evaluation and appraisal.* And this is exactly what we have explained in this chapter [about everything being balanced.]29

וְהִשְׁקִיתָ אֶת הָעֵדָה וְאֶת בְּעִירָם."

וּכְבָר יָצָאנוּ מֵעִנְיָן הַפֶּרֶק אֶלָּא שֶׁתֵּירַצְנוּ קוּשְׁיָא גְּדוֹלָה מֵקוּשְׁיוֹת הַתּוֹרָה, שֶׁרַבִּים דִּבְּרוּ בָזֶה, וְרַבִּים שׁוֹאֲלִים מַה הוּא הַחֵטְא שֶׁחָטָא, וְהִשְׁוֵה מַה שֶּׁאָמַרְנוּ אֲנַחְנוּ בָזֶה וּמַה שֶׁאָמְרוּ בוֹ אֲחֵרִים וְהָאֱמֶת יוֹרֶה דַרְכּוֹ. וְאֶחְזֹר לְעִנְיָנִי.

יב. וְאִם הָיָה הָאָדָם שׁוֹקֵל אֶת מַעֲשָׂיו תָּמִיד, וּמִתְכַּוֵּן לְמֻצַּע הֲרֵי יִהְיֶה בְּמַעֲלָה הָרָמָה בְּיוֹתֵר מִמַּעֲלוֹת הָאָדָם, וּבְכָךְ יִתְקָרֵב לִפְנֵי ה', וְיַשִּׂיג אֶת רְצוֹנוֹ, וְזוֹ הִיא דֶּרֶךְ הָעֲבוֹדָה הַשְּׁלֵמָה בְּיוֹתֵר.

וּכְבָר הִזְכִּירוּ חֲכָמִים, ז"ל, עִנְיָן זֶה, וְזֶה לְשׁוֹנָם בּוֹ, אָמְרוּ (סוטה ה:), "כָּל הַשָּׂם אוֹרְחוֹתָיו זוֹכֶה וְרוֹאֶה בִּישׁוּעָתוֹ שֶׁל הַקָּדוֹשׁ בָּרוּךְ הוּא, שֶׁנֶּאֱמַר (תהלים נ' כ"ג), וְשָׁם דֶּרֶךְ אַרְאֶנּוּ בְּיֵשַׁע אֱלֹקִים אַל תִּקְרֵי וְשָׂם אֶלָּא וְשָׁם," וְשׁוּמָא הוּא הַשִּׁעוּר וְהַהַעֲרָכָה. זֶהוּ הָעִנְיָן אֲשֶׁר בֵּאַרְנוּ בְּכָל הַפֶּרֶק הַזֶּה.

...the very highest caliber — Rambam's implication seems to be that such an individual would "be a person of the very highest caliber," even if he doesn't achieve that balance, and that it's the process as well as the humility and sensitivity involved that matters so.

...evaluation and appraisal — That is, the verse "I will show God's salvation to him who sets his way aright" can legitimately be read, "I will show God's salvation to him who calculates his way (and thus sets it) aright."

This concludes what we deem should be said about this.

זֶהוּ מַה שֶּׁרָאִינוּ שֶׁצָּרִיךְ בְּעִנְיָן זֶה.

SYNOPSIS

1. *Good deeds lie midway between two extreme ones; virtuous qualities lie midway between two extreme qualities; and specific qualities tend to foster specific deeds.*

2. *For example, temperance, which is a balanced trait, is a product of a virtuous quality and is good; indulgence and asceticism (the two polar opposite extremes of temperance) are bad. The same goes for other balanced versus extreme traits like generosity, as opposed to stinginess and extravagance; courage, as opposed to daring and cowardice; happiness, as opposed to brashness and dullness; humility, as opposed to arrogance and self-abasement; earnestness, as opposed to boastfulness and meekness; contentment, as opposed to indulgence and sloth; composure, as opposed to short-temperedness and apathy; shamefacedness, as opposed to audacity and bashfulness; and the like.*

3. *People often mistakenly consider character extremes to be good. They might consider daring people to be brave, indifferent people to be tolerant, lazy people to be content, and lethargic people to be temperate; and they might admire extravagant and boastful people. But that is wrong, because we're to strive for balance in our behavior. Nonetheless, it is important to understand that virtues and flaws only affix themselves onto us when we repeat the behavior patterns associated with them again and again.*

4. *Since no one is born with an inherently and utterly virtuous or flawed character, it is important to tend to your character much the way you would tend to your body when it goes off-kilter. For when the body is indeed off kilter, we reverse its course until it returns to a state of equilibrium, where we then allow it to stay. We should do that when it comes to our character, as well. So if one is self-abnegating, for example, he would be encouraged to be profligate until he has expunged the trait of self-abnegation, at which point he would be encouraged to allow himself some amenities. While if one is profligate, he would be encouraged to be somewhat self-abnegating, but he would not be encouraged to go to the other extreme (profligacy) quite as much in the process as he would be if he had been self-abnegating.*

5. As such, since it is easier to go from profligacy to merely allowing oneself some amenities than it is to go from utter self-denial to profligacy, just as it is easier to go from asceticism to temperance than it is to go from indulgence to temperance, we would thus have an indulgent person behave ascetically longer than we would have an ascetic be indulgent in the process of rectifying their personalities. We would have a cowardly person act daringly longer than we would have a daring person act cowardly; and we would have a meek person be boastful longer than we would have a boastful person act meekly.

6. The pious, however, wouldn't settle for equal balance. They would tend toward one extreme or another, depending on circumstances, in order to safeguard themselves against sin. They would be somewhat more ascetic than temperate; somewhat more daring than courageous; somewhat more earnest than boastful; somewhat more humble than meek, etc. Some pious individuals even fasted, awoke in the middle of the night to pray and study, avoided meat and wine and the like, but only for the sake of their moral wellbeing when those around them were corrupt, in which case, they feared being adversely affected.

7. Now, when fools who knew nothing of why the pious were doing what they did saw those individuals acting that way, they set out to do the same, assuming that this was how a person would draw close to God. But rather than doing good, they were actually doing harm.

8. The Torah means for us to live a normal life: to eat, drink, and have relations as permitted, in moderation; to live in society, and to wear standard clothing. It frowns upon extremes, and encourages us to achieve intellectual and personal virtues.

9. Hence, if one is foolish enough to believe that he should deny himself all pleasure in order to discipline himself, he is wrong. For what the Torah meant for us to do was to systematically withdraw from indulgence in order to implant the traits of temperance, generosity, and shamefacedness, as well as to discourage anger and bashfulness.

10. Therefore, one should always favor balanced actions over extreme ones, other than to heal himself. One should be introspective and self-aware. One should be like someone who senses he is becoming ill and remains constantly alert to his condition, making sure it

isn't deteriorating, who avoids anything that would do him harm and favors things that would make him well. Which is to say, one should try to rectify his flaws, for none of us are without them.

11. *In fact, even Moses wasn't without his flaws. He became angry at one point and referred to the Jewish nation as "rebels," when this was inappropriate. He thus profaned God's name and set a bad example for the rest of the nation (since they watched his every move and listened to everything he said, in order to learn from him), and he caused them to draw false conclusions about God's intentions.*

12. *Therefore, one should always judge his own actions and strive for balance in them, and then he will be a person of high caliber, and he will draw close to God and satisfy His wishes, and thus serve Him in the best of ways.*

5

בהפעלת כחות הנפש כלפי מטרה אחת

USING ALL OF ONE'S PERSONAL
CAPACITIES TO ONE END

THE PREVIOUS CHAPTER SPELLED OUT the gist of Rambam's vision of true,
Jewish piety. But there is yet another aspect of such piety, and that is that one
should engage in things of this world with the express end of using them as a
means of comprehending God. This will be discussed in the chapter below.

We can indeed live in the world, as we indicated in the last chapter, and
pursue a modicum of personal pleasure — but it should be done with the intent
to stay content and well enough to enjoy wisdom as a consequence. We can
likewise accumulate wealth — as long as we do that in order to develop virtues,
maintain our well-being, live long enough to comprehend God, and succeed
spiritually. It would thus also be all right to study secular literature in order
to sharpen one's mind enough to meet his spiritual goal. Nonetheless, pursuing
pleasure or even health for their own sakes is animal-like.

As such, we're told, we would do well to always remember that we are to use
all our personal capacities to understand God, to occupy ourselves with things
that encourage virtues, and to weigh everything in light of whether it will lead
to that goal or not.

Though only rare individuals can follow such a path fully — and such individuals are nearly on par with the prophets — Rambam underscores the fact
that we're all nonetheless bidden to do so.

1. It is proper for a person to subordinate all of his personal capacities to reason, the way we described in the previous chapter,* and to place a single goal before his eyes, which is to comprehend God Almighty as much as a human being can.*[1,2]

א. רָאוּי לְאָדָם לְשַׁעְבֵּד כָּל כֹּחוֹת נַפְשׁוֹ עַל פִּי הַמַּחֲשָׁבָה, כְּפִי שֶׁהִקְדַּמְנוּ בַּפֶּרֶק שֶׁלְּפָנֵי זֶה, וְיָשִׂים נֶגֶד עֵינָיו תַּכְלִית אַחַת, וְהִיא הַשָּׂגַת ה' יִתְהַדֵּר וְיִתְרוֹמֵם, כְּפִי יְכוֹלֶת הָאָדָם.

כְּלוֹמַר שֶׁיֵּדַע אוֹתוֹ, וְיָשִׂים כָּל פְּעֻלּוֹתָיו, תְּנוּעוֹתָיו, וּתְנוּחוֹתָיו, וְכָל

This is to say, one should know Him and direct all his actions, move-

---

...the way we described in the previous chapter — The point is that it's important to consciously and voluntarily defer to the idea of a balanced character (except when otherwise called for, as was discussed in chapter 4). For if we're ever to be truly pious, we're called upon to take self in hand where possible and set it aright, rather than settle for what's given.

...as much as a human being can — This chapter seems to interrupt the natural progression from the previous one (chapter 4) to the next (chapter 6). Rambam argues toward the end of chapter 4 that it is important to always be introspective and to keep alert enough to catch sight of one's faults and to rectify them — "since everyone has his flaws." He also cited other sources there that point out our flawed nature, as well. Yet he likewise indicated there that the philosophers (i.e., Aristotle and his adherents) hold that, while "it would be hard and hardly likely to find anyone with all the virtuous intellectual and character traits" — it nonetheless wouldn't be impossible. These two opposing worldviews will not be

explained until chapter 6, so what is the point of this chapter?

Essentially, this chapter focuses on the idea that we should use things of this world as a means of comprehending God. Apparently, then, this chapter is meant to underscore Rambam's statement at the very end of chapter 4, that the individual who is indeed introspective and always tries to rectify his ways will "be a person of the very highest caliber" and will in fact "draw close to God," since he will have engaged in "*the* most perfect form of divine service." This chapter, then, expands upon the idea of drawing close to God.

What is perhaps most significant about this chapter (as we'll see in sections 4 and 5 below) is that it focuses upon the uniquely *Jewish* way of serving God piously but on a more mundane level (just as the fourth chapter focused upon the uniquely Jewish perspective of what constitutes a pious disposition).

As such, we find that chapters 4, 5, and 6 each contrast Jewish and non-Jewish views of piety from a different perspective. As we'll see there, chapter 6 does it by focusing on the Jewish view that piety is achieved by fulfilling God's mitzvot as well as by being moral.

ments,* and utterances to that end, so that none of his actions is arbitrary — that is, not leading to this goal.

So, for example, when one eats, drinks, sleeps, cohabits, awakes, moves about, or rests, his only aim should be his health. But let the goal in being healthy is to remain robust* and well enough to acquire the knowledge and the personal and intellectual virtues that one needs to reach that goal.*

2. According to this, one's goals should not simply be to enjoy himself, to the point where he chooses only appetizing foods, drinks, and the like, but rather one

דְּבָרָיו, מוֹבִילִים אֶל הַתַּכְלִית הַזּוֹ, עַד שֶׁלֹּא תְהֵא בִּפְעֻלּוֹתָיו שׁוּם פְּעוּלָה לְבַטָּלָה כְּלַל, כְּלוֹמַר, פְּעוּלָה שֶׁאֵינָהּ מוֹבִילָה אֶל הַתַּכְלִית הַזֹּאת.

הַמָּשָׁל בָּזֶה, שֶׁיָּשִׂים הַכַּוָּנָה בַּאֲכִילָתוֹ וּשְׁתִיָּתוֹ וּשְׁנָתוֹ וְתַשְׁמִישׁוֹ וִיקִיצָתוֹ וּתְנוּעָתוֹ וּתְנוּחָתוֹ בְּרִיאוּת גּוּפוֹ בִּלְבָד, וְהַמַּטָּרָה בִּבְרִיאוּת גּוּפוֹ, כְּדֵי שֶׁתִּמְצָא הַנֶּפֶשׁ אֶת כֵּלֶיהָ בְּרִיאִים וּשְׁלֵמִים שֶׁתִּשְׁתַּמֵּשׁ בָּהֶם בַּלִּמּוּדִים וּקְנִיַּת הַמַּעֲלוֹת הַמִּדּוֹתִיּוֹת וְהַהֶגְיוֹנִיּוֹת, כְּדֵי שֶׁיַּגִּיעַ לְאוֹתָהּ הַתַּכְלִית.

ב. וּלְפִי דֶרֶךְ זוֹ לֹא תְהֵא מַטָּרָתוֹ אָז הַהֲנָאָה בִּלְבָד עַד שֶׁיִּבְחַר מִן הַמַּאֲכָל וְהַמִּשְׁתֶּה אֶת הַיּוֹתֵר עָרֵב, וְכֵן בִּשְׁאָר

---

movements — Lit., all his movements and rests.

to remain robust — Lit., that the *nefesh* should find its functions to be robust....

...to reach that goal — This section can be read two different ways: either from the perspective of the individual pursuing piety, or from our own.

Someone striving for piety might very well be inclined toward denying himself food, drink, intercourse, sleep, and the like to an extreme degree, in the hopes of achieving greater closeness to God. But as Rambam indicated in the previous chapter, that would be a mistake.

Instead, such a person should in fact "eat, drink, sleep, cohabits, awake, move about, [and] rest" to

the proper degree. Nonetheless, he should take comfort from the fact that he would thus achieve health — the kind of physical and spiritual health necessary "to acquire the knowledge and...virtues [he would] need to reach that goal" — the goal of achieving piety and drawing close to God. In contrast, those of us who perhaps wouldn't be inclined toward denying ourselves pleasures, who would in fact often indulge ourselves, would have to keep in mind the fact that we are indeed to "eat, drink, sleep, have intercourse, awake, move about, or rest" in moderation, and only so as "to remain robust and well enough to acquire the knowledge and the personal and intellectual virtues [we would] need to reach that goal" — the goal of comprehending God.[3]

should strive for what is most edifying. If it happens to be gratifying, too, so be it; and if it happens not to be, that does not matter. [Also], one should favor more appetizing things for medical reasons, for example if his appetite was weak he could whet it with well-seasoned and sweet foods; or if one suffers from melancholia* he could ward it off by listening to poems and music, by strolling in gardens and among fine buildings, or by sitting beside beautiful works of art and the like, in order to settle his spirit* and ward off his melancholia.*

הַהַנְהָגוֹת, אֶלָּא יְתַכַּוֵּן לְמַה שֶׁיּוֹתֵר
מוֹעִיל, וְאִם יִזְדַּמֵּן שֶׁיְּהֵא עָרֵב הֲרֵי טוֹב
וְאִם יִזְדַּמֵּן שֶׁיְּהֵא בִּלְתִּי עָרֵב אֵין בְּכָךְ
כְּלוּם אוֹ שֶׁיִּתְכַּוֵּן לְיוֹתֵר עָרֵב בְּהֶתְאֵם
לְמַדַּע הָרְפוּאִי, כְּגוֹן שֶׁנֶּחְלְשָׁה תַּאֲוָתוֹ
לְמַאֲכָל אָז יְעוֹרְרָהּ בְּמַאֲכָלֵי תַּאֲוָה
הָעֲרֵבִים וְהַמְּתוּבָּלִים. וְכֵן אִם גָּבְרָה
עָלָיו מָרָה הַשְּׁחוֹרָה יְסִירֶנָּה בִּשְׁמִיעַת
שִׁירִים וּמִינֵי נְגִינוֹת, וּבְטִיּוּל בְּגַנּוֹת
וּבִנְיָנֵי פְּאֵר, וִישִׁיבָה עִם צוּרוֹת נָאוֹת,
וְכַיּוֹצֵא בָזֶה מִמַּה שֶׁמְיַשֵּׁב אֶת הַנֶּפֶשׁ
וּמֵסִיר שַׁעֲמוּם הַמָּרָה הַשְּׁחוֹרָה
מִמֶּנָּה.

One's goal in all this though, should be his physical [and emotional] well-being; and his ultimate reason to be well should be to acquire knowledge.*

וְיִתְכַּוֵּן בְּכָל זֶה לְהַבְרוֹת אֶת גּוּפוֹ,
וְתַכְלִית בְּרִיאוּת גּוּפוֹ כְּדֵי שֶׁיֵּדַע.

---

suffers from melancholia — Literally, "if he is overtaken by the humor of black bile." See our discussion in supplementary note 8 to chapter 4 about medieval physiology, as well as about inborn prods to do or refrain from doing certain things.

his spirit — Lit., his *nefesh*. This is one of the few instances in which we translate *nefesh* as "spirit," since it fits the context so well.

ward off his melancholia — We in modernity seem to favor things like good food, poetry, music, leisurely strolls in gardens or museums, and so on very much. Are we more prone to anxiety and gloom (i.e., do we need to "settle our spirit" and "ward off

melancholy" more) than our ancestors were? And are we then justified in expending so much time, money, and energy on those kinds of things? Or do we have a lower anxiety and angst threshold than they did, perhaps; and pamper ourselves unnecessarily or even detrimentally?

The truth be known, either argument has its merits. And we would have to be greater sages than we are to pass judgment. Still, the reader would do well to consider how few of us resort to such "treatments," if you will, and then actually return to the essential task at hand — knowing and serving God — once we supposedly achieve equilibrium.

knowledge — I.e., knowledge of God.

Likewise, one's goal in encouraging himself to accrue money should be to use it to acquire edifying things, to maintain his well-being, and to extend his life long enough to comprehend God and know as much about Him as he can.*

וְכֵן כַּאֲשֶׁר יִתְעוֹרֵר וְיִתְעַסֵּק בִּרְכִישַׁת נְכָסִים, תִּהְיֶה מַטָּרָתוֹ בְּקִבּוּצוֹ כְּדֵי שֶׁיּוֹצִיאָנּוּ בִּדְבָרִים הַנַּעֲלִים, וְשֶׁיִּהְיֶה מָצוּי לְקִיּוּם גּוּפוֹ וְהַתְמָדַת מְצִיאוּתוֹ כְּדֵי שֶׁיַּשִּׂיג וְיֵדַע אֶת ה' כְּפִי שֶׁאֶפְשָׁר לָדַעַת.

In point of fact, the practice of medicine has a very large role in [acquiring personal and intellectual] virtues, knowing God, and comprehending what is true bliss.*

וּלְפִי דֶּרֶךְ זוֹ יִהְיֶה לִמְלֶאכֶת הָרְפוּאָה עִנְיָן רַב מְאֹד בְּמַעֲלוֹת וּבִידִיעַת ה', וּבְהַשָּׂגַת הָאוֹשֶׁר הָאֲמִתִּי, וְיִהְיֶה לִמּוּדָהּ וְהַהִתְעַסְּקוּת בָּהּ עֲבוֹדָה מִן

...to know as much about Him as he can — What this all comes to at bottom is following the dictates of reason rather than instinct or predisposition, as Rambam said. Yet while we all know in our heart the wisdom of all of this, instincts still tend to have their way, and we often allow our better judgment to be swayed.

Rambam's point seems to be, then, that the only solution would be to "place a single goal before one's eyes...to comprehend God Almighty," which is to say, to so preoccupy yourself with the all-consuming aim of knowing God, that you'd be far too busy to lapse, far too enchanted by your inquiries to spare the time for inanities.

Rambam seems to be addressing himself to those souls who are indeed pursuing piety, rather than to us (see our note above ["to reach that goal"]). For most of us aren't driven or inspired to know God. As Rambam himself indicates in section 6 below, setting one's sights on knowing God to the exclusion of everything else is "a very high

and formidable level that few attain." In fact, he places people who'd engage in that "on par with the prophets" — i.e., he implies that their pursuit of piety has succeeded to such a degree that they're prepared to undertake the pursuit of prophecy.

The rest of us, though, can take comfort in the fact that the Torah indeed allows us well-meaning, religious though perhaps impious individuals our food, drink, and the like. For as we saw in 4:8 above,[1] God "wants us to live normally and to follow a balanced path: to eat and drink what is permissible in balanced measure..." in our pursuit of less-than-pious religiousness.

Nevertheless, we're expected to sanctify those urges by channeling them into the service of God as best we can.[4]

...comprehending what is true bliss — That is to say, physicians and other such practitioners often find themselves in situations that can ennoble their character. Since they confront life and death regularly,

Studying and pursuing it is thus one of the greatest forms of [divine] service. It is not like weaving or carpentry [for example], because it enables us to put purpose into our actions and to make our actions truly human — things that foster virtues and [the realization of] many truths.

3. For someone who would go about eating appetizing, aromatic, and desirable foods that are [actually] harmful and can make a person seriously ill or even kill him is no different than an animal. This is not the behavior of a human being but rather that of a living creature who happens to be human, "like [one of] the beasts that perish" (Psalms 49:13).

His actions would only be human if he ate beneficial things and sometimes rejected pleasant things and ate unpleasant ones instead, in his pursuit of betterment. For that would be an act based on reason, which sets human behavior apart [from that of animals]. He'd likewise be behaving like a creature rather than a human if he cohabited whenever he wanted to, without giving thought to the harm or good it would do.*

In point of fact, everything one does should be done to better himself, as we said. But if his goal was to be merely healthy and free of

הַגְּדוֹלוֹת שֶׁבַּעֲבוֹדוֹת. וְלֹא תִהְיֶה אָז כְּמוֹ הָאֲרִיגָה וְהַנַּגָּרוּת, לְפִי שֶׁבָּה נְכַוֵּן אֶת פְּעוּלוֹתֵינוּ, וְיִהְיוּ פְּעוּלוֹתֵינוּ פְּעוּלוֹת אֱנוֹשִׁיּוֹת מְבִיאוֹת אֶל הַמַּעֲלוֹת וְאֶל הָאֲמִתִּיּוֹת.

ג. לְפִי שֶׁאָדָם אִם נִגַּשׁ וְאָכַל מַאֲכָל עָרֵב לַחֵיךְ רֵיחוֹ טוֹב מַאֲכָל תַּאֲוָה וְהוּא מַזִּיק וְאֶפְשָׁר שֶׁיְּהֵא גוֹרֵם לְמַחֲלָה מְסוּכֶּנֶת אוֹ אַף גַּם לְאִיבּוּד לְגַמְרֵי, הֲרֵי הוּא וְהַבְּהֵמָה שָׁוִין, וְאֵין זֶה מַעֲשֵׂה אָדָם מִצַּד הֱיוֹתוֹ אָדָם, אֶלָּא מַעֲשֵׂה אָדָם מִצַּד הֱיוֹתוֹ בַּעַל חַי (תהלים מ"ט י"ג), "נִמְשַׁל כַּבְּהֵמוֹת נִדְמוּ."

אֲבָל תִהְיֶה פְּעֻלָּתוֹ אֱנוֹשִׁית, אִם אָכַל אֶת הַמּוֹעִיל בִּלְבַד, וְאַף אִם יַנִּיחַ אֶת הָעָרֵב וְאוֹכֵל אֶת הַבִּלְתִּי עָרֵב לְפִי דְּרִישַׁת הַתּוֹעֶלֶת, וְזוֹ פְּעוּלָה בְּהִתְאֵם לַמַּחְשָׁבָה, וּבָזֶה יִבָּדֵל הָאָדָם בְּמַעֲשָׂיו מִזּוּלָתוֹ. וְכֵן אִם יִבְעַל כָּל זְמַן שֶׁיִּרְצֶה מִבְּלִי שֶׁיָּחוּשׁ לְהֶזֵק וּלְתוֹעֶלֶת, הֲרֵי פְּעוּלָתוֹ זוֹ מִצַּד הֱיוֹתוֹ בַּעַל חַי, וְלֹא מִצַּד הֱיוֹתוֹ אָדָם.

וְאֶפְשָׁר שֶׁתִּהְיֶה הַנְהָגָתוֹ תָּמִיד לְפִי הַתּוֹעֶלֶת, כְּמוֹ שֶׁבֵּאַרְנוּ, אֶלָּא שֶׁעוֹשֶׂה מַטָּרָתוֹ בְּרִיאוּת גּוּפוֹ וְשָׁלוֹמוֹ מִן

---

they can see the hand of God at work, and are consequently able to achieve a more spiritual perspective on life and to realize what truly matters and what doesn't.

...to the harm or good it would do — See supplementary note 17 to chapter 1, where we touched upon much of what is discussed here about essential humanity.

disease, one would not have acquired a virtue. For while one might prefer enjoying good health, another might prefer enjoying food or cohabitation* and neither of them have done anything toward achieving their true goal.*

The correct approach is to make the goal of everything one does his physical health and a long, sufficiently peaceful life, so as to remain sound enough* to pursue character and intellectual virtues without encumbrance.[5]

הַמַּחֲלוֹת בִּלְבַד, וְאֵין זוֹ מַעֲלָה, לְפִי שֶׁכְּמוֹ שֶׁהֶעְדִּיף זֶה הֲנָאַת הַבְּרִיאוּת, כֵּן הֶעְדִּיף הָאַחֵר הֲנָאַת הַמַּאֲכָל אוֹ הֲנָאַת הַתַּשְׁמִישׁ, וְכֻלָּם אֵין תַּכְלִית אֲמִתִּית לְמַעֲשֵׂיהֶם.

אֲבָל הַנָּכוֹן הוּא, שֶׁיַּעֲשֶׂה תַּכְלִית כָּל פְּעֻלּוֹתָיו בְּרִיאוּת גּוּפוֹ וְהַתְמָדַת מְצִיאוּתוֹ בְּשָׁלוֹם, כְּדֵי שֶׁיַּעַמְדוּ כְּלֵי כֹחוֹת הַנֶּפֶשׁ שֶׁהֵם אֶבְרֵי הַגּוּף שְׁלֵמִים, שֶׁאָז תִּשְׁתַּמֵּשׁ נַפְשׁוֹ בְּלִי מַעֲצוֹר בְּמַעֲלוֹת הַמִּדּוֹתִיּוֹת וְהַהֶגְיוֹנִיּוֹת.

ד. וְכֵן כָּל מַה שֶׁיִּלְמַד מִן הַלִּמּוּדִים וְהַמַּדָּעִים כָּל מַה שֶׁהוּא מֵהֶם דֶּרֶךְ לְאוֹתָהּ הַתַּכְלִית, הֲרֵי אֵין מַה לְדַבֵּר

4. The same goes for delving into [secular] areas of study or the sciences.* If doing so serves as a means to that end, then there is nothing to argue against. But when it comes to subjects that do not help one

---

For while one might prefer...food or cohabitation — That is, the former's pursuit of health would just be another sort of self-indulgence.

their true goal — I.e., a good and laudable goal that is rooted in what truly matters.

so as to remain sound enough — The text reads, "so that the agents of the *nefesh* — that is, all the organs of the body — will remain sound enough..."

or the sciences — ...as well as engaging in other things that are neither mitzvot nor sins per se, but sit somewhere in between.

For while there are 248 affirmative and proactive mitzvot (like giving charity, praying, doing favors, eating matzah on Passover, etc.) and 365 prohibitions (like not eating nonkosher food, not slandering, not lying, etc.), the great preponderance of the deeds of even the most pious and observant among us for the most part fall into neither category. They tend to fall within the category of the inner, heart-based acts of service of God that are depicted in *Chovot Ha-Levavot* (see that work's introduction, near end), since a great many of those 613 mitzvot play themselves out at particular times of the day or year, are only appropriate on specific occasions, or only come into effect when we're with others.

So the person in pursuit of piety would need to know what to do with the rest of his activities, so as to veer them toward the service of God, as well.

achieve that goal, like [solving arcane] problems in algebra, mechanics, *The Book of Cones* [a book of geometry written by the Greek mathematician Appolonius], engineering, or raising a lot of questions in geometry or hydraulics and the like — one's aim as far as they are concerned should be to sharpen his mind and to train himself in the art of theorems, so as to distinguish between valid and invalid proofs. For in fact, that will enable [a person] to comprehend God's essence.[6]

And the same is true for all a person's [secular, non-mitzvah] conversations. One should only speak about things that will either edify him or stave off personal or bodily harm; about learning virtues; or in praise of virtues or of great men, and in denunciation of flaws or wrongdoers.*

In fact, cursing flawed people* and denigrating their memories is an imperative and a virtue when one does it in order to lower them in

בו. וַאֲשֶׁר אֵין בּוֹ תּוֹעֶלֶת לְאוֹתָהּ הַמַּטָּרָה כְּגוֹן שְׁאֵלוֹת הָאַלְגְבְּרָה, וְהַהַשְׁנָאוֹת, וְסִפְרֵי הַתִּשְׁבֹּרֶת, וְהַתַּחְבּוּלוֹת, וְהָרִיבּוּי בִּשְׁאֵלוֹת הַהֶנְדָּסָה, וּמְשִׁיכַת הַכּוֹבְדִים וְהַרְבֵּה כָּאֵלֶּה, תִּהְיֶה הַמַּטָּרָה בָּהֶם חִדּוּד הַשֵּׂכֶל וְהֶרְגֵּל כֹּחַ הַהִגָּיוֹן לְדַרְכֵי הַהוֹכָחָה, כְּדֵי שֶׁתּוּשַׂג לְאָדָם תְּכוּנַת יְדִיעַת הַהֶיקֵּשׁ הַמּוֹפְתִי מִזּוּלָתוֹ, וְיִהְיֶה לּוֹ זֶה דֶרֶךְ שֶׁיַּגִּיעַ בּוֹ לִידִיעַת אֲמִתַּת מְצִיאוּתוֹ יִתְעַלֶּה.

וְכֵן דִּבְרֵי הָאָדָם כֻּלָּם לֹא יְזְדַּקֵּק לְדַבֵּר אֶלָּא בְּמַה שֶׁיָּבִיא לְעַצְמוֹ בּוֹ תּוֹעֶלֶת אוֹ יְסַלֵּק נֶזֶק מִנַּפְשׁוֹ אוֹ מִגּוּפוֹ, אוֹ בִּלְמִידַת מַעֲלָה, אוֹ בְּשֶׁבַח מַעֲלָה, אוֹ אָדָם גָדֹל, אוֹ בִגְנוּת מִגְרַעַת אוֹ רָשָׁע.

לְפִי שֶׁקְּלָלַת בַּעֲלֵי הַמִּגְרָעוֹת וְגִינוּי זִכְרָם אִם הָיְתָה הַמַּטָּרָה בְּכָךְ

The point is made here, though, that the study of science and other such things can either be very helpful, as when it supports one's understanding of God; very harmful, as when it questions God's ways in the world or His very existence; or very distracting, as when it does neither, but beguiles and distracts the mind. As such, it would do well to ensure that we only engage in such things when they help us achieve our ultimate goal.

...in denunciation of flaws or wrongdoers — That is to say, since we spend a great deal of our time speaking, it would do us well to know what to speak about, in our pursuit of piety.[7]

flawed people — I.e., very evil people, as opposed to the rest of us, who indeed have our flaws, but also have our good points.

the eyes of others who would then learn a lesson* and not do what those others did. Has not God Himself said, "[Do not do] the sorts of things done in the land of Egypt where you dwelt; and [do not do] the sorts of things done in the land of Canaan, [where I am bringing you]" (Leviticus 18:3)? He also recounted what the Sodomites did; and everywhere in Scripture where evil people are defamed and their memory is denigrated and righteous people are praised and glorified is all for the very same reason, as I have told you, to have people follow their ways and avoid the ways of wrongdoers.

5. In fact, when a person makes this* his goal he will [automatically, and as a direct consequence of his priorities] do and say a lot less; for a person whose goal is this will not be moved to adorn his walls with gold or hem his clothing with gold [trim, for example] — unless he thus intended to settle his *nefesh* in order that it become healthy and free of illness, and be clear and pure enough to grasp his studies.

For as our Sages said, "A beautiful home, a beautiful wife, beautiful dishes, and a well-made bed [are good] for scholars" (*Shabbat* 25b) because they "broaden a man's mind" (*Berachot* 57b).

לְהַשְׁפִּילָם בְּעֵינֵי בְנֵי אָדָם, כְּדֵי שֶׁיִּקְחוּ בָהֶם תּוֹכָחוֹת וְלֹא יַעֲשׂוּ כְּמַעֲשֵׂיהֶם הֲרֵי זֶה חוֹבָה וְזוֹ מַעֲלָה. הֲלֹא תִרְאֶה אָמְרוּ יִתְעַלֶּה (ויקרא י"ח ג'), "כְּמַעֲשֵׂה אֶרֶץ מִצְרַיִם אֲשֶׁר יְשַׁבְתֶּם בָּהּ וּכְמַעֲשֵׂה אֶרֶץ כְּנַעַן," וְסִפּוּר הַסְּדוֹמִים, וְכָל מַה שֶּׁבָּא בַמִּקְרָא בִּגְנוּת הָאֲנָשִׁים בַּעֲלֵי הָרָעוֹת וְהַמִּגְרָעוֹת, וְגִנּוּי זִכְרָם וְשֶׁבַח הַצַּדִּיקִים וְרוֹמְמוּתָם, אֵין הַכַּוָּנָה בָהֶם אֶלָּא כְּמוֹ שֶׁאָמַרְתִּי לְךָ, כְּדֵי שֶׁיֵּלְכוּ בְנֵי אָדָם בְּדַרְכָּם שֶׁל אֵלּוּ, וְיִתְרַחֲקוּ מִדַּרְכָּם שֶׁל אֵלֶּה.

ה. וְכַאֲשֶׁר יָשִׂים הָאָדָם מַטָרָתוֹ עִנְיָן זֶה יִהְיֶה פָנוּי מֵהַרְבֵּה מִמַּעֲשָׂיו וְיִתְמַעֵט מִדְּבָרָיו הַרְבֵּה מְאֹד, כִּי מִי שֶׁמַּטָרָתוֹ עִנְיָן זֶה לֹא יִתְעוֹרֵר לְקַשֵּׁט אֶת הַקִּירוֹת בְּזָהָב אוֹ לַעֲשׂוֹת סֶרֶט שֶׁל זָהָב בַּבֶּגֶד, זוּלָתִי אִם נִתְכַּוֵּן בְּדָבָר זֶה לְיַשֵּׁב אֶת נַפְשׁוֹ כְּדֵי שֶׁתַּבְרִיא וּלְסַלֵּק מִמֶּנָּה חָלְיָהּ, כְּדֵי שֶׁתִּהְיֶה בְהִירָה וְזַכָּה לְקַבֵּל אֶת הַמַּדָּעִים.

כְּדֶרֶךְ שֶׁאָמְרוּ (שבת כ"ה:), "דִּירָה נָאָה וְאִשָּׁה נָאָה וְכֵלִים נָאִים וּמִטָּה מוּצַעַת לְתַלְמִידֵי חֲכָמִים" (ברכות נ"ז:) "מַרְחִיבִים דַּעְתּוֹ שֶׁל אָדָם."

---

engaging in things that would ultimately lead to that.

For the *nefesh* grows tired and its thoughts become befuddled when it constantly delves into difficult things, much the way the body tires when one does heavy work — unless he rests and relaxes, and allows it to return to equilibrium.* In much the same way, the *nefesh* needs to rest and relax its senses, for example by gazing upon paintings and other attractive things until it is no longer fatigued.* In fact, "when the Sages would grow weary from studying, [they would joke]."* So it seems to me neither wrong nor unnecessary to decorate and adorn buildings, vessels, or clothing in such a context.*

לְפִי שֶׁהַנֶּפֶשׁ תִּלְאֶה וְתִטַּמְטֵם הַמַּחֲשָׁבָה בְּהַתְמָדַת רְאִיַּת דְּבָרִים הַקָּשִׁים, כְּמוֹ שֶׁיֶּחֱלֶה הַגּוּף בְּהִתְעַסְקוֹ בַּעֲבוֹדוֹת הַמְיַגְּעוֹת עַד שֶׁיָּנוּחַ וְיָנְפַשׁ, וְאָז יַחֲזוֹר לְאֵיתָנוֹ, כַּךְ גַּם הַנֶּפֶשׁ צְרִיכָה לְהִשָּׁקֵט וּלְהִתְעַסֵּק בְּנַחַת חוּשִׁים, כְּגוֹן הַהִסְתַּכְּלוּת בְּצִיּוּרִים וּדְבָרִים הַנָּאִים, עַד שֶׁתִּסְתַּלֵּק מִמֶּנָּה הַלֵּאוּת, כְּמוֹ שֶׁאָמְרוּ, "כִּי חַלְשֵׁי רַבָּנָן מִגִּרְסָא." וְחוֹשְׁשַׁנִי לוֹמַר כִּי לְפִי אוֹפַנִּים אֵלֶּה לֹא יִהְיוּ אֵלּוּ רָע, וְלֹא פְּעֻלּוֹת לְבַטָּלָה, כְּלוֹמַר, הַהִתְעוֹרְרוּת לְצִיּוּרִים וְכִיּוּרִים בְּבִנְיָנִים, בְּכֵלִים וּבַבְּגָדִים.

...return to equilibrium — Rambam provides us here with a marvelous illustration of his concept of equilibrium, as spoken of in chapter 4. At bottom, it comes to challenging your inner strength to its limits, then easing off until you'd have gotten enough of your "wind" back to face the challenge again. You would then find you would have to exert yourself less the next time, because you'd have developed "muscles" in the process.

Let's use an example. Suppose you were stingy. As Rambam argues in 4:2, you'd need to be extravagant for a while, then settle back into the more equibalanced way, which is generous. What that comes to, taking our illustration into consideration, is challenging your natural inclination to be stingy to its limits by being just the opposite — extravagant — for a while, then easing off and being merely generous, thanks to your newly honed "generosity-muscle."

...until it is no longer fatigued — Apparently Rambam is discussing delicate, balanced, quiet, and tranquil paintings and sculptures, rather than the more discordant, suggestive, and disquieting works we're often faced with in modernity, which do anything but "quiet and relax" the senses.

"they would joke" — The exact source of this quote cannot be found, but it is analogous to one in *Shabbat* 30b that reads, "Rabbah would begin [his lectures] to the scholars by saying something humorous, which would then make the scholars cheerful."

in such a context — I.e., with this in mind.

6. But know that this is a very high and formidable level [of piety and dedication] that few attain, and only after a great deal of preparation at that. In fact, I would consider anyone who proved to be like that on par with the prophets* — that is to say, anyone who uses all his personal capacities with God as his sole impetus; who never does or says anything, great or small, that either would not foster a character virtue itself or encourage one; and who concentrates upon and thinks about every move [he makes] and every action [he takes] to determine if it would accomplish his goal (which he would then do) or not.

Yet in point of fact, this is what God meant for us all to set as our goal* when He told us to "love God, your Lord, with all your heart, with your entire being"* (Deuteronomy 6:5);

ו. וְדַע שֶׁהַדַּרְגָּה הַזּוֹ הִיא דַּרְגָּה גְבוֹהָה מְאֹד וְקָשָׁה, לֹא יַשִּׂיגוּהָ אֶלָּא מְעַטִּים וְאַחֲרֵי הַכְשָׁרָה רַבָּה מְאֹד, וְאִם יִזְדַּמֵּן מְצִיאוּת אָדָם שֶׁאֵלֶּה הֵם תָּאֲרָיו אֵינִי חוֹשֵׁב שֶׁהוּא פָּחוֹת מֵהַנְּבִיאִים, כְּלוֹמַר, שֶׁמַּפְעִיל כָּל כֹּחוֹת נַפְשׁוֹ וְעוֹשֶׂה מַטְרָתָם ה' יִתְעַלֶּה בִּלְבַד, וְלֹא יַעֲשֶׂה פְּעוּלָה גְדוֹלָה אוֹ קְטַנָּה, וְלֹא יְבַטֵּא שׁוּם מִלָּה אֶלָּא אִם אוֹתָהּ הַפְּעֻלָּה אוֹ אוֹתָהּ הַמִּלָּה מְבִיאָה לִידֵי מַעֲלָה אוֹ לְדָבָר שֶׁמֵּבִיא לִידֵי מַעֲלָה, וְהוּא מִתְבּוֹנֵן וְחוֹשֵׁב בְּכָל פְּעוּלָה וּתְנוּעָה, וְרוֹאֶה אִם הִיא מְבִיאָה לְאוֹתָהּ הַתַּכְלִית אוֹ אֵינָהּ מְבִיאָה, וְאַחַר כַּךְ יַעֲשֶׂנָה.

וְזֶה הוּא מַה שֶּׁדּוֹרֵשׁ יִתְעַלֶּה מִמֶּנּוּ שֶׁתְּהֵא זוֹ מַטְרָתֵנוּ בְּאָמְרוֹ (דברים ו' ה'), "וְאָהַבְתָּ אֵת ה' אֱלֹקֶיךָ בְּכָל לְבָבְךָ וּבְכָל נַפְשְׁךָ," כְּלוֹמַר, בְּכָל חֶלְקֵי

As we alluded to in the third note above, sections 4 and 5 here serve to make the point that from a Jewish perspective, piety isn't based on eschewing delicacies, health, wealth, or engagement in the mundane world (see sections 2 and 3). As Rambam illustrates, from a Jewish perspective, piety allows for all that. Nonetheless, it requires that one pursue them *in moderation*, and with one end in mind: "to comprehend God Almighty as much as a human being can" (section 1).

on par with the prophets — This

seems to be both a warning and a consolation to those in pursuit of piety: a warning, in that it speaks of how few ever attain such a level; and a consolation, in that it indicates that once a person does indeed reach such a level, he is already on par with the prophets.[8]

...to set as our goal — Rambam's point is that this is the universal ideal — rather than mere goodness or "niceness," as many in polite (though often banal) modernity would think.[9]

which is to say, to set only one goal for the whole of your being* — and that is to "love God, your Lord."[10]

The prophets [i.e., King Solomon] also warned us about this and said, "Know Him in all your ways" (Proverbs 3:6), which our Sages explained means, "...even when it comes to a sin" (Berachot 63a); which is to say that one is to do what is involved with one end in mind: the ultimate truth,* even if it is a sin in a certain sense. And they presented this whole matter in the most concise language possible.

Our Sages encapsulated this whole principle perfectly in as few words as possible. (In fact, consider how few words they used to express so great and mighty an idea, about which whole books have been written without exhausting the subject, and you will realize just how divinely inspired they undoubtedly were.) They charged us later on in this tractate (i.e., Pirkei Avot 2:15) to do "all our deeds for the sake of Heaven," which is what we have been explaining in this chapter.

This, then, is the extent of what we saw fit to mention here, in light of these introductory remarks.

נַפְשְׁךָ, שֶׁתָּשִׂים תַּכְלִית כָּל חֵלֶק מֵהֶם תַּכְלִית אַחַת, וְהִיא לְאַהֲבָה אֶת ה' אֱלֹקֶיךָ.

וּכְבָר זֵרְזוּ גַם הַנְּבִיאִים עֲלֵיהֶם הַשָּׁלוֹם עַל עִנְיָן זֶה וְאָמַר (משלי ג' ו'), "בְּכָל דְּרָכֶיךָ דָעֵהוּ," וּפֵרְשׁוּ חֲכָמִים, וְאָמְרוּ (ברכות ס"ג.), "אֲפִילוּ בִּדְבַר עֲבֵירָה," כְּלוֹמַר, שֶׁתָּשִׂים לְאוֹתָהּ הַפְּעֻלָּה תַּכְלִית כָּלְפֵּי הָאֱמֶת, וְאַף עַל פִּי שֶׁיֵּשׁ בָּהּ עֲבֵירָה מֵאֵיזוֹ בְּחִינָה שֶׁהִיא כְּבָר כָּלְלוּ חֲכָמִים, עֲלֵיהֶם הַשָּׁלוֹם, כָּל הָעִנְיָן הַזֶּה בִּלְשׁוֹן הַקָּצָר בְּיוֹתֵר שֶׁיָּכוֹל לִהְיוֹת.

וְהִקִּיפוּ אֶת עִנְיַן הֶקֵּף שָׁלֵם מְאֹד מְאֹד, עַד שֶׁכַּאֲשֶׁר אַתָּה מִתְבּוֹנֵן בְּקוֹצֶר אוֹתָם הַמִּלִים אֵיךְ נֶאֶמְרוּ עַל הָעִנְיָן הַגָּדוֹל הֶעָצוּם הַזֶּה בִּכְלָלוּתוֹ שֶׁכְּבָר חֻבְּרוּ בּוֹ חִבּוּרִים וְלֹא הִקִּיפוּ אֶת כֻּלוֹ, תֵּדַע שֶׁהוּא נֶאֱמַר בְּכֹחַ אֱלֹקִי בְּלִי שׁוּם סָפֵק כְּלָל, וְהוּא אָמְרָם בְּצַנְאוֹתֵיהֶם בַּמַּסְכְתָּא זוֹ (אבות ב' י"א), "וְכָל מַעֲשֶׂיךָ יִהְיוּ לְשֵׁם שָׁמַיִם." וְזֶהוּ הָעִנְיָן שֶׁבֵּיאַרְנוּהוּ בְּפֶרֶק זֶה.

וְזֶהוּ מַה שֶׁרָאִינוּ שֶׁרָאוּי לְהַזְכִּיר כָּאן לְפִי הַהַקְדָּמוֹת הָאֵלוּ.

---

your entire being — Lit., with all your *nefesh*.

the whole of your being — Lit., each and every capacity of your *nefesh*.

the ultimate truth — This phrase is often an idiomatic expression for God in Arabic (the language in which *Shemoneh Perakim* was originally written), and could be translated as such here.[11]

Synopsis

1. *Aside from subordinating one's personal qualities in the ways spoken of before, one should strive to comprehend God as much as he can. One should make that his life's goal, and do whatever he does purposefully and with it in mind.*

2. *As such, one should strive for what is edifying. If what is edifying happens to be gratifying, too, then so be it. In addittion, one could enjoy gratifying or attractive things for one's health, or to be well enough to acquire knowledge. One would also do well to accrue money only in order to own uplifting things, to maintain his well-being, and to extend his life long enough to comprehend God. In point of fact, the field of medicine affords a person the opportunity to grow intellectually and personally, to know God, and thus, to comprehend what true bliss is.*

3. *A person who goes about eating satisfying but harmful foods is no different than an animal. For a true human being — a person of reason — would only do things that would edify him and keep him healthy. However, he would not make health itself his goal, for that is no different than pursuing any other form of self-indulgence. He would try to stay healthy in order to pursue personal and intellectual virtues without encumbrance.*

4. *The same goes for studying non-Torah subjects: One may do so as long as those studies bring him closer to his ultimate goal. But one should only study things like geometry, engineering, and the like, since they sharpen the mind enough to discriminate between valid and invalid theorems, which will help one understand God. Similarly, when one speaks, he should speak about wisdom and personal virtues and against wrongdoing.*

5. *One would tend to do and say much less if he makes comprehending God his goal in life; and the only reason one would relax and occupy himself with extraneous things would be to stay healthy and have a clear mind.*

6. *The sort of individual who uses all his personal capacities toward understanding God, who only occupies himself with things that are themselves virtuous or foster a virtue, and who measures each action to determine if it will lead to that end or not is on par with the prophets. In point of fact, though, that is exactly what God requires of each one of us!*

6

בהבדל בין החסיד והכובש את יצרו

THE DIFFERENCE BETWEEN THE EMINENT PERSON AND ONE WHO CONTROLS HIS DESIRES

T HIS CHAPTER SEEMS TO APPEAR out of "the blue." For we have just learned how to heal our beings and about the direction in which we are to lead our lives. Now, for some reason, Rambam offers a short discourse on the abstract notion of whether it is better to consciously, selflessly stop oneself from succumbing to temptation, or to be the sort of person who could never contemplate committing that sin. Let us first follow his argument, then try to determine why it is here.

Ramban informs us that many philosophers held that one who is not tempted by sin in the first place is loftier, because someone who struggles with his baser impulses still has those impulses, despite his actual behavior. Then he cites our Sages' view, which is just the opposite.

Is this an out-and-out clash of ideals? We are told it's not, because the two are referring to two distinct types of sin. The philosophers are concerned with universally recognized sins, such as murder, theft, and robbery, while the Sages have in mind deeds which the Torah — and only the Torah — defines as sins, such as eating milk and meat together, wearing a mixture of wool and linen, and the like.

Hence, he concludes, while everyone agrees that it is better to be the sort of person who would never think of stealing, murdering, and the like, there is more to personal piety than that. For the Torah offers that the conscious, purposeful decision not to wear sha'atnez or eat meat and milk together after a struggle is more precious than any sort of easy and quiet, natural compliance with no struggle.

But other than the fact that it is a vital philosophical conflict, why does Rambam present this to us here and now?

Perhaps it is to convince us to accept such restrictions upon ourselves because they are rooted in faith and in divine authority and to be prepared to engage in them despite any conflict we might experience in the process. And also because, as we will discover, this is a uniquely Jewish devotional path.

---

1. The philosophers explained that one who controls his desires, although he may do lofty things, nonetheless does good while longing and yearning to do bad.[1] It is just that he struggles with his longings and withstands the promptings of his personal bents,* desires, and disposition and does good deeds while suffering in the process.* In contrast, the eminent person's* actions are prompted by his [inherently noble] desires and disposition, and he does good deeds because he longs and yearns to do so.

א. אָמְרוּ הַפִּילוֹסוֹפִים, שֶׁהַכּוֹבֵשׁ אֶת יִצְרוֹ, וְאַף עַל פִּי שֶׁהוּא עוֹשֶׂה מַעֲשִׂים נַעֲלִים הֲרֵי הוּא עוֹשֶׂה אֶת הַטּוֹב בּוֹ בִּזְמַן שֶׁהוּא שׁוֹאֵף לְמַעֲשִׂים הָרָעִים, וּמִשְׁתּוֹקֵק לָהֶן, וְנֶאֱבַק עִם שְׁאִיפוֹתָיו וְנוֹגֵד בִּפְעֻלּוֹתָיו אֶת מַה שֶּׁמְעוֹרְרִים אוֹתוֹ אֵלָיו כֹּחוֹתָיו וְתַאֲווֹתָיו וּתְכוּנוֹת נַפְשׁוֹ, וְעוֹשֶׂה הַמַּעֲשִׂים הַטּוֹבִים וְהוּא מִצְטַעֵר בַּעֲשִׂיָּתָם. אֲבָל הֶחָסִיד הֲרֵי הוּא יִמָּשֵׁךְ בְּמַעֲשָׂיו אַחַר מַה שֶּׁמְעוֹרֶרֶת אוֹתוֹ אֵלָיו תַּאֲוָתוֹ וּתְכוּנָתוֹ, וְעוֹשֶׂה הַטּוֹבוֹת, וְהוּא שׁוֹאֵף וּמִשְׁתּוֹקֵק לָהֶן.

---

personal bents — We've translated this term as "capacities" and "aptitudes" above, but decided upon "personal bents" here, because it works best in this context.

...suffering in the process — I.e., he is thrown into turmoil and inner conflict as a consequence of the battle between his ideals and his urges.

the eminent person's — Although the term *chasid* is usually translated as "a pious person," our use of the term *eminent person* will be explained in the following note ("one who controls his desires").

Thus, the philosophers determined that the eminent person is loftier and more perfect than the one who controls his desires.*

וּמוּסְכָּם מִכָּל הַפִּילוֹסוֹפִים, שֶׁהֶחָסִיד יוֹתֵר נַעֲלֶה וּמוּשְׁלָם מִן הַכּוֹבֵשׁ אֶת יִצְרוֹ.

one who controls his desires — This paragraph calls for some explanation.

As we said, the astute reader would have to ask why Rambam inserted this chapter in *Shemoneh Perakim* in the first place, and why at this point in particular. After all, it doesn't seem to touch upon the subject of personal improvement per se, and it doesn't appear to follow on the heels of the last chapter. It seems, instead, to concern itself with the arcane academic issue of "Who is loftier — the inherently good soul, or the one who struggles to become good?"

But as we indicated in the second note to chapter 5 above, this chapter is actually a continuation of the fourth chapter. We contend that this chapter underscores one of Rambam's major points, and that it serves as an elegant prelude to the next one. But let's explain a few things that need to be explained first.

As we also indicated in the notes to chapter 5, the "philosophers" referred to here are Aristotle and his proponents, whom we've encountered before in this work — most significantly, as far as we're concerned here, at the end of chapter 4. We were told there that they claimed that "it would be hard and hardly likely" — though not impossible — "to find anyone with all the virtuous intellectual and character traits."

That is to say that the ancient Greeks contended that there are indeed some rare individuals who were born with all the virtuous intellectual and character traits. They described them as "heroic" (i.e., larger than life, superhuman), "godly," inherently perfect souls. They claimed that such individuals wouldn't even *think* of doing anything lowly; they'd only do inherently good and noble things. They termed them the "great-souled" or "eminent" ones.

As Rambam depicts it here, the philosophers also contended that the person who subdues his baser instincts (his *yetzer hara*, in Hebrew) is indeed praiseworthy — after all, despite his longings and the "promptings of his personal bents, desires, and disposition," and notwithstanding the subsequent anguish and inner turmoil he experiences, he nevertheless manages to conquer his instincts and to let his ideals hold sway.

But they maintain that he is still and all not as praiseworthy or as inherently good and noble as the eminent person. For the latter doesn't even have to contend with baser instincts, simply because he doesn't have any, and he just naturally wants to do good and noble things. In contrast, the person who conquers his *yetzer hara* is, after all, inherently flawed, and has to fight his natural inclinations all the time just to approach the moral altitude the eminent individual occupies effortlessly.

Rambam, on the other hand, doesn't hold out eminence as the ideal — or even as possible.

His point, instead, is that emi-

They added, though, that someone who controls his desires is on par with an eminent person in many ways,* but his level is decidedly lower than his because he [i.e., the one who controls his desires] still longs to do bad, and even

אֲבָל אָמְרוּ, שֶׁהַכּוֹבֵשׁ אֶת יִצְרוֹ שָׁוֶה לְחָסִיד בְּהַרְבֵּה עִנְיָנִים, אֶלָּא שֶׁמַּעֲלָתוֹ פְּחוּתָה מִמֶּנּוּ בְּהֶחְלֵט מִפְּנֵי שֶׁהוּא מִתְאַוֶּה לְמַעֲשֵׂה הָרַע, וְאַף עַל

nence is fictitious. The very idea of it is supremely un-Jewish. The Jewish moral ideal is piety (as we've been discussing all along), and pious people are humans who bear inherent human frailties, and nonetheless strive to perfect themselves while boldly contending with inner conflict and moral turmoil in the process. They repent of their ways and redirect their energies toward returning to God again after having lapsed.

After all, as Rambam put it elsewhere in this work, "No one is born with an inherently virtuous or flawed character" (4:4), "everyone has his flaws" (4:10), and "it is no more possible to be born either inherently lofty or flawed than it is to be born automatically adept at a trade" (8:1). As he declared most forthrightly, "One who weighs his actions all the time and strives for balance" — i.e., someone who realizes his faults and tries to mend them when he comes upon them — "will become a person of the very highest caliber" — and would be considered pious. Indeed, such an individual would "draw close to God, and have satisfied His wishes" in the process, and he'd have engaged in "*the* most perfect form of divine service" (4:12).

Rambam will shortly cite traditional sources that seem to set eminence as the ideal — let alone as *possible*. But he'll then prove later on

that the true Jewish perspective is that piety is earned rather than inherent; that it's rooted in mitzvah observance as well as in morality; and that full and inborn blamelessness is not only a human impossibility, but it's not even the ideal.

Thus we contend that the person termed "one who controls his desires" in this chapter is, in fact, the pious person spoken of throughout the work.

In fact, Rambam makes the point in the very next chapter that even the prophets — who had to have been pious — also had their flaws and had to control their desires (7:2). They also struggled and had their failings (albeit fewer in number and in magnitude than ours), which also flies in the face of the philosophers' views. This point will be developed in the next chapter, though; and it's what connects this chapter with that one so elegantly.

In point of fact, this chapter is connected to the next one in yet another way. Recall that we said above that this chapter is a continuation of chapter 4. There, section 11 speaks of Moses' character fault. That theme is discussed again in chapter 7:4 below.[2]

...in many ways — After all, he ultimately does many of the same lofty things that the pious person does.

though he does not do it this is itself an inherently bad [element of his] disposition.*

In fact, [King] Solomon said much the same when he declared, "The soul of the wrongdoer yearns for wrongdoing" (Proverbs 21:10), and when he referred to the joy the eminent person experiences when doing good as opposed to the suffering [i.e., the inner conflict and struggle] a noneminent person experiences doing the very same thing with, "It is a joy to the righteous to do justice; but a torment to the evildoers" (ibid., 15).

Thus, the Torah and the philosophers seem to agree.*

פִּי שֶׁאֵינוֹ עוֹשֵׂהוּ בְּכָל אוֹפֶן תְּשׁוּקָתוֹ
לוֹ תְכוּנָה רָעָה הִיא בְּנָפֶשׁ.

וּכְבָר דִּבֵּר שְׁלֹמֹה כַּגוּוֹן זֶה, אָמַר
(שם כ"א י') "נֶפֶשׁ רָשָׁע אִוְּתָה רָע"
וְאָמַר בְּשִׂמְחַת הֶחָסִיד בְּמַעֲשֶׂה
הַטּוֹב וְצַעַר מִי שֶׁאֵינוֹ חָסִיד בַּעֲשִׂיָּתוֹ
לָשׁוֹן זֶה (שם כ"א ט"ו) "שִׂמְחָה
לַצַּדִּיק עֲשׂוֹת מִשְׁפָּט וּמְחִתָּה לְפֹעֲלֵי
אָוֶן." זֶהוּ מַה שֶׁנִּרְאֶה מִדִּבְרֵי תּוֹרָה
הַמַּתְאִים לְדִבְרֵי הַפִילוֹסוֹפִים.

ב. וְכַאֲשֶׁר חָקַרְנוּ עַל דִּבְרֵי חֲכָמִים
בְּעִנְיָן זֶה, מָצָאנוּ לָהֶם שֶׁהַשּׁוֹאֵף
אֶת הָעֲבֵרוֹת וּמִשְׁתּוֹקֵק לָהֶן יוֹתֵר
נַעֲלֶה וְשָׁלֵם מִמִּי שֶׁאֵינוֹ שׁוֹאֵף לָהֶן
וְאֵינוֹ מִצְטַעֵר בַּעֲזִיבָתָן, עַד שֶׁאָמְרוּ,
שֶׁכָּל מַה שֶׁיִּהְיֶה הָאָדָם יוֹתֵר גָּדוֹל
וְשָׁלֵם תִּהְיֶה תַּאֲוָתוֹ לַעֲבֵירוֹת וְצַעֲרוֹ
בַּעֲזִיבָתָם יוֹתֵר חָמוּר, וְהֵבִיאוּ בְּזֶה

2. But when we examine what the Sages say about this, we find that they deem one who wants and yearns to sin [but doesn't] loftier and more perfect than one who does not yearn [to sin] and does not suffer in restraining himself from doing those things [if there were such a person]. In fact, they said that the greater and more perfect a person is, the stronger his craving for sins, and the greater his suffering* in denying them to himself! They cited

...inherently bad disposition — That is to say, the philosophers contend that the "naturally pious" person is even more perfect in the ideal sense than one who strives to perfect himself, simply because the former has never been "tainted," and because the one who controls his desires is still and all less of a person, inasmuch as his inclinations are untoward despite his doing many of the same lofty things the eminent person does.

Once again, though, Rambam contends that "eminence" does not exist.[3]

seem to agree — But as we indicated above, the apparent agreement between King Solomon and the philosophers is actually illusory.

the greater his suffering — As we indicated in the notes to section 1 above, "suffering" suggests being thrown into turmoil and inner

personal examples and concluded that "the greater the man, the greater his desires [for evil]"* (Sukkah 52a).

Not only did they say that, but they also said that the more the person who controls his desires suffers in the process, the greater his reward. As they put it, "One's reward is commensurate with his suffering"* (Pirkei Avot 5:26).

They even commanded us to control our desires, and warned us never to say, "I personally would not want to commit that sin even if the Torah did not forbid it." Similarly, they said, "Rabbi Shimon ben Gamliel said: A person should never say, 'I just cannot eat meat and milk [together], wear sha'atnez,* or have forbidden relations.' Instead [he should say], 'I can, but what can I do — my Father in Heaven forbade me to!' "* (Sifra, Parashat Kedoshim).

מַעֲשִׂיּוֹת וְאָמְרוּ (סוכה נ"ב.), "כֹּל הַגָּדוֹל מֵחֲבֵרוֹ יִצְרוֹ גָּדוֹל מִמֶּנּוּ."

וְלֹא דִי בָזֶה, אֶלָּא שֶׁאָמְרוּ, שֶׁשְׂכַר הַכּוֹבֵשׁ אֶת יִצְרוֹ גָּדוֹל לְפִי עֵרֶךְ צַעֲרוֹ בִּכְבִישָׁתוֹ אֶת יִצְרוֹ, וְאָמְרוּ (אבות ה' כ"ו) "לְפוּם צַעֲרָא אַגְרָא."

וְעוֹד יוֹתֵר מִזֶּה, שֶׁהֵם צִוּוּ שֶׁיְּהֵא הָאָדָם כּוֹבֵשׁ אֶת יִצְרוֹ, וְהִזְהִירוּ שֶׁיֹּאמַר, אֲנִי מִטִּבְעִי אֵינִי מִתְאַוֶּה לַעֲבֵירָה זוֹ וַאֲפִילוּ לֹא אֲסָרַתָּהּ הַתּוֹרָה, וְהוּא אָמְרָם (ספרא סוף פרשת קדושים), "רַבָּן שִׁמְעוֹן בֶּן גַּמְלִיאֵל אוֹמֵר, לֹא יֹאמַר אָדָם אִי אֶפְשִׁי לֶאֱכוֹל בָּשָׂר בְּחָלָב, אִי אֶפְשִׁי לִלְבּוֹשׁ שַׁעַטְנֵז, אִי אֶפְשִׁי לָבוֹא עַל הָעֶרְוָה, אֶלָּא אֶפְשִׁי וּמָה אֶעֱשֶׂה וְאָבִי שֶׁבַּשָּׁמַיִם גָּזַר עָלַי."

---

conflict as a consequence of the battle between one's ideals and his urges.

the greater his desires — That is, the tradition embraces inner moral and spiritual struggle and subsequent victory. It not only recognizes the humanity of the pious but also acknowledges the depths to which their inner struggles go, and deems them to be greater, the greater their challenge.

his suffering — That is, the tradition also underscores the values of the struggle to the participant.

wear sha'atnez — See the Torah's injunction not to let "a garment mixed of linen and wool (i.e., sha'atnez) come upon you" (Leviticus 19:19).

my Father in Heaven forbade me to — That is, the tradition even charged us to admit the challenge as we confront it.

All in all, what Rambam is pointing out in this section is that the Jewish tradition doesn't hold out as the ideal individuals never faced with sin, those who are innately untarnished and safeguarded from all that from birth. Rather, the Jewish tradition offers as the ideal the human being who

3. Now, a cursory reading of the two viewpoints* would lead us to believe that they contradict each other, but that is not so. In fact, both are correct, and they do not disagree at all.

For what the philosophers consider bad — the sort of acts that would make the person who does not want to commit them loftier[4] than the one who does, but controls his desires so as not to do so — are the sorts of things commonly accepted as bad, like murder, theft, robbery, fraud, harming an innocent person, ingratitude, holding one's parents in contempt, and such. In fact, they are the sorts of prohibitions about which our Sages said, "Had they not already been written [i.e., codified in the Torah], they would have to be" (*Yoma* 67b). (Some modern scholars* who caught the disease of the Mutakallimun* refer to these as "reason-based" mitzvot.)*

ג. וּלְפִי פַּשְׁטֵי שְׁנֵי הַמַּאֲמָרִים בָּעִיּוּן רִאשׁוֹן הֲרֵי שְׁנֵי הַמַּאֲמָרִים סוֹתְרִים זֶה אֶת זֶה, וְאֵין הַדָּבָר כֵּן, אֶלָּא כּוּלָם אֱמֶת וְאֵין מַחֲלוֹקֶת בֵּינֵיהֶם כְּלָל.

וְהוּא שֶׁהָרָעוֹת שֶׁהֵם אֵצֶל הַפִּילוֹסוֹפִים רָעוֹת הֵם, אֲשֶׁר בָּהֶם אָמְרוּ, שֶׁמִּי שֶׁאֵינוֹ שׁוֹאֵף לָהֶם יוֹתֵר נַעֲלֶה מִן הַשּׁוֹאֵף לָהֶם וְכוֹבֵשׁ אֶת יִצְרוֹ מֵהֶם, וְהֵם הַדְּבָרִים הַמְפֻרְסָמִים אֵצֶל כָּל אָדָם שֶׁהֵם רָעוֹת כְּגוֹן שְׁפִיכַת דָּמִים, וּגְנֵיבָה, וְגֵזֶל, וְאוֹנָאָה, וְהַהֶזֵּק לְמִי שֶׁלֹּא עָשָׂה רָע, וּגְמִילַת הַמֵּטִיב בְּרָעָה, וְהַזִּלְזוּל בַּהוֹרִים, וְכַיּוֹצֵא בָּהֶן, וְהֵם הַמִּצְווֹת שֶׁעֲלֵיהֶן אוֹמְרִים חֲכָמִים עֲלֵיהֶם הַשָּׁלוֹם (יומא ס"ז): דְּבָרִים שֶׁאִלְמָלֵא לֹא נִכְתְּבוּ רְאוּיִין הָיוּ לְכָתְבָן," וְקוֹרִין אוֹתָם מִקְצַת חֲכָמֵינוּ הָאַחֲרוֹנִים, אֲשֶׁר חָלוּ בְּמַחֲלַת כַּת "הַמְדַבְּרִים" הַמִּצְווֹת הַשִּׂכְלִיּוֹת.

There is no doubt that the person* who would long and yearn to commit any one of these sins would be flawed. For a lofty person would not want to commit a single one of them, nor would he suffer by restraining himself from them.*

But the sorts of acts which the Sages said that anyone who controls his desires rather than commit them is greater and his reward is higher [than that of the "eminent" person, who doesn't have to control his desires at all] are [what the

וְאֵין סָפֵק שֶׁהַנֶּפֶשׁ הַשּׁוֹאֶפֶת לְאֵיזוֹ מֵהֶן וּמִשְׁתּוֹקֶקֶת לוֹ, שֶׁהִיא נֶפֶשׁ בַּעֲלַת מִגְרַעַת, וְשֶׁהַנֶּפֶשׁ הַנַּעֲלֶה לֹא תִּתְאַוֶּה לְאַחַת מִן הָרָעוֹת הַלָּלוּ כְּלָל, וְלֹא תִצְטַעֵר בְּהִמָּנְעָהּ מֵהֶם.

אֲבָל הַדְּבָרִים אֲשֶׁר בָּהֶן אָמְרוּ חֲכָמִים, שֶׁהַכּוֹבֵשׁ אֶת יִצְרוֹ מֵהֶם יוֹתֵר גָּדוֹל, וּשְׂכָרוֹ יוֹתֵר עָצוּם, הֵם

Lord" at the end.

They then assert that "laws" are acts that are naturally objectionable, such as idolatry, licentiousness, murder, robbery, and blasphemy. These will be referred to as "reason-based" mitzvot below, because they're commonly understood to be bad. (Rambam adds fraud, harming an innocent person, ingratitude, holding one's parents in contempt, etc., on his own here.)

"Ordinances," on the other hand, are acts that wouldn't logically seem to be either good or bad, like sha'atnez, chalitzah (see Deuteronomy 25:5–10), the Red Heifer (see Leviticus 14:1–32), and the sending off of the scapegoat (see Leviticus 16:1–28). These will soon be referred to as "authority-based" mitzvot because they're to be observed in faithful acquiescence to the authority of the Torah, despite the fact that they don't seem to be either bad or good.

We are not to think the latter are of little value, though. After all, the verse ends with "I am God, your Lord," which means to say that God

ordained them for a reason of His own.

As to "loftiness," it is a neutral term meant to refer to the character of a person of high caliber who is neither "eminent" nor "pious" as the philosophers or the Jewish tradition understand those terms. We'll explain its significance shortly.

the person — Lit., the *nefesh*.

by restraining himself from them — That is to say, anyone who would want to worship idols, act licentiously, murder, rob, blaspheme, act fraudulently, harm an innocent person, be ungrateful, hold his parents in contempt, and the like, would certainly be of low caliber — let alone neither "eminent" or "pious," since, as Rambam says, "a lofty person" — a decent and well-meaning person with values — "would not want to commit a single one" of these crimes, "nor would he suffer at all by denying them to himself." He would never even entertain the thought or need to renounce it.

aforementioned "modern scholars" refer to as] the "authority-based mitzvot.* And this is true, for were it not for the Torah, they would not be [considered] bad at all. Hence, they are the ones the Sages said one should allow himself to long for* and only deny them to himself because the Torah itself deters us from them.*

הַמִּצְוֹת הַשִּׁמְעִיּוֹת, וְזֶה אֱמֶת, שֶׁלּוּלֵי הַתּוֹרָה לֹא הָיוּ רָעוֹת כְּלָל, וּלְפִיכָךְ אָמְרוּ, שֶׁצָּרִיךְ הָאָדָם לְהַשְׁאִיר אֶת עַצְמוֹ חוֹשֵׁק לָהֶן וְלֹא יָשִׂים הַמּוֹנְעוֹ מֵהֶם, אֶלָּא הַתּוֹרָה.

In fact, observe that their very

וְהִתְבּוֹנֵן חָכְמָתָם, עֲלֵיהֶם הַשָּׁלוֹם, וּבְמַה הִמְשִׁילוֹ, לְפִי שֶׁלֹּא אָמַר, "לֹא יֹאמַר אָדָם אִי אֶפְשִׁי לַהֲרוֹג אֶת הַנֶּפֶשׁ, אִי אֶפְשִׁי לִגְנוֹב, אִי אֶפְשִׁי לְכַזֵּב אֶלָּא אֶפְשִׁי וּמַה אֶעֱשֶׂה," אֶלָּא הִזְכִּיר

examples reveal just how wise the Sages were. For they did not say, "A person should never say, 'I just cannot murder, steal, lie...I can, but what can I do...?' " What they cited were "authority-based" prohibi-

---

"authority-based" mitzvot — I.e., mitzvot we observe in faithful acquiescence to the authority of the Torah.

to long for — I.e., allow oneself to question their rationality and to struggle with the temptation to transgress them.

...deters us from them — That is to say, the person who would entertain the notion of not complying with so-called "auothority-based" mitzvot like *shaatnez, chalitzah*, the Red Heifer, the sending off of the scapegoat, and the like — who would then struggle with that inclination, and eventually comply not to sin in the end, after all — is indeed "loftier" than someone who would merely not murder, rob, and so on. The values he is submitting to are rooted in faith and the authority of God's Torah, rather than in common decency. Such a person would certainly not stoop to committing clearly indecent things.

But there is another, quite important point to be made here as well. The purpose of this chapter is to add yet another dimension to Rambam's understanding of Jewish piety. Not only is an individual who follows the Jewish path of piety balanced and even-handed, as well as learned, and not only does he do all he does with the aim of comprehending God in the end, but a pious Jewish individual gains piety also by engaging in uniquely Jewish, Torah-based mitzvot that have nothing to do with what is commonly thought of as necessary to be pious.

For, besides being especially good, civil, moral, and outstanding, pious Jewish souls go to great pains to submit to God's higher, albeit difficult to understand requirements of us. Accordingly, he does more "good" in the world than does a non-Jewish pious person — even when the latter seems to be more abstemious and selfless.

tions like the ones against meat and milk,* wearing *sha'atnez*, and forbidden relations.

For they [i.e., authority-based mitzvot] are the sorts of mitzvot that God refers to as His "ordinances,"* about which our Sages said, "You have no right to doubt any of the ordinances I [God] decreed for you" (*Yoma* 67b) — even though [as the Talmud continues] gentiles retort against them and the Satan denounces them, for example the Red Heifer, the scapegoat, and the like.* (Thus, those mitzvot which [the aforementioned] modern scholars refer to as "reason-based" ones are [called] "mitzvot," in the Sages' words.)*

It has become clear from all that we have said which sins make the person who does not long to commit them greater [i.e., loftier] than the one who does long to commit them but controls his desires to do

עִנְיָנִים שֶׁכּוּלָם שִׂמְעִיּוֹת, בָּשָׂר בְּחָלָב, לִבִישַׁת שַׁעַטְנֵז, וַעֲרָיוֹת.

וּמִצְוֹת אֵלּוּ וְכַיּוֹצֵא בָּהֶן הֵן שֶׁקּוֹרֵא אוֹתָן ה' "חֻקּוֹתַי." וְאָמְרוּ (יומא ס"ז:), "חֻקִּים שֶׁחָקַקְתִּי לְךָ וְאֵין לְךָ רְשׁוּת לְהַרְהֵר בָּהֶן," וְאוּמּוֹת הָעוֹלָם מְשִׁיבִין עֲלֵיהֶן, וְהַשָּׂטָן מְקַטְרֵג עֲלֵיהֶן, כְּגוֹן פָּרָה אֲדוּמָה וְשָׂעִיר הַמִּשְׁתַּלֵּחַ וְכוּ'. וְאוֹתָן שֶׁקּוֹרִין אוֹתָן הָאַחֲרוֹנִים שִׂכְלִיּוֹת נִקְרָאִין מִצְוֹת, כְּמוֹ שֶׁבֵּאֲרוּ חֲכָמִים.

הִנֵּה נִתְבָּאֵר מִכָּל מַה שֶׁאָמַרְנוּ, אֵיזוֹ עֲבֵרוֹת יִהְיֶה מִי שֶׁאֵינוֹ מִשְׁתּוֹקֵק לָהֶן יוֹתֵר גָּדוֹל מִן הַמִּשְׁתּוֹקֵק לָהֶן וְכוֹבֵשׁ יִצְרוֹ מֵהֶם, וְאֵיזוֹ מֵהֶם בְּהֵפֶךְ.

---

meat and milk — I.e., eating or cooking meat and milk together, or profiting from the combination of the two some other way.

ordinances — I.e., apparently unfathomable decrees that accomplish some unknown end.[5]

the Red Heifer, the scapegoat, and the like — See our note on p. 103 above ("'reason-based' mitzvot") for an explanation of this in context.

I.e., while you indeed "have no right to *criticize* any of the ordinances I [God] decreed for you...." and so, to fail to fulfill them as a consequence, you would still be considered pious if you *questioned* them, but ob-

served them in the end. For a pious person might very well entertain the thought of violating an "ordinance" or "authority-based" mitzvah for a moment because its worth or purpose is unclear. Yet he would never actually violate it, since ultimately it is a mitzvah, albeit an inexplicable one.

...in the Sages' words — As happened in various instances in the course of Jewish scholastic history, Rambam's text of *Yoma* 67b was slightly at variance with our own. His text apparently referred to the things commonly recognized as good or bad as "mitzvot," while ours refers to them as "acts" or "things."

so, and which are the ones about which the opposite is true. That is both a marvelous novel point and a wondrous suggestion as to how to reconcile those two statements [i.e., those of the philosophers and those of the Sages]; and the terminology proves our point in both instances.

וְזוֹ נְקוּדָה נִפְלָאָה וְתֵירוּץ נִפְלָא לִשְׁנֵי הַמַּאֲמָרִים וְגַם הַלָּשׁוֹן מוֹרֶה עַל נְכוֹנוּת מַה שֶּׁבֵּיאַרְנוּ.

וּבָזֶה נִשְׁלַם עִנְיַן הַפֶּרֶק הַזֶּה.

We have thus completed the subject of this chapter.

Synopsis

1. *According to the philosophers, one who subdues his evil inclination does good even when he is not inclined to and suffers in the process, while an "eminent" person does good because he is naturally inclined to. They concluded that the "eminent" person is thus loftier. In fact, the Torah seems to agree with this.*

2. *However, the Sages disagreed. They declared that one who longs to sin but doesn't is loftier than one who doesn't long to; and that the greater the struggle, the greater the reward. They even charged us not to deny that struggle.*

3. *Now while the two perspectives seem to contradict each other, they actually don't. Because what the philosophers saw as bad are things everyone agrees are bad — for example, murder, theft, robbery, abuse, and the like. And indeed, anyone inclined toward any of them is flawed. In contrast, the things the Sages referred to as "bad" were deeds one wouldn't ordinarily see as such — like eating milk and meat together, wearing sha'atnez, and the like. The Sages' point is that since the latter sorts of deeds are mandated by the Torah, as such, the person who observes them is loftier than someone who doesn't.*

7

במסכים ועניינם
ON THE PARTITIONS AND
THEIR MEANING

L IKE THE PREVIOUS ONE, this chapter also seems incongruous. For it alludes to certain "partitions" and focuses on prophecy.
   In fact, though, Rambam already referred to prophecy in his introduction and in chapter 5, so in one sense he is merely expanding upon the
subject here.

Yet he stresses another point here, as well. This touches upon his earlier theme
that the Jewish concept of piety isn't tinged with the same unreal and inhuman
expectations as non-Jewish conceptions of it.

As Rambam points out here, though they were certainly exalted and truly
pious, prophets weren't without their human frailties and faults (each of which
served as a partition or barrier to the true comprehension of God). In fact Moses, the greatest of all prophets, indeed had his faults (see 4:11). Nonetheless, in
the end, he — and he alone — had so perfected himself that the only thing that
proved to be a "fault" on his part and thus separated him from God to some
degree was his mortality (referred to as a single "diaphanous" — so subtle as to
be negligible — partition).

1. There are many *references* in the Midrash, the Aggadah, and the Talmud to the fact that some prophets*

א. הַרְבֵּה יִמָּצֵא בְּמִדְרָשׁוֹת וּבְהַגָדוֹת, וּמֵהֶם גַּם בַּתַּלְמוּד, שֶׁיֵּשׁ מִן הַנְּבִיאִים

---

prophets — Axiomatic to the Jewish faith is belief in the fact that God reveals His wishes to humanity in a unique fashion known as prophecy. In fact, were it not for prophecy, there would be no Judaism; for Torah, which is its sum and substance, is a product of prophetic revelation.

So we believe that there have been certain unique, sagacious individuals who have indeed communed with God and divulged His Will, and that the greatest of them was Moses (whom we'll soon discuss).

Thus, one might expect a prophet to be an utterly flawless superhuman being, wholly removed from common faults and foibles, who is barely of this world.

Much to our surprise, though, Rambam points out in section 2 below that indeed, while "a prophet could not prophesy unless he had acquired all the *intellectual* virtues," as we'd expect, he'd nonetheless only be presumed to have acquired "most" — not all — of "the *more significant*" personal virtues. Which is to say that he might even have his share of minor character flaws, and yet enjoy divine revelation!

This, too, differs from the non-Jewish unrealistic view of prophets — as well as of the pious. After all, Solomon, David, Elijah, Jacob, and Samuel will all prove to have had minor flaws (see section 2 below), and even Moses apparently had his struggles (see 4:11 and our supplemental note 28 there).

To be sure, Rambam's point is

that one's flaws do separate him from God, and are thus tragic, woesome impediments to what matters most. Nonetheless, his other contention is that prophets were humans with personal proclivities, as are we. Yet they became prophets despite that. So what sets them apart from us?

The first difference is the fact that they pursued and attained piety. After all, as Rambam noted in his introduction (section 2), "piety leads to prophecy."

They were also the kind of people who "used all [their] personal capacities with God as [their] sole impetus; who would never do or say anything, great or small, that either would not foster a character virtue itself or encourage one; and who... concentrate[d] upon and thought about every move [they] would make, every action [they] would take, to determine if it would accomplish [their] goal (which [they] would then do) or not" (5:6).

They'd struggle to control their desires — i.e., any untoward urges they might have to lapse into sin and error (see chapter 6). After all, they were disposed toward certain faults, as this chapter indicates. But they strove, repented when that was called for (see our note on p. 99 of chapter 6 ["one who controls his desires"]), and managed to emerge victorious.

And though Rambam doesn't touch upon this here as he does elsewhere, they also had to have been born with various uncommon faculties and abilities and to have acquired certain recondite, esoteric skills.[1]

saw God from behind many partitions,* others saw Him from behind just a few (depending on their closeness to God* and on their level of prophecy), and that Moses saw God from behind a single sheer, diaphanous partition.* As the Sages put it, he "peered through a clear 'aspaklaria'* (Yevamot 49b), which is a windowpane made of a diaphanous material like crystal or glass (as we explained at the end of Keilim*).

The point here about the difference between the prophets, as we'll explain, hinges upon what we said in the second chapter.* There are intellectual virtues and personal virtues, as well as intellectual flaws (like ignorance, gullibility, and slow-wittedness) and personal flaws (like indulgence, arrogance,

מִי שֶׁרוֹאֶה אֶת ה' מֵאֲחוֹרֵי מַסְכִּים מְרוּבִּים, וּמֵהֶם מִי שֶׁרוֹאֵהוּ מֵאֲחוֹרֵי מַסְכִּים מְעַטִים, לְפִי עֶרֶךְ קִרְבָתָם לִפְנֵי ה' וְרוּם מַעֲלָתָם בַּנְּבוּאָה, עַד שֶׁאָמְרוּ (יבמות מ"ט:) שֶׁמֹּשֶׁה רַבֵּינוּ רָאָה אֶת ה' מֵאֲחוֹרֵי מָסָךְ אֶחָד בָּהִיר, כְּלוֹמַר שָׁקוּף, וְהוּא אָמְרָם, "הִסְתַּכֵּל בַּסְפַּקְלַרְיָא הַמְּאִירָה עֵינָיִם."
וְ"סְפַּקְלַרְיָא" שֵׁם הָרְאִי הֶעָשׂוּי מֵחוֹמֶר שָׁקוּף כְּיַהֲלוֹם וּכְזְכוּכִית, כְּמוֹ שֶׁנְּבָאֵר בְּסוֹף כֵּלִים (פרק ל' משנה ב').

וְהַכַּוָּנָה בְּעִנְיָן זֶה מַה שֶׁאֲבָאֵר לְךָ, וְהוּא שֶׁכְּבָר בֵּאַרְנוּ בַּפֶּרֶק הַשֵּׁנִי, שֶׁהַמַּעֲלוֹת מֵהֶם הִגְיוֹנִיּוֹת וּמֵהֶם מִדּוֹתִיּוֹת, וְכֵן הַמִּגְרָעוֹת מֵהֶן מִגְרָעוֹת בְּהִגְיוֹן כְּגוֹן הַסַּכְלוּת, וְהַפְּתַיּוּת, וּקְשִׁי הַהֲבָנָה, וּמֵהֶם מִדּוֹתִיּוֹת כְּגוֹן

---

partitions — The word partitions can be read literally as screens, or figuratively, as barriers or impediments.

depending on their closeness to God — I.e., depending on their degree of piety.

...sheer, diaphanous partition — See the end of the fourth note to chapter 6 above ("one who controls his desires"), about the connection between this chapter and the ones just before it.

"Seeing" God as spoken of here refers to grasping Him in one's mind (see section 4 below). Hence, since we're about to find that a prophet's — or anyone's — character as well as his intellectual flaws can restrict his abili-

ty to "see" or grasp God, it follows that one's character plays an essential role in grasping God. Thus, inasmuch as our chief aim in life is to "comprehend God Almighty as much as a human being can" (5:1), it now becomes clear why having a lofty character is so very important to our spiritual station.

a clear "aspaklaria" — The whole passage reads, "While the [other] prophets peered through a dusky aspaklaria, Moses peered through clear aspaklaria."

at the end of Keilim — I.e., at the end of Rambam's comments to Mishnah Keilim.

in the second chapter — See section 2 there.

wrath, indignation, audacity, and avarice). There are many others, which we cited by category in the fourth chapter. Each such flaw acts as a partition between man and God, as the prophet explained when he said, "Your sins alone have separated you from your God" (Isaiah 59:2). Which is to say that our sins (i.e., the above-cited bad qualities) act as partitions separating us from God.*

2. It is important to know that a prophet could not prophesy unless he had acquired all of the intellectual virtues, and most of the more significant personal ones. As the Sages put it, "Prophecy only manifests itself in a wise, strong, and wealthy individual" (*Shabbat* 92a).

"Wisdom" clearly encompasses all of the intellectual virtues, without a doubt. "Wealth" refers to the personal virtue of contentment, since the Sages referred to people who are content as "wealthy" when they said, "Who is wealthy? One who is happy with his portion" (*Pirkei*

הַתַּאֲוָתָנוּת, וְהַגַּאֲוָה, וְהָרַגְזָנוּת, וְהֶחָרוֹן, וְהָעַזּוּת, וְאַהֲבַת הַמָּמוֹן וְדוֹמֵיהֶם, וְהֵם רַבִּים מְאֹד, וּכְבָר בֵּאַרְנוּ חֹק יְדִיעָתָם בְּפֶרֶק הָרְבִיעִי. וְכֹל הַמִּגְרָעוֹת הַלָּלוּ הֵם הַמָּסַכִּים הַמַּבְדִּילִים בֵּין הָאָדָם לְבֵין ה' יִתְעַלֶּה, אָמַר הַנָּבִיא בְּבָאֲרוֹ אֶת זֶה (ישעיה נ"ט ב'), "כִּי אִם עֲוֹנֹתֵיכֶם הָיוּ מַבְדִּילִים בֵּינֵכֶם לְבֵין אֱלֹקֵיכֶם". אָמַר, שֶׁעֲוֹנוֹתֵינוּ וְהֵם הָרָעוֹת הַלָּלוּ כְּמוֹ שֶׁהִזְכַּרְנוּ, הֵם הַמָּסַכִּים הַמַּבְדִּילִים בֵּינֵינוּ וּבֵינוֹ יִתְעַלֶּה.

ב. וְדַע, שֶׁכָּל נָבִיא אֵינוֹ מִתְנַבֵּא אֶלָּא אַחַר שֶׁנִּקְנוּ לוֹ כָּל הַמַּעֲלוֹת הַהִגְיוֹנִיּוֹת וְרוֹב הַמַּעֲלוֹת הַמִּדּוֹתִיּוֹת, וְהַחֲמוּרוֹת שֶׁבָּהֶן, וְהוּא אָמְרָם (שבת צ"ב.), "אֵין הַנְּבוּאָה שׁוֹרָה אֶלָּא עַל חָכָם גִּבּוֹר וְעָשִׁיר."

"חָכָם" הוּא כּוֹלֵל כָּל הַמַּעֲלוֹת הַהִגְיוֹנִיּוֹת בְּלִי סָפֵק, "וְעָשִׁיר" הִיא מִן הַמַּעֲלוֹת הַמִּדּוֹתִיּוֹת, כְּלוֹמַר, עַיִן טוֹבָה, לְפִי שֶׁהֵם קוֹרְאִים לְבַעַל עַיִן טוֹבָה — עָשִׁיר, וְהוּא אָמְרָם בְּהַגְדָּרַת הֶעָשִׁיר (אבות פרק ד' משנה א'), "אֵיזֶהוּ עָשִׁיר הַשָּׂמֵחַ

...separating us from God — It's clear that while each one of us is separated from God to one degree or another, God is never separated from us. For the use of the image of a partition, or a screen, clearly implies a light in front of it being blocked by that partition.

Indeed, God's "light" — His shin-

ing, undeniable presence — is ever-present. Our experience of it, however, is impaired by our faults. The person of full faith and divine longing would be devastated by the very thought of that, much the way someone who is within easy reach of his beloved yet is denied contact with her would be.

Avot 4:1) and thus defined wealth as the state of being satisfied with whatever one has, and untroubled by what he does not.* "Strength" also refers to a personal virtue, i.e., conducting oneself according to [the dictates of] reason, as we explained in the fifth chapter. As they put it, "Who is strong? One who controls his desires"* (ibid.).

Now, a prophet did not have to have all the personal virtues and be utterly devoid of flaws. For [King] Solomon was a prophet, as the verse attests to by the statement that "God appeared to Solomon at Gibbon" (1 Kings 3:5), yet we find in him an explicit character flaw, i.e., he was overindulgent — and clearly so, since he had many

בְּחֶלְקוֹ," כְּלוֹמַר, שֶׁהוּא מִסְתַּפֵּק בַּמֶּה שֶׁהִמְצִיא לוֹ הַזְּמַן וְאֵינוֹ מִצְטַעֵר עַל מַה שֶּׁלֹּא הִמְצִיא לוֹ. וְכֵן "גִּבּוֹר" גַּם הוּא מִן הַמַּעֲלוֹת הַמִּדּוֹתִיּוֹת, כְּלוֹמַר, שֶׁהוּא מַדְרִיךְ אֶת כֹּחוֹתָיו בְּהֶתְאֵם לַמַּחְשָׁבָה, כְּמוֹ שֶׁבֵּיאַרְנוּ בְּפֶרֶק הַחֲמִישִׁי, וְהוּא אָמְרָם (שם), "אֵיזֶהוּ גִבּוֹר הַכּוֹבֵשׁ אֶת יִצְרוֹ."

וְאֵין מִתְּנָאֵי הַנָּבִיא שֶׁיִּהְיוּ בּוֹ הַמַּעֲלוֹת הַמִּדּוֹתִיּוֹת בִּכְלָלוּתָן עַד שֶׁלֹּא יְהֵא בּוֹ שׁוּם מִגְרַעַת כְּלָל, שֶׁהֲרֵי שְׁלֹמֹה הָיָה נָבִיא כְּמוֹ שֶׁהֵעִיד הַכָּתוּב (מלכים א' ג' ה'), "בְּגִבְעוֹן נִרְאָה ה' וְכוּ'," וּמָצִינוּ בוֹ בְּפֵרוּשׁ מִגְרַעַת מִדּוֹתִית, וְהִיא הַתַּאֲוְתָנוּת וְהוּא

...what he does not — It's sometimes said that only the wealthy can "afford" to be good. After all, they have everything they need and want (or so it seems), so they needn't lapse into pettiness and ill-intention. Yet there are impossibly greedy, unhappy wealthy people in the world, and delightfully poor but glad individuals, too.

The difference apparently lies in being content, as Rambam points out here, rather than restless and always dissatisfied.

Ironically, though, a sort of restlessness and dissatisfaction define piety — as well as prophecy. Yet the difference lies in this: the pious are *spiritually* restless (they always want to advance), and they're dissatisfied with their *spiritual* standing; while we are materially restless and materi-

ally dissatisfied.

controls his desires — The first point to be made is that the reference to controlling one's desires obviously alludes to the previous chapter and underscores our point in our note on p. 99 ("one who controls his desires"), about the connection between these two chapters.

But the question can be raised as to how "strength" per se figures into controlling one's desires and not lapsing into impulsiveness. It would seem to allude to the fact that the person who cares enough about his spiritual well-being and relationship with God to counter the pressures put upon us all to fit in and to live shallow lives that are devoid of depth, ideals, and Godly longings would indeed *have* to be strong.[2]

wives, which derives from an overindulgent disposition. In fact, it is said explicitly, "Did Solomon not sin through them [i.e., through his many wives]?" (Nehemiah 13:26).

[King] David, of blessed memory, was also a prophet, as he said, "The Rock of Israel spoke to me" (2 Samuel 23:3). Yet we find that he was hard-hearted, and though he [only] used it toward other nations and in slaying heretics, while he was compassionate toward the [rest of the] Jewish people, it is nonetheless explained in the Book of Chronicles that God found him unsuitable to build the Holy Temple because he had had so many killed. As He said to David, "You shall not build a house to My Name, for you have spilled much blood..." (1 Chronicles 22:8).[3]

And we find that Elijah, of blessed memory, possessed the quality of anger, though he only used it toward heretics. Nonetheless, our Sages said that God re-

רַבּוּי הַנָּשִׁים, שֶׁזֶּה מִפְּעוּלוֹת תְּכוּנַת הַתַּאֲוָתָנוּת, וְאָמַר מְפוֹרָשׁ (נחמיה י"ג כ"ו), "הֲלֹא עַל אֵלֶּה חָטָא שְׁלֹמֹה וְכוּ'."

וְכֵן דָּוִד עָלָיו הַשָּׁלוֹם, נָבִיא אָמַר (שמואל ב' כ"ג ג'), "לִי דִבֶּר צוּר יִשְׂרָאֵל" וּמְצָאנוּהוּ בַּעַל לֵב קָשֶׁה, וְאַף עַל פִּי שֶׁנִּשְׁתַּמֵּשׁ בְּכָךְ בַּגּוֹיִם וּבַהֲרִיגַת הַכּוֹפְרִים וְהָיָה רַחֲמָן לְיִשְׂרָאֵל, הֲרֵי בֵּיאֵר בְּדִבְרֵי הַיָּמִים שֶׁה' לֹא מְצָאוֹ רָאוּי לִבְנְיַן בֵּית הַמִּקְדָּשׁ בִּגְלַל רוֹב הֲרוּגָיו, וְאָמַר לוֹ (דברי הימים א' כ"ב ח'), "לֹא תִבְנֶה בַיִת לִשְׁמִי כִּי דָמִים רַבִּים שָׁפַכְתָּ וְכוּ'."

וּמְצָאנוּ לְאֵלִיָּהוּ זִכְרוֹנוֹ לִבְרָכָה מִדַּת הַכַּעַס, וְאַף עַל פִּי שֶׁנִּשְׁתַּמֵּשׁ בָּה בַּכּוֹפְרִים וַעֲלֵיהֶם הָיָה כּוֹעֵס, הֲרֵי בֵּאֲרוּ חֲכָמִים ז"ל (סנהדרין קי"ג), שֶׁה' סִלְּקוֹ וְאָמַר לוֹ, שֶׁאֵין רָאוּי לִבְנֵי אָדָם מִי שֶׁיֵּשׁ בּוֹ מִן הַקִּנּוּי כְּמוֹ שֶׁיֵּשׁ בְּךָ, לְפִי שֶׁהוּא יְאַבְּדֵם. וְכֵן מָצָאנוּ שְׁמוּאֵל חָרֵד מִשָּׁאוּל, וְיַעֲקֹב נִתְיָרֵא מִפְּגִישַׁת עֵשָׂו.

כָּל הַמִּדּוֹת הָאֵלּוּ וְכַיּוֹצֵא בָּהֶן הֵם הַמָּסַכִּים שֶׁל הַנְּבִיאִים, עֲלֵיהֶם הַשָּׁלוֹם, וְכָל מִי שֶׁהָיָה בּוֹ מֵהֶם שְׁתֵּי

moved him [from the world] and told him that someone with as much zeal as he had would be unsuitable for the people, for he would destroy them (*Sanhedrin* 113a–b). We likewise find that Samuel was fearful of Saul,* and that Jacob was afraid to encounter Esau.*

These and other such traits were the prophets' partitions [i.e., they are what separated them from God]. And any prophet exhibiting two

---

Samuel was fearful of Saul — See 1 Samuel 16:12.

Jacob was afraid to encounter Esav — See Genesis 32:8.

or three such "unbalanced" traits* was said to see God from behind two or three portions.

3. Do not be surprised by the fact that some personal failings would lessen the quality of one's prophecy. For we find that some character flaws — like anger — actually blocked prophecy completely.

As our Sages said, "Anyone who becomes angry…, if he is a prophet, his ability to prophesy* departs from him" (*Pesachim* 66b), which they deduced from the fact that Elisha could not prophesy when he became angry, until he removed his anger when he said, "Now bring me a musician"* (2 Kings 3:15).

The same is true for worry and anxiety, for our forefather Jacob's divine inspiration left him as long as he was mourning for Joseph, until he was told that Joseph was alive. As it is said, "And the spirit of Jacob their father was revived" (Genesis 45:27), which the Targum* (which

מִדּוֹת אוֹ שָׁלֹשׁ שֶׁאֵינָן מְמוּצָעוֹת, כְּמוֹ שֶׁבֵּאַרְנוּ בְּפֶרֶק הָרְבִיעִי, אוֹמְרִים עָלָיו, שֶׁהוּא רָאָה אֶת ה' מֵאַחוֹרֵי שְׁנֵי מַסֵּכִים אוֹ שְׁלֹשָׁה.

ג. וְאַל תִּתְמַהּ עַל כַּךְ שֶׁחֶסְרוֹן בְּמִקְצַת מִדּוֹת מְמַעֵט בְּמַעֲלַת הַנְּבוּאָה, לְפִי שֶׁמָּצָאנוּ מִקְצַת הַמִּגְרָעוֹת הַמִּדּוֹתִיּוֹת מוֹנְעוֹת אֶת הַנְּבוּאָה לְגַמְרֵי כְּגוֹן הַכַּעַס. אָמְרוּ (פסחים ס"ו:), "כָּל הַכּוֹעֵס אִם נָבִיא הוּא נְבוּאָתוֹ מִסְתַּלֶּקֶת מִמֶּנּוּ," וְלָמְדוּ מֵאֱלִישָׁע שֶׁנֶּעֱדַר מִמֶּנּוּ הֶחָזוֹן כַּאֲשֶׁר כָּעַס עַד שֶׁהֵסִיר כַּעְסוֹ וְהוּא אוֹמְרוֹ (מלכים ב' ג' ט"ו) "וְעַתָּה קְחוּ לִי מְנַגֵּן."

וְכֵן הַדְּאָגָה וְהַדָּאֲבוֹן לְפִי שֶׁיַּעֲקֹב אָבִינוּ כָּל יְמֵי אֶבְלוֹ עַל יוֹסֵף נִסְתַּלְּקָה מִמֶּנּוּ רוּחַ הַקּוֹדֶשׁ עַד שֶׁנִּתְבַּשֵּׂר שֶׁהוּא חַי, אָמַר (בראשית מ"ה כ"ז), "וַתְּחִי רוּחַ יַעֲקֹב אֲבִיהֶם," וְאָמַר הַתַּרְגּוּם הַמְפָרֵשׁ אֶת הָעִנְיָנִים הַמְקֻבָּלִים מִמֹּשֶׁה רַבֵּינוּ, "וּשְׁרַת רוּחַ קוּדְשָׁא עַל יַעֲקֹב אֲבוּהוֹן." וְלָשׁוֹן הַחֲכָמִים, (שבת ל:), "אֵין הַנְּבוּאָה שׁוֹרָה לֹא מִתּוֹךְ עַצְלוּת וְלֹא מִתּוֹךְ עַצְבוּת אֶלָּא מִתּוֹךְ דְּבַר שִׂמְחָה."

explains what was received by our master Moses) rendered, "Divine inspiration dwelt upon Jacob their father [once again]." For as our Sages put it, "Prophecy does not dwell where there is laziness or sadness — only where there is happiness" (*Shabbat* 30b).[4]

"unbalanced" traits — See chapter 4.

his ability to prophesy — Lit., his prophecy.

Now bring me a musician — I.e., he

asked for music to be played so as to mollify his anger, and to thus gain back his ability to prophesy.

the Targum — I.e., Onkelos, whose translation of the Torah from Hebrew to Aramaic was known as *Targum*.

4. Now, when our master Moses realized that there was not a single remaining partition he had not rent, and that he had achieved personal and intellectual perfection, he asked to comprehend God as He truly is, because there was no impediment left.* Thus he said, "Please show me Your Glory"* (Exodus 33:18).

But God told Moses that this was impossible, since he was an intellect fixed in matter,* i.e., he was human. And He said, "No man can see Me and live [i.e., while alive]" (ibid., 20).[5]

Hence, the only thing still standing between [Moses] and

ד. וּלְפִי שֶׁיָּדַע מֹשֶׁה רַבֵּינוּ, שֶׁלֹּא נִשְׁאַר לְפָנָיו מָסָךְ שֶׁלֹּא קָרְעוֹ, וְשֶׁכְּבָר נִשְׁלְמוּ בּוֹ הַמַּעֲלוֹת הַמִּדּוֹתִיּוֹת כֻּלָּן וְהַמַּעֲלוֹת הַהֶגְיוֹנִיּוֹת כֻּלָּן, בִּקֵּשׁ שֶׁיַּשִּׂיג אֶת ה' כְּפִי אֲמִתַּת מְצִיאוּתוֹ כֵּיוָן שֶׁלֹּא נִשְׁאַר לוֹ שׁוּם מוֹנֵעַ וְאָמַר (שמות ל"ג י"ח), "הַרְאֵנִי נָא אֶת כְּבוֹדֶךָ."

אָז הוֹדִיעוֹ ה' יִתְעַלֶּה שֶׁזֶּה בִּלְתִּי אֶפְשָׁרִי מִכֵּיוָן שֶׁהוּא שֵׂכֶל מָצוּי בְּחוֹמֶר, כְּלוֹמַר, מֵחֲמַת הֱיוֹתוֹ אָדָם, וְהוּא אָמְרוֹ (שמות ל"ג כ'), "כִּי לֹא יִרְאַנִי הָאָדָם וָחָי."

וְלֹא נִשְׁאַר בֵּינוֹ וּבֵין הַשָּׂגַת ה' יִתְעַלֶּה כְּפִי אֲמִתַּת מְצִיאוּתוֹ אֶלָּא מָסָךְ אֶחָד בָּהִיר, וְהוּא הַשֵּׂכֶל הָאֱנוֹשִׁי שֶׁאֵינוֹ נִפְרָד, וְהֵיטִיב לוֹ ה' וְנָתַן לוֹ

the comprehension of God as He truly is was a single sheer partition — the fact that his human intellect was still fixed in matter. God none-

...there was no impediment left — What is most telling about this is the fact that Moses perceived that he had to *ask* to comprehend God at that point. We might think that he would surely be spontaneously granted his wish because he had achieved personal and intellectual perfection. But we would all do well to realize that God Almighty longs for our prayers; and that He often withholds things we would assume are due us, in order to prod us to surrender ourselves to His Presence, and to ask Him for His help.

...Your Glory — Yet notice 4:11 above, which speaks of Moses' character flaw! See our supplementary note 28 to chapter 4, which explains

the apparent contradiction.

Nonetheless, the point must be made that Moses wasn't "eminent," as described in chapter 6. He wasn't "born with all the virtuous intellectual and character traits" as the Greeks believed certain people were (see our note on p. 99 ["one who controls his desires"]). He *became* the person he eventually came to be in time, after struggle and great effort. Let that serve as a lesson for us all.

intellect fixed in matter — That is to say that man isn't to be characterized as "a speaking animate being" in contradistinction to *non*-speaking animate beings, as many of the ancients held. Rather, we are minds and souls ensconced in bodies.

theless showed him favor after he made that request by granting him greater comprehension [of Himself] than he had had before, and by letting him know that he could not possibly realize such a goal as long as he was corporeal.[6]

And He referred to true comprehension [of God] as "seeing a face," because when a person sees his friend face-to-face he would never confuse him for anyone else, since his friend's image is so ingrained in his heart. But if he were to see him from behind, even though he recognizes him, he may nonetheless not be sure it was him, or perhaps mistake him for someone else. The same is true when it comes to comprehending God as He truly is. For [the person capable of that] would so fully grasp God's Being

מִן הַהֶשֵּׂג אַחַר שֶׁשָּׁאַל יוֹתֵר מִמַּה שֶׁהָיְתָה לוֹ קוֹדֶם שֶׁשָּׁאַל, וְהוֹדִיעוֹ שֶׁהַתַּכְלִית בִּלְתִּי אֶפְשָׁרִית לוֹ כָּל זְמַן שֶׁהוּא בַּעַל גּוּף.

וְכִנָּה אֶת אֲמִתּוּת הַהַשָּׂגָה בִּרְאִיַּת פָּנִים, לְפִי שֶׁהָאָדָם כַּאֲשֶׁר רוֹאֶה פְּנֵי חֲבֵרוֹ תִּקְבַּע לוֹ בְּלִבּוֹ צוּרָה שֶׁאֵינָה מִתְחַלֶּפֶת לוֹ בְּזוּלָתוֹ, אֲבָל אִם רָאָה אֲחוֹרָיו, וְאַף עַל פִּי שֶׁהוּא מַכִּירוֹ בְּאוֹתָהּ הָרְאִיָּה, אֲבָל אֶפְשָׁר שֶׁיִּסְתַּפֵּק בּוֹ וְאֶפְשָׁר שֶׁיִּתְחַלֵּף לוֹ בְּזוּלָתוֹ. כָּךְ הַשָּׂגָתוֹ יִתְעַלֶּה לְפִי הָאֱמֶת הוּא שֶׁתִּוָּשֵׂג בְּנֶפֶשׁ מֵאֲמִתַּת מְצִיאוּתוֹ, בְּאוֹפֶן שֶׁלֹּא יְשׁוּתַּף בְּאוֹתָהּ הַמְּצִיאוּת זוּלָתוֹ מִשְּׁאָר הַנִּמְצָאִים, עַד שֶׁיִּמְצָא אֶת מְצִיאוּתוֹ [יִתְעַלֶּה] קְבוּעָה בְּנַפְשׁוֹ בְּאוֹפֶן שׁוֹנֶה מִמַּה שֶׁיִּמְצָא בְּנַפְשׁוֹ מִמְּצִיאוּת שְׁאָר הַנִּמְצָאִים. וְאֵין יְכוֹלֶת בְּהַשָּׂגַת הָאָדָם לְהַשִּׂיג עַד כְּדֵי הַשָּׂגָה זוֹ, אֲבָל הוּא עָלָיו הַשָּׁלוֹם הִשִּׂיג פָּחוֹת מִזֶּה מְעַט, וְהוּא שֶׁכִּנָּה בּוֹ (שמות ל"ג כ"ג), "וְרָאִיתָ אֶת

that he would never confuse Him for anyone else,* since God's Being would be so ingrained in him that it would be utterly distinct from anything else's, as far as he was concerned.* Now, while no human could ever achieve that degree of comprehension, [Moses], of blessed memory, achieved an only slightly lesser degree of it, which is what God was referring to when He said, "You will [only] see My back"

...confuse Him for anyone else — In theory, for as Rambam is about to say, "no human could ever achieve that degree of comprehension."

...concerned — That is to say that the person who would truly comprehend God's essence would be as sure it was God he was experiencing at the time as another person would be sure it was his friend he was seeing when he came upon him full-face. In contrast, anyone who was said to have "seen" (i.e., comprehended) God from "behind" (i.e., indirectly) couldn't be sure that he had actually comprehended Him.[7]

(Exodus 33:23).[8] And I will explain all this in further detail in *Sefer HaNevuah*.*

Since the Sages, of blessed memory, knew that these two categories of flaws — i.e., personal ones and intellectual ones — act as partitions to separate man from God and therefore serve to differentiate the prophets by rank, they said that some of them [i.e., some of the Sages] had such wisdom and loftiness that "they were worthy of having the Divine Presence dwell upon them just as our master Moses did" (*Sukkah* 28a). Nonetheless, do not overlook the fact that the Sages only likened them to him and never equated them to him, God forbid. They said similar [things] about others, too, like Yehoshua, in the same way.

We have thus explained all we intended to in this chapter.

אֲחוֹרָי." וְעוֹד אַשְׁלִים עִנְיָן זֶה בְּסֵפֶר הַנְּבוּאָה.

וּלְפִי שֶׁיָּדְעוּ חֲכָמִים, עֲלֵיהֶם הַשָּׁלוֹם, כִּי שְׁנֵי מִינֵי מִגְרָעוֹת אֵלּוּ, כְּלוֹמַר, הַהֶגְיוֹנִיּוֹת וְהַמִּדּוֹתִיּוֹת, הֵם הַמָּסַכִּים הַמַּבְדִּילִים בֵּין הָאָדָם לְבֵין ה', וּבָהֶם נִבְדָּלִים מַעֲלוֹת הַנְּבִיאִים, אָמְרוּ עַל אֲחָדִים מֵהֶם לְפִי מַה שֶׁרָאוּ מֵחָכְמָתָם וּמִדּוֹתֵיהֶם (סוכה כ"ח.), "רְאוּיִים הֵם שֶׁתִּשְׁרֶה עֲלֵיהֶם שְׁכִינָה כְּמֹשֶׁה רַבֵּינוּ," וְאַל יֵעָלֵם מִמְּךָ עִנְיַן הַדִּמְיוֹן לְפִי שֶׁהֵם דִּמּוּ אוֹתָם לוֹ, לֹא שֶׁהִשְׁווּ אוֹתָם לוֹ חָלִילָה לְה'. וְכֵן אָמְרוּ עַל אֲחֵרִים, כִּיהוֹשֻׁעַ, עַל הַדֶּרֶךְ שֶׁאָמַרְנוּ.

וְזֶהוּ הָעִנְיָן אֲשֶׁר נִתְכַּוַּנּוּ לְבָאֲרוֹ בְּפֶרֶק זֶה.

Sefer HaNevuah — See our note on this book on p. 38 of chapter 1.

Synopsis

1. *There have always been qualitative differences between prophets. Some were said to "see" God from behind several screens, others from behind just a few, while Moses was said to have "seen" Him from behind a single, diaphanous one. The difference between them is based upon the principle that every intellectual or personal flaw a person suffers from, and each sin he commits, acts as a barrier between himself and God.*

2. *Nonetheless, a person could not become a prophet until he had achieved all of the intellectual virtues and most of the more significant personal ones, like contentment and the ability to let reason rule over impulse. But a prophet did not have to have all the personal virtues and be devoid of flaws, for we find that Solomon, David, Elijah, Samuel, and Jacob each suffered from one personal flaw or another, even though they were prophets.*

3. *Some personal flaws (like anger, sorrow, and anxiety) can actually cause prophecy to be withheld for a time, until they are corrected.*

4. *When Moses realized that he had achieved personal and intellectual perfection, he asked to comprehend God. But God would not allow him to, because he was still a mortal being, which proved to be the only barrier separating him from God. No other prophet ever compared to him.*

8

באופי הטבעי האנושי
ON HUMAN NATURE

This final chapter returns to a number of themes addressed earlier on, and delves into one or two that are even more profound.

Addressing the idea of our being beholden to no one and nothing else in our personal choices, as discussed in chapter 2, Rambam allows here that, while we are certainly predisposed to certain traits, the truth is, we can nonetheless transcend any untoward predisposition — with some effort. In the end, we will ultimately have to answer for who we came to be, despite our provocations. As such, we're obliged to contend with our flaws and do teshuvah for our sins, since no one caused us to embrace them other than ourselves.

Some are under the mistaken impression that certain human experiences were "meant to be" from the beginning, and that we're powerless in the face of them. But the only things that can be said to be fixed are the ones that have nothing to do with ethical choices, like natural phenomena.

Rambam then goes on to deal with certain statements in the Torah which seem to suggest that God impels behavior. But he assures us that while, indeed, certain individuals were prevented from doing teshuvah for their misdeeds and suffered as a consequence, that was only so because they'd committed serious sins earlier on, and were thus being punished.

Nonetheless, as a rule, Rambam assures us, unless God punishes you by taking away your free will in one instance or another, you yourself choose your behavior. So it would behoove you to strive for goodness.

This then raises the question of how anyone could do or be anything on his own if God already knows what he'll decide beforehand. Doesn't that suggest that certain things will come to be despite us?

Rambam's response to this complex subject is that we simply cannot fathom God's knowledge — let alone His foreknowledge — since His knowledge is an inseparable part of His Being. As we said in the previous chapter, we mortals can never hope to understand Him (or His knowledge). Suffice it to say, though, that the tradition assures us that our behavior is in our hands alone, and that God never compels us to act one way or another (except under the extraordinary circumstances stated above).

1. It is not possible for man to be born either inherently lofty or inherently flawed, just as it is impossible for him to be born instinctively adept at a trade. But it is possible to be predisposed to a particular virtue or fault, and to find it easier to do certain things over others.*

א. אִי אֶפְשַׁר שֶׁיְּהֵא הָאָדָם מֵרֵאשִׁיתוֹ בְּטִבְעוֹ בַּעַל מַעֲלָה אוֹ בַּעַל מִגְרַעַת, כְּשֵׁם שֶׁאִי אֶפְשָׁר שֶׁיְּהֵא אָפִי הָאָדָם בְּטִבְעוֹ בַּעַל מְלָאכָה מִן הַמְּלָאכוֹת הַמַּעֲשִׂיּוֹת, אֲבָל אֶפְשָׁר שֶׁיְּהֵא אָפִיוֹ בְּטִבְעוֹ מוּכָן לְמַעֲלָה אוֹ מִגְרַעַת, שֶׁיְּהוּ פְּעוּלוֹת אֵלּוּ יוֹתֵר קַלִּים עָלָיו מִפְּעוּלוֹת זוּלָתָם.

certain things over others — This last chapter addresses the great theme of free will versus predetermination; i.e., whether we choose to do the things we do and to be the person we are, or God chooses beforehand.

Rambam's answer will prove to be a sort of compromise — or better yet, a *balance* between the two extremes of complete free will and complete predetermination. He contends that ultimately God determines who we are from the outset, but we determine what we will do with what we are from then on.

As such, everyone enjoys a certain number of innate physical, intellectual, and personal boons and impediments. We're each asked to use those boons to our best advantage, and to overcome our impediments.

His point will also be that, while some people can be born skilled in carpentry, for example, intellectually advanced, or inherently generous, no one is born a full-fledged carpenter, scholar, or philanthropist. Every inborn skill and predisposition has to be honed and perfected. Otherwise, it remains a mere potential, and thus a failing in the end, because it was never brought to fruition. For as Rambam put it at the end of chapter 1 in reference to the *nefesh*, if a person never achieves his potential, "then [his] aptitude to achieve it would have been for naught."

On Human Nature / 121

So, for example, [a person] whose constitution tended toward dryness and whose brain matter was clear and barely moist by nature [i.e., a "cool, calm, and collected" individual, as we might put it] would find it easier to remember and understand things than a more phlegmatic person would, one whose brain matter was very moist.*

But if someone who was predisposed toward this virtue [i.e., toward remembering and understanding things easily] did not study at all and was not encouraged to do so, he would undoubtedly remain ignorant* [despite his native gifts]; while if [someone else] with a duller, quite moist nature were taught and trained, he

הַמָּשָׁל בָּזֶה, כְּגוֹן שֶׁהָיָה מִזְגוֹ נוֹטֶה אֶל הַיּוֹבֶשׁ יוֹתֵר וְתִהְיֶה מַהוּת מוֹחוֹ זַכָּה, מְעֻטֶּת הַלַּחְיוֹת, הֲרֵי אָדָם זֶה יֵקַל עָלָיו הַזִּכְרוֹנוֹת וַהֲבָנַת הָעִנְיָנִים יוֹתֵר מֵאָדָם בַּעַל מָרָה לְבָנָה וּמְרֻבָּה הַלַּחְיוֹת בְּמוֹחוֹ.

אֲבָל אִם יֻנַּח אוֹתוֹ שֶׁיֵּשׁ בּוֹ הַהֲכָנָה בְּמִזְגוֹ כְּלַפֵּי הַמַּעֲלָה הַזּוֹ בְּלִי לִמּוּד כְּלָל, וּבְלִי לְעוֹרֵר בּוֹ שׁוּם כֹּחַ, הֲרֵי הוּא יִשָּׁאֵר סָכָל בְּלִי סָפֵק. וְכֵן אִם יְלַמְּדוּ וְיַשְׂכִּילוּ אוֹתוֹ גַּם הַטִּבְעִיִּים רֹב הַלַּחְיוֹת הֲרֵי הוּא יִלְמַד וְיָבִין, אֲבָל בְּקֹשִׁי וִיגִיעָה. וְעַל הָאוֹפֶן הַזֶּה עַצְמוֹ יִהְיֶה אָדָם מֶזֶג לִבּוֹ יוֹתֵר חַם מִמַּה שֶּׁרָאוּי מְעַט וְאָז יִהְיֶה אַמִּיץ, כְּלוֹמַר, שֶׁיֵּשׁ בּוֹ הַהֲכָנָה לָאַמִּיצוּת, וְאִם יְלֻמַּד לָאַמִּיצוּת יִהְיֶה אַמִּיץ בְּקַלּוּת. וְאַחַר מֶזֶג לִבּוֹ קַר יוֹתֵר מִן הָרָאוּי הֲרֵי יֵשׁ בּוֹ הֲכָנָה לְמֹרֶךְ וּלְפַחַד, שֶׁאִם לֻמַּד לְכַךְ וְהֻרְגַּל בָּזֶה יְקַבְּלֵהוּ בְּקַלּוּת. וְאִם

could learn and understand things [despite his not having a knack for it], though [it would admittedly be only] with diffficulty and effort. In the same fashion, someone who is inappropriately hot by nature [i.e., a "hot-blooded" individual] could be brave, since he is predisposed to it, and he would easily become so, if he were taught how to, while someone overly cold by nature who is thus predisposed to cowardice and fear would easily become cowardly and fearful if he were trained in it and acted that

---

was very moist — Hippocrates and his medieval adherents believed that health and disposition were rooted in the balance or imbalance of one's bodily humors (yellow bile, black bile, phlegm, and blood), and by their degree of moistness or dryness. Rambam's point here is that a "clear," "dry" constitution would more easily allow for

intelligence than a "moist," "phlegmatic" one, and that this is simply a given in one's makeup.

he would undoubtedly remain ignorant — Because, as we indicated above, while we're each granted certain advantages from the start, we need to cultivate them if they're ever to reach fruition.

way consistently. Yet if he were directed towards courage, he could undoubtedly become brave, though with difficulty, if he consistently did brave things.

2. The only reason I explained this to you was to prevent you from accepting the inanities that astrologers hold to be true. For they imagine that a person's birthdate determines whether he will be lofty or flawed, and that one is compelled to act accordingly.*

It is important to know, however, that the Torah agrees with Greek philosophy which substantiates conclusively that man's actions are in his own hands, no one compels him to do anything, and nothing other than himself* ever

יַטֵּהוּ לְאֲמִיצוּת הֲרֵי בְּקוֹשִׁי יִהְיֶה אַמִּיץ, אֲבָל יִהְיֶה אִם יוּרְגַּל בְּכָךְ בְּלִי סָפֵק.

ב. וְלֹא בֵּיאַרְתִּי לְךָ אֶת זֶה אֶלָּא כְּדֵי שֶׁלֹּא תַחֲשׁוֹב שֶׁאוֹתָם הַהֲזָיוֹת שֶׁבּוֹדִים אוֹתָם בַּעֲלֵי מִשְׁפְּטֵי הַמַּזָּלוֹת שֶׁהֵם אֱמֶת, שֶׁהֵם מְדַמִּים שֶׁמּוֹלְדוֹת בְּנֵי אָדָם עוֹשׂוֹת אוֹתָם בַּעֲלֵי מַעֲלָה אוֹ בַּעֲלֵי מִגְרַעַת, וְשֶׁהָאָדָם מוּכְרָח עַל אוֹתָן הַפְּעוּלוֹת עַל כָּל פָּנִים.

אֲבָל אַתָּה דַע, שֶׁדָּבָר מֻסְכָּם הוּא מִתּוֹרָתֵינוּ וּפִילוֹסוֹפִית יָוָן בַּמֶּה שֶׁאֲמַתּוּהוּ הוֹכָחוֹת הָאֲמִתִּיּוֹת, שֶׁכָּל פְּעֻלּוֹת הָאָדָם מְסוּרוֹת בְּיָדוֹ, אֵין עָלָיו הֶכְרֵחַ בָּהֶם וְאֵין לוֹ מוֹשֵׁךְ חִיצוֹנִי כְּלָל

...to act accordingly — Although we're not quite as enamored of astrology in our day as people were in Rambam's day, we certainly take genetics, psychology, and sociology seriously. And while scholars in those fields don't suggest that our choices per se are determined by our genes or psychological and environmental background, many laypeople do, and have thus come to accept levels of evil, crime, perversion, and the like that were once almost universally objectionable.

"What else could he do?" some actually muse in the face of wrongdoing, "After all, it's almost as if he *had* to!"

Rambam vehemently argues against that, and proclaims that, while indeed we're colored by our background and have to contend

with untoward predispositions, still and all, we're free to strive toward betterment, despite it. Ultimately, we're the masters of our own moral substance. In light of chapter 2 above, this means that we can indeed control our emotions, and can adopt sound or unsound ideas and philosophies of life.

We'd also do well to realize that if we're compelled to do wrong, then we're also compelled to do good, and wouldn't deserve credit for our victories any more than for our failings. Yet few of us in modernity deny anyone credit for his achievements (even though they'd have been beyond his control, too, according to this logic).

nothing other than himself — Lit., there is no external factor that....

inclines him toward a character virtue or flaw (other than a predisposition, which as we explained would make him find a specific thing easier or harder to do). Nonetheless, it will never happen that one is compelled [to] or restrained [from behaving one way or another].

For if man was compelled to act the way he does, then all the Torah's imperatives and prohibitions would be in vain and utterly meaningless, since man would not be free to do as he wishes.*

All study, education, and labor- or craft-related training would be in vain, too, since (according to this theory) man would have something other than himself* compelling him to do something in particular, to be familiar with a particular subject, or to exhibit a particular trait.*

Reward and punishment — whether society's* or God's* — would be utterly unfair. For if a person ("Shimon") killed another ("Reuven") because he was forced to or compelled to kill, and his victim was forced or compelled to be killed, then why should [the killer], Shimon,

הַמַּטֵּהוּ כְּלַפֵּי מַעֲלָה אוֹ מִגְרַעַת, אֶלָּא אִם כֵּן הִיא הֲכָנָה מַזְגִּית בִּלְבַד, כְּמוֹ שֶׁבֵּיאַרְנוּ, וְיִהְיֶה קַל לוֹ דָּבָר מִסְיָם אוֹ קָשֶׁה. אֲבָל שֶׁיְּהֵא מוּכְרָח אוֹ מָנוּעַ — אֵין זֶה בְּשׁוּם פָּנִים וְאוֹפֶן.

וְאִלּוּ הָיָה הָאָדָם מוּכְרָח בְּמַעֲשָׂיו כִּי אָז הָיוּ בְּטֵלִים הַצִּוּוּי וְהָאַזְהָרָה הַתּוֹרָנִיִּים, וְהָיָה כָּל זֶה לְבַטָּלָה בְּהֶחְלֵט, כֵּיוָן שֶׁאֵין הַבְּחִירָה בְּיַד הָאָדָם בְּמַה שֶׁיַּעֲשֶׂה.

וְכֵן מִתְחַיֵּיב מִזֶּה בִּטּוּל הַלִּמּוּד וְהַחִנּוּךְ, וְלִמּוּדֵי כָּל הַמְלָאכוֹת הָאוּמָנוּתִיּוֹת וְהָיָה נַעֲשָׂה כָּל זֶה לְבַטָּלָה, כֵּיוָן שֶׁעַל כָּל פָּנִים יֵשׁ לְאָדָם בְּהֶכְרֵחַ מוֹשֵׁךְ חִיצוֹנִי הַמּוֹשְׁכוֹ — לְפִי דַּעַת הַסּוֹבְרִים כֵּן — לְמַעֲשֶׂה פְּלוֹנִי שֶׁיַּעֲשֶׂה אוֹתוֹ וּלְמַדַּע פְּלוֹנִי שֶׁיֵּדָעֶנּוּ וּלְמִדָּה פְּלוֹנִית שֶׁתְּהֵא בּוֹ.

וְהָיָה גַּם הַשָּׂכָר וְהָעוֹנֶשׁ עֲוֶל מָחְלָט, בֵּין מֵאִתָּנוּ זֶה לָזֶה וּבֵין מֵאֵת ה' לָנוּ, כִּי שִׁמְעוֹן זֶה שֶׁרָצַח אֶת רְאוּבֵן, אִם הָיָה זֶה אָנוּס וּמֻכְרָח לַהֲרֹג וְזֶה אָנוּס וּמֻכְרָח לֵיהָרֵג, אִם כֵּן מַדּוּעַ נַעֲנִישׁ אֶת שִׁמְעוֹן? וְעוֹד הֵיאַךְ יִתָּכֵן

...as he wishes — Which is to say, how could you be charged by God to do or not do something when the ability to comply was intrinsically out of your hands?

something other than himself — Lit., something external to himself.

...to exhibit a particular trait — That is, it would be useless to try to grow and change if your fate was already fixed.

society's — Lit., the sort we administer to each other.

God's — Lit., that of God toward us.

be punished? And how could it ever be said that God, Who is just and fair, punished someone for doing something he was compelled to do and could not help but do, even if he did not want to? Besides, any precautions we would take [against homelessness, poverty, disease, etc.], like building houses, procuring food, running away when frightened,* and the like, would be meaningless, since what was decreed to be simply had to be.

But that is nonsense, utterly meaningless, and runs counter to reason and to emotion;[1] it tears down [i.e., it threatens to invalidate] the wall of Torah; and it deems God unjust, Heaven forfend![2]

לוֹמַר עָלָיו יִתְעַלֶּה צַדִּיק וְיָשָׁר הוּא, שֶׁיַּעֲנִישֵׁהוּ עַל מַעֲשֶׂה שֶׁהוּא מוּכְרָח לַעֲשׂוֹתוֹ עַל כָּל פָּנִים, וַאֲפִילוּ אִם רָצָה שֶׁלֹּא לַעֲשׂוֹתוֹ, לֹא יָכוֹל? וְעוֹד וְהָיוּ בְּטֵלִים כָּל הַהִתְכּוֹנְנוּיוֹת עַד סוֹפָן, בִּנְיַן הַבָּתִּים, וּקְנִיַת הַמְּזוֹנוֹת, וְהַבְּרִיחָה בִּזְמַן הַפַּחַד וְזוּלָתָן, כֵּיוָן שֶׁכָּל מַה שֶׁנִּגְזַר שֶׁיִּהְיֶה מוּכְרָח לִהְיוֹת.

וְכָל זֶה הֶבֶל וּדְבָרִים בְּטֵלִים בְּהֶחְלֵט, וְנֶגֶד הַמֻּשְׂכָּל וְהַמֻּרְגָּשׁ, וְהֶרֶס חוֹמַת הַתּוֹרָה, וּלְהַנִּיחַ כִּי ה' יִתְעַלֶּה עַוָּל, חָלִילָה לוֹ מִכָּךְ.

ג. אֲבָל הָאֱמֶת שֶׁאֵין בּוֹ סָפֵק שֶׁכָּל מַעֲשֵׂי הָאָדָם מְסוּרִים בְּיָדוֹ, אִם רָצָה עוֹשֶׂה וְאִם רָצָה לֹא יַעֲשֶׂה, לְלֹא הֶכְרֵחַ וְלֹא כְּפִיָּה עָלָיו בְּכָךְ, וּלְפִיכָךְ נַעֲשָׂה חִיּוּבֵי הַצִּוּוּי.

3. But the truth of the matter, beyond any doubt, is that all of man's actions are in his own hands. If he wants to do something, he can; and if he does not want to, he does not have to. There is no compulsion or force working upon him,* and that is what establishes the authority of the mitzvot.

---

when frightened — I.e., when faced with a threat.

working upon him — The subject at hand is human free will versus "Divine compulsion" — that is, whether we're free to do as we see fit, or whether God (so to speak) transports us from place to place of His own volition, has us do what He wants us to do, and then carries us along to our next mission, despite ourselves.

Hence, the question is, "How free are we to act out on our own wills?" Or, put another way, "Where does God's will end and mine begin? Where does my will end and God's begin?"

Rambam seems to be saying quite firmly that man is utterly free to act on his own — that he's "as free as a bird" and able to do what he wants, when he wants, as he wants. But in truth, man *isn't* as free as a bird. In fact, no matter how hard he tries, or how determined he is, he could never fly on his own. Nor could he live to two hundred, become invisible, etc. God Almighty *does* manifest and express His Will all the time, which, by definition, is utterly and uniquely invincible and unstoppable.

Yet man is nonetheless completely free in one area and domain — in his moral decisions. Those decisions affect both the world's and one's own spiritual standing.

Here, then, is one of the great truths, as Rambam seems to be setting it out: each one of us stands alone in life, existentially, and is accountable for his or her being, no one else. And we're each very real. For if we were so essentially vacant that God not only provided us with body and soul, but with a predetermined personal will and direction as well, then what would we be but well-stocked drones of no consequence?

Thus, unlike any other living creatures, we're free to act out on our moral decisions. But we'd do well to realize that not only do we have to contend with the consequences of those decisions, we'll also have to answer for them.

For while an animal has to contend with the fact that it moves from here to there, it will never have to *answer* for itself if something bad happened as a result. The animal doesn't have the inner incandescence and rushing will that would credit or fault it with its deeds. If a cat knocked something over that fell on someone and hurt him, we'd say, "What would you expect of a cat?"

But no one would say, "What would you expect of a person?" under the same circumstances, unless he believed a person is preformulated from birth, and could not help

but act a certain way.

Rambam's point is that there is a part of us that *decides*, thinks, wants something to happen, and goes about engaging in things as much as possible to make it happen. This part will have to account for its decisions to God, just as any person in power has to account for his or her decisions.

What this all seems to come down to is a person's depiction of his and others' immediate or long range future, and his decisions about what to do after arriving at that depiction. He'll either like what he expects or he won't, and he'll react accordingly, in order to encourage or discourage that future as much as he wants to. The immediate future in toto will be affected accordingly, which will then affect the next future, and so on. And the world will be changed as a consequence of that first person's depictions and reactions.

For in fact, each one of us extends towards the future, and God Almighty allows for our active contribution to it. The agent for all that is our (hopefully reasoned) decisions about what to do — the use of our free will. For everything else around us and everything else in the world will be swept up in the future we have brought about, and can only contend with it dumbly and passively, while we have it within us to color it; give it contour and heft, width and dapple; to make the future formidable, or haggard and meaningless; or to have it play itself out another way.

In a manner of speaking, then, we're each mystery writers who must answer to our "Publisher" as to why our "characters" do what they do, why they simply don't do something else with their natures — or *despite* their natures, why they didn't do

After all, [God Himself] has said, "Behold, I have placed before you today life and goodness, death and evil...[therefore choose life*]" (Deuteronomy 30:15–19), and thus placed the choice in our hands.[6] And there is necessarily punishment for transgression* and reward for obedience,* [as it says], "[You will receive blessing] if you obey [the mitzvot of God, your Lord], and [you will be cursed] if you disobey"* (ibid. 11:26–28), and there is an obligation to study and to teach, [as it is said,] "Teach them to your children" (ibid. 11:19), and "...learn them, observe them, and do them" (ibid. 5:1). [There is an obligation] as well to do everything else connected to studying and observing mitzvot.*

וְאָמַר (דברים ל' ט"ו), "רְאֵה נָתַתִּי לְפָנֶיךָ הַיּוֹם אֶת הַחַיִּים וְאֶת הַטּוֹב וְאֶת הַמָּוֶת וְאֶת הָרָע," (שם ל' י"ט) "וּבָחַרְתָּ בַּחַיִּים." וְנָתַן אֶת הַבְּחִירָה בָּזֶה בְּיָדֵינוּ. וְחִיּוּבֵי הָעוֹנֶשׁ לְעוֹבֵר וְהַגְּמוּל לְנִשְׁמַע (ראה דברים י"א כ"ז-כ"ח), "אִם תִּשְׁמְעוּ וְאִם לֹא תִשְׁמָעוּ." וְחִיּוּבֵי לִלְמֹד וּלְלַמֵּד (שם י"א י"ט), "וְלִמַּדְתֶּם אוֹתָם אֶת בְּנֵיכֶם וְכוּ'," (שם ה' א') "וּלְמַדְתֶּם אוֹתָם וּשְׁמַרְתֶּם לַעֲשׂוֹתָם," וּשְׁאָר כָּל מַה שֶׁנֶּאֱמַר בְּלִמּוּד וּבְקִיּוּם הַמִּצְוֹת.

---

something further back in the work that would have worked or effected the story better, and the like.[3]

There is another point to be made, though, that's quite ironic.

The prophets, whom Rambam focused on shortly before this — the most spiritually developed human beings — were in a state that could only be described as "beyond free will" when they prophesied. For they were so taken over by God's presence at that point, they simply couldn't *help* but obey His every wish.

As such, it follows that while free will is vitally important for our spiritual progress, it's nonetheless a means to an end, which is the achievement of a state of consciousness *beyond* free will, of being utterly and selflessly attuned to God's wishes.[4]

choose life — I.e., God suggests that we choose life, but we are not

compelled to if we do not see fit. That is our decision alone.[5]

for transgression — Lit., for the transgressor.

for obedience — Lit., for one who obeys.

if you disobey — The full text reads, "Behold, I have set before you today a blessing and a curse. A blessing, if you obey God your Lord's mitzvot.... And a curse, if you disobey God your Lord's mitzvot."

...observing mitzvot — That is to say, since we're responsible for our actions and we will have to answer for them, it behooves us to know just what we're responsible for, so that we can do what's right. Furthermore, we're expected to teach others about what God expects of them as well.

One is also obligated to take all the precautions [against harm or damage] enumerated in the Book of Truth,* which says, "Make a guardrail for your roof...lest someone fall from there"* (Deuteronomy 22:8); "[Let him go back to his house,] for he may die in battle"* (ibid. 20:5–7); "[If you make your neighbor's garment* as security, bring it back to him by sundown. for that is his only covering...] What would he then sleep with?"* (Exodus 22:26); [and] "Do not take lower or upper millstones as a pledge"* (Deuteronomy 24:6). And there were many other statements in the Torah and the Books of the Prophets on this subject, i.e., taking precautions.*

וְכֵן נַעֲשׂוּ חִיּוּבִיִּים כָּל הַהִתְכּוֹנְנֻיּוֹת, כְּמוֹ שֶׁפֵּרֵשׁ בְּסֵפֶר הָאֱמֶת וְאָמַר (שם כ"ב ח'), "וְעָשִׂיתָ מַעֲקֶה לְגַגֶּךָ כִּי יִפֹּל הַנֹּפֵל," (שם כ' ה'-ז') "פֶּן יָמוּת בַּמִּלְחָמָה," (שמות כ"ב כ"ו) "בַּמֶּה יִשְׁכָּב," (דברים כ"ד ו') "לֹא יַחֲבֹל רֵחַיִם וָרָכֶב," וְרַבִּים מְאֹד בַּתּוֹרָה וּבְסִפְרֵי הַנְּבוּאָה מֵעִנְיָן זֶה, כְּלוֹמַר, הַהִתְכּוֹנְנֻיּוֹת.

See the end of section 6 below, as well, which says that, "Since the ability to willfully do either good or bad things at any time is an essential part of our beings, *it is necessary that we be instructed in the right path....*"[7]

the Book of Truth — I.e., the Torah.

...lest someone fall from there — The full verse reads, "Make a guardrail for your roof when you build a new house so as not to bring blood upon your house, lest someone fall from there."

he may die in battle — The full text reads, "The officers will speak to the people, saying, 'Which man has built a new house and not dedicated it? Let him go back to his house, for he may die in battle, and another may dedicate it [instead of him]. Which man has planted a vineyard and not eaten from it? Let him also go back to his house, for he may die in battle, and another may eat from it. And which man has betrothed a wife and not taken her? Let him go back to his house, for he may die in battle, and another may take her."

what would he then sleep with — The full text reads, "If you take your neighbor's garment as security, bring it back to him by sundown. For that is his only covering, it is the garment for his skin. What would he then sleep with [if you do not return it]?"

...as a pledge — The full text reads, "Do not take lower or upper millstones as a pledge, for [one who does that] takes a man's life [i.e., his livelihood] as a pledge."

taking precautions — In other words, since man is free to act as he will, he is liable to bring about harm to others. It is thus reasonable as well as incumbent upon us to take precautions against that.

As to the Sages' statement that "everything is in the hands of Heaven but the fear of Heaven" (*Berachot* 33b) — that, too, is correct. In fact, it [even] follows along with our explanation [as we'll soon see].

אֲבָל הַלָּשׁוֹן שֶׁמָּצָאנוּ לַחֲכָמִים, וְהוּא אָמְרָם (ברכות ל"ג.), "הַכֹּל בִּידֵי שָׁמַיִם חוּץ מִיִּרְאַת שָׁמַיִם," הוּא נָכוֹן וְהוּא אָמוּר עַל הַדֶּרֶךְ שֶׁבִּיאַרְנוּ.

4. Now, people often mistakenly believe that a person is compelled to do certain things that are actually open to choice, for example marrying a particular woman or acquiring a certain amount of money by stealing, but that is incorrect. For it is a mitzvah to marry a woman permissible to you by means of a *ketubah* and *kiddushin**** in order to have children, and God does not compel the observance of mitzvot.* In

ד. אֶלָּא שֶׁהִרְבֵּה טוֹעִים בּוֹ בְּנֵי אָדָם וְחוֹשְׁבִים עַל מִקְצָת פְּעוּלוֹת הָאָדָם אֲשֶׁר הוּא בְּחִירִי בָּהֶם שֶׁהוּא מוּכְרָח עֲלֵיהֶם, כְּגוֹן לִישָׂא פְּלוֹנִית אוֹ שֶׁיִּהְיֶה הַמָּמוֹן הַזֶּה בְּיָדוֹ בְּגֶזֶל. וְזֶה אֵינוֹ נָכוֹן, לְפִי שֶׁהָאִשָּׁה הַזּוֹ אִם לְקָחָהּ בַּכְּתֻבָּה וְקִדּוּשִׁין וְהִיא מוּתֶּרֶת לוֹ, וְנָשָׂאָהּ לִפְרִיָּה וְרִבְיָה הֲרֵי זוֹ מִצְוָה, וְאֵין ה' גּוֹזֵר עַל עֲשִׂיַּת מִצְוָה. וְאִם הָיוּ נִשּׂוּאֶיהָ בְּרֶשַׁע הֲרֵי זוֹ עֲבֵירָה, וְאֵין ה' גּוֹזֵר עַל עֲבֵירָה.

וְכֵן זֶה שֶׁגָּזַל מָמוֹן שֶׁל פְּלוֹנִי, אוֹ גְנָבוֹ אוֹ רִמָּהוּ אוֹ כָּפַר בּוֹ וְנִשְׁבַּע לוֹ עַל מָמוֹנוֹ, אִם נֹאמַר שֶׁה' גָּזַר עַל זֶה שֶׁיָּבוֹא לְיָדוֹ מָמוֹן זֶה וְשֶׁיֵּצֵא מִיַּד אוֹתוֹ הַשֵּׁנִי, הֲרֵי

addition, if there were some wrongdoing in marrying her [i.e., if someone were to marry a woman who was forbidden to him], it would be a transgression, and God does not decree that a person transgress.

The same would be true if one stole money from a person or robbed or defrauded him, then denied it and took an oath about the money [declaring it to be his own]. If one claimed that God decreed that the money be taken from the other person's hands and placed in his,* it

---

by means of a *ketubah* and *kiddushin* — I.e., with a marriage contract and following a betrothal period.

...the observance of mitzvot — Notice the point being made here. While God does indeed beckon, call upon, charge, and enjoin us to do His mitzvot, He nonetheless doesn't coerce, harass, or prevail upon us to carry through with them. We alone choose whether or not to do them.

placed in his — That is, if one claimed that God decreed that the money be taken from the other person's hands and placed in his, so he wasn't really stealing so much as fulfilling God's will....

would be saying that God decreed a transgression and that is simply not so.*

Rather, all of a person's actions are in his own hands, and through them obedience and disobedience will undoubtedly be demonstrated. For as we explained in the second chapter, Torah-based imperatives and prohibitions only apply to the deeds one is free to act upon or not.* As such, the fear of Heaven,* which is not in the hands of Heaven but is rather given to man, as we have explained, lies in this part of the *nefesh.**

גָּזַר עַל עֲבֵירָה, וְאֵין הַדָּבָר כֵּן.

אֶלָּא כָּל פְּעֻלּוֹת הָאָדָם שֶׁהֵם מְסוּרוֹת בְּיָדוֹ בָּהֶן בְּלִי סָפֵק תִּמָּצֵא הַמִּשְׁמַעַת וְהַמֶּרִי, לְפִי שֶׁכְּבָר בֵּיאַרְנוּ בְּפֶרֶק הַשֵּׁנִי, שֶׁהַצִּוּוּי וְהָאַזְהָרָה הַתּוֹרָנִיִּים אֵינָם אֶלָּא בִּפְעֻלּוֹת שֶׁיֵּשׁ לָאָדָם בָּהֶן בְּחִירָה לַעֲשׂוֹתָן, אוֹ שֶׁלֹּא לַעֲשׂוֹתָן, וּבְחֵלֶק הַזֶּה מִן הַנֶּפֶשׁ תִּהְיֶה יִרְאַת שָׁמַיִם אֵינָהּ בִּידֵי שָׁמַיִם, אֶלָּא מְסוּרָה לִבְחִירַת הָאָדָם, כְּמוֹ שֶׁבֵּיאַרְנוּ.

ה. וְהִנֵּה אָמְרָם "הַכֹּל" אֵין הַכַּוָּנָה בְּךָ אֶלָּא עַל הַדְּבָרִים הַטִּבְעִיִּים אֲשֶׁר אֵין לָאָדָם בְּחִירָה בָּהֶם כְּגוֹן הֱיוֹתוֹ אָרוֹךְ

5. And the [Sages'] statement that "*everything* [is in the hands of Heaven]," is not intended literally; what they were referring to were natural phenomena which man has no control over, like being tall or

---

that is simply not so — That is to say, some believe that marriages are "made in heaven" and that some people are "meant" to have money regardless of how either comes about. But that is like believing that one's "destiny" is etched in the stars. In fact, marriage and income are both rooted in ethics and mitzvot, and everyone is accountable for his or her own part in either.

Although marriages are very likely to come about because the people involved share the same tastes, run in the same social circles, are approximately as attractive as each other, meet the right age and social criteria, etc., there are presumably a number of potential partners fitting those categories, so no one person is impelled to marry another.

It might also be argued that certain people are simply craftier, more cunning, and have more "street sense" than others, and are thus more likely to take advantage of the latter and take their money. In the end, though, no one is impelled to either commit a crime or to be a victim of one.

to act upon or not — I.e., they only apply to those capacities of your *nefesh* that allow you the freedom to do as you choose — your emotions and intellect (see 2:1).

the fear of Heaven — Which is synonymous with man's willingness to either obey or disobey God.

this part of the *nefesh* — I.e., in the emotions and the intellect.

short, whether it will rain or be dry, whether the air will be foul or pure, and everything else that occurs in the [natural] world, rather than through man's actions.*

But the point the Sages made, that obedience or disobedience [i.e., the fear of Heaven] are not the decree of God or by His will, but rather by man's will, were deduced from the words of Jeremiah, who said, "Neither bad nor good comes from the mouth of the Most High" (Lamentations 3:38), where "bad" refers to bad deeds, and "good" refers to good deeds. That means to say that God does not decree whether a person will do bad deeds or good deeds.

That being so, it is only right that man mourns for and regrets all his sins and transgressions, since he has done wrong of his own volition. As [Jeremiah] said, "What should a living man mourn for, a mortal man? For his sins" (ibid., 39).

He then goes on to say that the cure for this illness therefore lies in our own hands. For just as we disobeyed by choice, so, too, can we turn aside from our bad deeds.* Hence he concluded with, "Let us search and examine our ways, and return to God. Let us lift up our hearts with our hands to God in Heaven" (ibid., 40–41).

אוֹ קָצָר, אוֹ יְרִידַת גֶּשֶׁם אוֹ בַּצּוֹרֶת, אוֹ עֲכִירוּת הָאֲוִיר אוֹ זַכּוּתוֹ וְכַיּוֹצֵא בָּזֶה מִכָּל מַה שֶּׁיֵּשׁ בָּעוֹלָם, חוּץ מִתְּנוּעוֹת הָאָדָם וּתְנוּחוֹתָיו.

אֲבָל עִנְיָן זֶה שֶׁבֵּיאֲרוּהוּ חֲכָמִים, שֶׁהַמִּשְׁמַעוֹת וְהַמֶּרִי אֵינָם בִּגְזֵירָתוֹ יִתְעַלֶּה וְלֹא בִּרְצוֹנוֹ אֶלָּא הֵם בִּרְצוֹן אוֹתוֹ הָאָדָם נִמְשְׁכוּ בָּזֶה אַחֲרֵי דִבְרֵי יִרְמְיָהוּ, וְהוּא אָמְרוֹ (איכה ג' ל"ח), "מִפִּי עֶלְיוֹן לֹא תֵצֵא הָרָעוֹת וְהַטּוֹב," כִּי "רָעוֹת" הֵם הַמַּעֲשִׂים הָרָעִים וְ"טוֹב" הַמַּעֲשִׂים הַטּוֹבִים, אָמַר שֶׁאֵין ה' גּוֹזֵר שֶׁיַּעֲשֶׂה הָאָדָם מַעֲשִׂים רָעִים וְלֹא שֶׁיַּעֲשֶׂה מַעֲשִׂים טוֹבִים.

וְכֵיוָן שֶׁהַדָּבָר כֵּן הֲרֵי בֶּאֱמֶת רָאוּי לוֹ לְאָדָם לְהִתְאוֹנֵן וּלְהִצְטַעֵר עַל מַה שֶּׁעָשָׂה מִן הָעֲווֹנוֹת וְהָאֲשָׁמוֹת כֵּיוָן שֶׁהוּא עָשָׂה הָרַע בִּרְצוֹנוֹ, אָמַר (שם ג' ל"ט), "מַה יִּתְאוֹנֵן אָדָם חַי גֶּבֶר עַל חֲטָאָיו."

וְחָזַר וְאָמַר, כִּי רְפוּאַת חוֹלִי זֶה בְּיָדֵינוּ, שֶׁכְּשֵׁם שֶׁמָּרִינוּ בִּרְצוֹנֵינוּ, כָּךְ יְכוֹלִים אָנוּ לָשׁוּב וְלַחֲזֹר מִמַּעֲשֵׂינוּ הָרָעִים, וּלְפִיכָךְ אָמַר אַחֲרֵי זֶה (שם ג' מ'-מ"א), "נַחְפְּשָׂה דְרָכֵינוּ וְנַחְקֹרָה וְנָשׁוּבָה עַד ה', נִשָּׂא לְבָבֵנוּ אֶל כַּפַּיִם, אֶל קֵל בַּשָּׁמָיִם."

---

rather than through man's actions — Lit., rather than through man's movements or rests.

...our bad deeds — This section encapsulates a lot of what has been said already. It points out that while God certainly controls the circumstances into which we've been placed and the sort of people we are,

6. Now, there is a very popular notion among people which can even be found in the words of the Sages and in other literature, to the effect that man's rising up, his sitting down, and all his movements are dependent on God's will and His desire. This is true, but only in a specific way.

For if you were to throw a stone in the air, and it came back down, it would be correct to say it did that because God wanted it to, since God designated* that the earth in its entirety would be in the center,* and that any time a part of it would be thrown upward, it would [automatically] return to the center (the way particles of fire always flicker upward in deference to God's will that fire [always] do that).*

ו. אֲבָל הַדָּבָר הַמְפֻרְסָם אֵצֶל בְּנֵי אָדָם, וְאֶפְשָׁר לִמְצוֹא בְּדִבְרֵי חֲכָמִים וּבִלְשׁוֹנוֹת הַכְּתוּבִים כְּמוֹתוֹ, וְהוּא שֶׁעֲמִידַת הָאָדָם וִישִׁיבָתוֹ וְכָל תְּנוּעוֹתָיו בִּרְצוֹן ה' יִתְעַלֶּה וּבְחֶפְצוֹ, וְזֶה דָּבָר נָכוֹן, אֲבָל בְּאוֹפֶן מְסֻיָּם.

וְהוּא, כְּגוֹן הַזּוֹרֵק אֶבֶן לָאֲוִיר וְיָרְדָה לְמַטָּה, אִם נֹאמַר עָלֶיהָ שֶׁבִּרְצוֹן ה' יָרְדָה לְמַטָּה, הוּא דָּבָר נָכוֹן לְפִי שֶׁה' רָצָה שֶׁתִּהְיֶה הָאָרֶץ בִּכְלָלוּתָהּ בְּמֶרְכָּז, וּלְפִיכָךְ כָּל זְמַן שֶׁנִּזְרַק חֵלֶק מִמֶּנָּה לְמַעְלָה הֲרֵי הוּא נָע אֶל הַמֶּרְכָּז. וְכֵן כָּל חֵלֶק מֵחֶלְקֵי הָאֵשׁ נָע לְמַעְלָה בְּאוֹתוֹ הָרָצוֹן שֶׁהָיָה כְּלוֹמַר שֶׁתִּהְיֶה הָאֵשׁ נָעָה לְמַעְלָה.

---

nonetheless, we ourselves determine how we'll react to all that and the sorts of people we'll be in the end.

For we have it within us to either acquiesce to our harmful dispositions, and thus succumb to the illness of self that this entails, or to grow past them, correct any errors we've made along the way, and go on to perfect ourselves and achieve piety despite — or perhaps even as a consequence of — them.

designated — Lit., willed.

in the center — We might first think that Rambam is expressing the geocentric view of the universe that held sway at the time he wrote this, which was replaced by the heliocentric view introduced by

Copernicus (1403–1473). Apparently, however, he is referring instead to the classical idea that things always return to their "center" or source (soil, in this case, to the earth; fire, in the case to follow, to the sun, etc.).[8]

that fire [always] do that — This, too, touches upon free will, as discussed above.

Based on the principles presented here and as we know fully well ourselves, inanimate objects have natures that allow us to predict things about them. I can fully expect a rock to fall when I drop it, and I can plan accordingly. I can also fully expect food to eventually spoil, etc.

In fact, humans also have natures that allow us to predict things about them. For example, we generally

But it is not true to say that God wants that particular moving piece* of earth to fall at that very moment.

The Mutakallimun* disagree. I have heard them contend that God's will manifests itself in everything at each and every moment.[9] But this is not our belief. Rather, [we hold that] God already expressed His will in the course of the six days of creation, and that things act in accordance with their nature from then on, as it is said, "What was will always be, and what has been done will always be done; for there is nothing new under the sun" (Ecclesiastes 1:9).

לֹא שֶׁה' רָצָה עַתָּה בְּעֵת תְּנוּעַת הַחֵלֶק זֶה מִן הָאָרֶץ שֶׁיָּנוּעַ לְמַטָּה.

וּבָזֶה חוֹלְקִים "כַּת הַמְדַבְּרִים," לְפִי שֶׁשָּׁמַעְתִּים אוֹמְרִים, שֶׁהָרָצוֹן בְּכָל דָּבָר הוּא בְּכָל עֵת וְעֵת תָּמִיד, וְלֹא כֵן אֱמוּנָתֵנוּ אָנוּ, אֶלָּא הָרָצוֹן הָיָה בְּשֵׁשֶׁת יְמֵי בְרֵאשִׁית וְשֶׁכָּל הַדְּבָרִים יִנְהֲגוּ לְפִי טִבְעֵיהֶם תָּמִיד, כְּמוֹ שֶׁאָמַר (קהלת א' ט'), "מַה שֶּׁהָיָה הוּא שֶׁיִּהְיֶה וּמַה שֶּׁנַּעֲשָׂה הוּא שֶׁיֵּעָשֶׂה וְאֵין כָּל חָדָשׁ תַּחַת הַשָּׁמֶשׁ."

וּלְפִיכָךְ הֻצְרְכוּ חֲכָמִים לוֹמַר, בְּכָל הַנִּסִּים אֲשֶׁר הֵם מִחוּץ לְטֶבַע, שֶׁהָיוּ וְשֶׁיִּהְיוּ כְּפִי שֶׁהֻבְטַח בָּהֶם, כֻּלָּם כְּבָר קֹדֶם הָרָצוֹן בָּהֶם בְּשֵׁשֶׁת יְמֵי בְרֵאשִׁית, וְנִתַּן בְּטֶבַע אוֹתָם הַדְּבָרִים אָז שֶׁיִּתְחַדֵּשׁ בָּהֶם מַה שֶּׁנִּתְחַדֵּשׁ. וְכַאֲשֶׁר נִתְחַדֵּשׁ בִּזְמַן הָרָאוּי חָשְׁבוּ

That explains why the Sages found it necessary to say that all the supernatural miracles that have occurred [in the past] and all those that we are promised will come about [in the future]were already designated to come about in the course of the six days of creation, when the miraculous events were implanted in the nature of the things involved in them.* And when these miraculous events come about at the proper* time, they might seem to have been instigated right there

---

sleep at night and work to earn a living in the daytime. We plan for that and make predictions based on those facts our whole lives long. But none of us can actually make predictions based on someone's *inner* life, since we cannot be sure he'll be the same person today as he was yesterday. He can always decide to act otherwise, and spin about the course of his and our own whole life in a moment.

moving piece — Lit., moving part.

Metakallimun — See supplementary note 12 to chapter 1.

involved in them — I.e., involved in the miracles. So for example, the phenomenon of splitting was implanted into the very makeup of the Red Sea when it was created.

proper — I.e., designated.

and then, but in fact they were not.*

They [the Sages] expounded upon this at length in the *Midrash Kohelet* and elsewhere, and said as a consequence that "the world always pursues its usual course" (*Avodah Zarah* 54b). And you will find that [the Sages], may peace be upon them, always avoided ascribing God's will to particular things at particular moments.

As such, were we to say that a person was standing or sitting "in deference to God's will" we would be referring to the fact that he has the inborn [God-given] ability to

בּוֹ שֶׁהוּא דְּבַר אִיכָא עַתָּה, וְאֵין הַדָּבָר כֵּן.

וּכְבָר הִרְחִיבוּ בָּעִנְיָן זֶה הַרְבֵּה בְּמִדְרָשׁ קֹהֶלֶת וְזוּלָתוֹ, וּמִמַּה שֶׁאָמְרוּ בָּעִנְיָן זֶה (עבודה זרה נ"ד), "עוֹלָם כְּמִנְהָגוּ הוֹלֵךְ," וְתִמְצָאֵם עֲלֵיהֶם הַשָּׁלוֹם, תָּמִיד בְּכָל דִּבְרֵיהֶם מִתְרַחֲקִים מִלְּהַנִּיחַ כִּי הָרָצוֹן בְּכָל דָּבָר וְדָבָר וּבְכָל עֵת וָעֵת.

וְעַל דֶּרֶךְ זוּ אוֹמְרִים בְּאָדָם אִם עָמַד וְיָשַׁב, שֶׁבִּרְצוֹן ה' עָמַד וְיָשַׁב, כְּלוֹמַר, שֶׁנִּתַּן בְּטִבְעוֹ בְּרֵאשִׁית מְצִיאוּת הָאָדָם שֶׁיַּעֲמֹד וְיֵשֵׁב בִּרְצוֹנוֹ, לֹא שֶׁהֵ' רָצָה עַתָּה בְּעֵת עֲמִידָתוֹ שֶׁיַּעֲמֹד אוֹ שֶׁלֹּא יַעֲמֹד, כְּמוֹ שֶׁלֹּא רוֹצֶה עַתָּה בְּעֵת נְפִילַת הָאֶבֶן הַזּוּ שֶׁתִּפּוֹל אוֹ שֶׁלֹּא תִּפּוֹל.

stand or sit at will — not to the notion that God wanted him to stand or not at that moment. It would be analogous to the way we would say that God does not will a particular stone to fall or not as it is falling.

---

in fact they were not — That is to say, since specific actions aren't predetermined, and everything follows the laws of nature instead, we're forced to say that a miracle is a "natural phenomenon," too, rather than a supernatural one, and that a miracle is actually a playing out of a unique characteristic implanted in a thing's nature from the first.

In modern terms, a miracle would be something quirky that occurred suddenly and unexpectedly, but is perfectly explainable. It is fairly similar to the way adrenaline functions in our everyday lives. While the average person could never imagine lifting a car, for ex-

ample, since that would be simply "unnatural," he'd nonetheless be able to do it "miraculously," should someone he loves become trapped under it, thanks to his adrenaline. For the "miracle" of adrenaline is certainly a part of our physiology, but it's an extraordinary part of it that only comes into play under specific circumstances.

Thus, both the miracle of the splitting of the Red Sea and the miracle of adrenaline are expressions of an extraordinary aspect of nature. The point to be remembered, though, is that both were purposefully "programmed" by God to come about the way they did.[10]

In short, the principle that you need to know is that just as God designated man to stand vertically, to be broad-chested, and to have fingers, so too, did He designate him to move about or stay in place at will, and to act freely, without anything compelling him to or preventing him from doing so.*

This was explained in the Book of Truth and enunciated in its context as follows: "Behold, man has become like one of us, knowing good from evil" (Genesis 3:22). As the Targum clearly explained, the intent of the statement, "like one of us, knowing good from evil," serves to indicate that man is unique in the world this way, in that he is the only being who can distinguish between good and evil on his own and can do whichever he pleases without impediment. And since that is so, he just might "stretch out his hand

נִמְצָא כְּלָל הַדְּבָרִים שֶׁאַתָּה תֵּדַע,
שֶׁכְּמוֹ שֶׁרָצָה ה' שֶׁיְּהֵא הָאָדָם בַּעַל
קוֹמָה זְקוּפָה, וְחָזֶה רָחָב, וּבַעַל
אֶצְבָּעוֹת, כַּךְ רָצָה שֶׁיְּהֵא מִתְנוֹעֵעַ וְנָח
מִצַּד עַצְמוֹ, וְיַעֲשֶׂה פְּעוּלוֹת בִּבְחִירָתוֹ,
וְאֵין דָּבָר הַמַּכְרִיחוֹ עֲלֵיהֶם וְלֹא מוֹנֵעַ
אוֹתוֹ מֵהֶן.

כְּמוֹ שֶׁבִּיאֵר בְּסֵפֶר הָאֱמֶת וְאָמַר
בְּפֵרוּשׁוֹ עִנְיָן זֶה (בראשית ג' כ"ב)
"הֵן הָאָדָם הָיָה כְּאַחַד מִמֶּנּוּ לָדַעַת
טוֹב וָרָע," וּכְבָר בִּיאֵר הַתַּרְגּוּם אֶת
פֵּירוּשׁוֹ שֶׁעִנְיָנוֹ מִמֶּנּוּ לָדַעַת טוֹב וָרָע,
כְּלוֹמַר, שֶׁהוּא נַעֲשֶׂה אֶחָד בָּעוֹלָם,
כְּלוֹמַר, סוּג שֶׁאֵין כָּמוֹהוּ סוּג אַחֵר
הַדּוֹמֶה לוֹ בְּעִנְיָן זֶה הַמָּצוּי לוֹ, וּמַה
הוּא, שֶׁהוּא עַצְמוֹ וּמִצַּד עַצְמוֹ יֵדַע
הַטּוֹבוֹת וְהָרָעוֹת וְיַעֲשֶׂה אֵיזֶה מֵהֶן
שֶׁיִּרְצֶה וְאֵין מוֹנֵעַ אוֹתוֹ מִכָּךְ, וְכֵיוָן
שֶׁהַדָּבָר כֵּן פֶּן יִשְׁלַח יָדוֹ וְיִקַּח מִזֶּה
וְאָכַל וָחַי לְעוֹלָם.

וְכֵיוָן שֶׁזֶּה חִיּוּבִי בִּמְצִיאוּת הָאָדָם,
כְּלוֹמַר שֶׁיַּעֲשֶׂה בִּרְצוֹנוֹ פְּעוּלוֹת הַטּוֹב
וְהָרַע מָתַי שֶׁיִּרְצֶה, צָרִיךְ לְלַמְּדוֹ דֶּרֶךְ
הַטּוֹב וִיצֻוֶּה וְיֻזְהַר וְיֵעָנֵשׁ וְיִגָּמֵל, וְיִהְיֶה

and take from this [the Tree of Life], eat, and live forever" (ibid.).

Since the ability to willfully do either good or bad things at any time is an essential part of our beings, it is necessary that we be instructed in the right path, commanded [to do certain things] and warned [against others], punished [for disobeying] and rewarded [for obey-

---

...from doing so — Let's explain this rather complicated theme as simply as we can.

Some argue that one's every move is dictated by God, but that is simply not true. For although gravitational pull has been implanted by God in nature, the act of acceding to it at any moment by any one thing hasn't been dictated by Him. Similarly, the ability to choose between one's actions has likewise been implanted in his nature by God, yet He doesn't dictate what one will actually do at any one moment. That lies in a person's own hands.

ing], and all this is just. In addition, we are obligated to accustom ourselves to do good things and achieve character virtues, and avoid doing bad things in order to undo any flaws we might already have, rather than say that we cannot change them. Because any circumstance can be turned around from good to bad, or from bad to good — the decision is in our own hands. In fact, because of this fact alone we have been able to say all we have about obedience and disobedience.*

7. But there is something else to explain on this subject. For there are several verses that lead people to imagine that God preordains and compels disobedience, which is absurd.* So we will indeed explain them, since people discuss them so much.

An example would be [God's] statement to Abraham, "They will serve them [the Egyptians], and they [the Egyptians] will afflict them [i.e., your descendants]" (Genesis 15:13). Based on that, some say, "Apparently [God] decreed that the Egyptians were to harm Abraham's descendants! Why, then, did He punish them? Weren't they forced to enslave them, as it was decreed?"

כָּל זֶה צֶדֶק. וְנִתְחַיֵּיב לְהַרְגִּיל אֶת עַצְמוֹ
בִּפְעוּלוֹת הַטּוֹב עַד שֶׁיּוּשְׂגוּ לוֹ הַמַּעֲלוֹת
וְיִתְרַחֵק מִפְּעוּלוֹת הָרַע עַד שֶׁיָּסוּרוּ
מִמֶּנּוּ הַמִּגְרָעוֹת אִם הָיוּ בּוֹ כְּבָר וְאַל
יֹאמַר יֶשְׁנָם כְּבָר בּוֹ בְּמַצָּב שֶׁאִי אֶפְשָׁר
לְשַׁנּוֹתָם, כִּי כָּל מַצָּב אֶפְשָׁר לְשַׁנּוֹתוֹ
מִטּוֹב לְרַע וּמֵרַע לְטוֹב, וְהַבְּחִירָה בְּיָדוֹ
בְּכָךְ וְעַל פִּי עִנְיָן זֶה וּבִגְלָלוֹ הֵבֵאנוּ כָּל
מַה שֶׁהִזְכַּרְנוּ מֵעִנְיְנֵי הַמִּשְׁמַעַת וְהַמֶּרִי.

ז. וְהִנֵּה נִשְׁאַר לָנוּ דָּבָר אֶחָד לְבָאֲרוֹ
בְּעִנְיָן זֶה, וְהוּא שֶׁנֶּאֶמְרוּ מִקְצַת
פְּסוּקִים שֶׁמְּדַמִּים בָּהֶם בְּנֵי אָדָם,
שֶׁהַ' גּוֹזֵר עַל הַמֶּרִי וְשֶׁהוּא מַכְרִיחַ
בָּהֶם, וְדָבָר זֶה בָּטֵל, וְלָכֵן נְבָאֲרֵם, לְפִי
שֶׁהִרְבָּה נָשְׂאוּ וְנָתְנוּ בָּהֶם בְּנֵי אָדָם.

מֵהֶם אָמְרוּ לְאַבְרָהָם (בראשית
ט"ו י"ג), "וַעֲבָדוּם וְעִנּוּ אוֹתָם," אָמְרוּ,
הִנֵּה כְּבָר גָּזַר עַל הַמִּצְרִים לְהָרַע לְזֶרַע
אַבְרָהָם וּמַדּוּעַ הֶעֱנִישָׁם? וְהֵם מָכְרָחִים
עַל כָּל פָּנִים לְשַׁעְבְּדָם כְּמוֹ שֶׁגָּזַר?

...obedience and disobedience —
That is, given that we're free to act of our own volition and are thus culpable for our own deeds, it is only logical and fair that we'd be warned to do or not do certain things (i.e., that we'd be informed as to what is right and what is wrong, and charged with doing the right things). Thus we take upon ourselves to do good and

undo bad in our beings. Otherwise Torah observance and the pursuit of piety would be absurd.

...which is absurd — Just as there are people who believe that God preordains compliance (see section 4 above), there are others who believe that He preordains noncompliance, as well.

But the answer is as follows. It is as if God had said, "Some people yet to be born will be rebellious, others obedient, some righteous, and others wrongdoers." That is simply a fact.* God's saying that does not compel any one person to necessarily be a wrongdoer has or anyone else to necessarily be righteous. Rather, whoever happens to be a wrongdoer has chosen to be one, and if he wants to be righteous he could have chosen to do so, without anything preventing him. Likewise, any righteous person could have been a wrongdoer, if he had wanted to, without anything preventing him.

God's declaration was not directed toward anyone in particular, who might then claim that it was decreed on him [to do wrong]. Rather, He spoke in general terms, and every individual is free to make his own decision in accordance with his nature. Likewise, each and every Egyptian who harmed and oppressed the Israelites could have chosen not to harm them, if he so wanted, for it was not decreed on any individual to do harm.

The same response applies to God's statement [to Moses], "Behold, you are about to lie with your forefathers, and the people will rise up

וּתְשׁוּבַת שְׁאֵלָה זוֹ, שֶׁזֶּה דּוֹמֶה כְּמוֹ אִלּוּ אָמַר יִתְעַלֶּה כִּי אֲשֶׁר יִוָּלְדוּ בֶּעָתִיד יִהְיוּ בָהֶם מַמְרִים וְנִשְׁמָעִים וְצַדִּיקִים וּרְשָׁעִים, וְזֶה אֱמֶת, וְלֹא בִּדְבַר זֶה יִתְחַיֵּב פְּלוֹנִי הָרָשָׁע שֶׁיְּהֵא רָשָׁע עַל כָּל פָּנִים, וְלֹא פְּלוֹנִי הַצַּדִּיק שֶׁיְּהֵא צַדִּיק עַל כָּל פָּנִים, אֶלָּא כָּל מִי שֶׁהָיָה מֵהֶם רָשָׁע הֲרֵי זֶה בִּרְצוֹנוֹ, וְאִלּוּ רָצָה לִהְיוֹת צַדִּיק הָיָה הַדָּבָר בְּיָדוֹ, וְאֵין לוֹ מוֹנֵעַ. וְכֵן כָּל צַדִּיק אִלּוּ רָצָה לִהְיוֹת רָשָׁע לֹא הָיָה לוֹ מוֹנֵעַ.

לְפִי שֶׁהַהוֹדָעָה לֹא בָאָה עַל כָּל אֶחָד וְאֶחָד עַד שֶׁיֹּאמַר כְּבָר נִגְזַר עָלַי, אֶלָּא בָּאָה בִּסְתָם וְנִשְׁאַר כָּל אָדָם בִּרְצוֹנוֹ כְּפִי עִקַּר הָאוֹפִי הַטִּבְעִי. וְכָךְ כָּל אֶחָד וְאֶחָד מֵהַמִּצְרִים שֶׁהֵרֵעוּ וְהֵצֵרוּ לְיִשְׂרָאֵל אִלּוּ רָצָה שֶׁלֹּא לְהָרַע לָהֶם הֲרֵי הָיְתָה הַבְּחִירָה בְּיָדוֹ בְּכָךְ, לְפִי שֶׁלֹּא גָזַר עַל אָדָם מְסֻיָּם לְהָרַע.

וּתְשׁוּבָה זוֹ עַצְמָהּ הִיא הַתְּשׁוּבָה בְּאָמְרוֹ (דברים ל"א ט"ז), "הִנְּךָ שׁוֹכֵב עִם אֲבוֹתֶיךָ וְקָם הָעָם הַזֶּה

...simply a fact — That is to say, God's statement to Abraham seems to indicate that He had already determined that the Egyptians would oppress the Israelites. Rambam's point is that this is not so. God was merely recounting what was going to happen when the Israelites encountered the Egyptians in a world in which injustice and wrongdoing exist.

and stray after the alien gods of the land" (Deuteronomy 31:16). It is tantamount to God saying, "Do such-and-such to whoever serves idols,"* for if no one had served idols, then there would have been no reason for all the threats and all the curses.

In fact, the same is true of all the punishments in the Torah. After all, we would not say that because there is a sentence of stoning in the Torah someone who profaned the Sabbath was compelled to do so, any more than we would say that because there are curses in the Torah [against one who worships idols] anyone who worshiped idols and thus subjected himself to these curses was preordained to worship idols. Rather, whoever worshiped idols did so of his own volition and subjected himself to punishment,* as it is written, "Since they chose their own ways [and delight in their abominations], I will choose [their afflictions and bring their fears upon them]" (Isaiah 66:3–4).

וְזָנָה אַחֲרֵי אֱלֹהֵי נֵכַר הָאָרֶץ," כִּי אֵין הֶבְדֵּל בֵּין זֶה וּבֵין אָמְרוֹ, שֶׁכָּל הָעוֹבֵד עֲבוֹדָה זָרָה נַעֲשָׂה בּוֹ כַּךְ וְכָךְ, לְפִי שֶׁאִלּוּ לֹא הָיָה שָׁם לְעוֹלָם מִי שֶׁיַּעֲבוֹר הָיוּ כָּל הָאִיּוּמִים לְבַטָּלָה, וְהָיוּ כָּל הַקְּלָלוֹת כּוּלָן לְבַטָּלָה.

וְכָךְ כָּל הָעוֹנָשִׁין שֶׁבַּתּוֹרָה וְלֹא בִּגְלַל מְצִיאוּת דִּין הַסְּקִילָה בַּתּוֹרָה נֹאמַר שֶׁזֶּה שֶׁחִלֵּל אֶת הַשַּׁבָּת מוּכְרָח לְחַלְּלוֹ. וְלֹא בַּמְּצִיאוּת הַקְּלָלוֹת נֹאמַר שֶׁאוֹתָם אֲשֶׁר עָבְדוּ עֲבוֹדָה זָרָה וְחָלוּ בָּהֶם אוֹתָם הַקְּלָלוֹת נִגְזַר עֲלֵיהֶם לְעָבְדָהּ, אֶלָּא בִּרְצוֹנוֹ עָבַד כָּל מִי שֶׁעָבַד וְחָל עָלָיו הָעוֹנֶשׁ (ישעיה ס"ו ג'-ד'), "גַּם הֵמָּה בָּחֲרוּ בְּדַרְכֵיהֶם גַּם אֲנִי אֶבְחַר וְכוּ'."

...serves idols — God's statement to Moses, "Behold, you are about to lie with your forefathers, and the people will rise up and stray after the alien gods," is immediately followed by His revelation that His "anger will be kindled against them on that day," and that He'd forsake them and "hide [His] face from them." And as a consequence, they'd "be devoured, and many evils [would] befall them" (Deuteronomy 31:16–17).

Rambam's point is that we're not to mistakenly take the quote to mean that the people were *destined* to suffer great harm, and that Moses was

being informed of the inevitable. Instead, we're to understand God to be saying that *if* the people were to serve alien gods, they were to be punished in the ways He was about to enunciate.

...subjected himself to punishment — In other words, the fact that the Torah enunciates punishments for specific sins doesn't imply that someone is necessarily going to commit them. Those punishments are cited in the event that someone takes it upon himself to commit the sins.

Still and all, God's statement that He had "hardened Pharaoh's heart" (Exodus 14:4), and the fact that He later punished him and had him destroyed, needs to be addressed here. We will actually deduce an important principle from it.*

Therefore, reflect upon what I have to say about this as opposed to what others have said, and decide for yourself who is right.*

8. Now, if the only sin Pharaoh and his servants had committed was not setting Israel free, that would certainly be problematic, since God Himself prevented them from freeing the Israelites. As it is written, "For I [God] hardened his heart and the heart of his servants" (Exodus 10:1). After all, how could God have asked Pha-

אֲבָל אָמְרוּ (שמות י"ד ד'), "וְחִזַּקְתִּי אֶת לֵב פַּרְעֹה," וְאַחַר כָּךְ הֶעֱנִישׁוֹ וְהִשְׁמִידוֹ, הִנֵּה זֶה מָקוֹם שֶׁיֵּשׁ לְדַבֵּר בּוֹ, וְיוּשַׂג בּוֹ יְסוֹד גָּדוֹל.

וְלָכֵן הִתְבּוֹנֵן בִּדְבָרַי בָּעִנְיָן זֶה וְשִׂים לְבָּךְ בּוֹ, וְהַשְׁוֵהוּ לִדְבָרַי כָּל מִי שֶׁדִּבֵּר בּוֹ וּבְחַר לְעַצְמְךָ אֶת הַטּוֹב.

ח. וְהוּא, שֶׁפַּרְעֹה וַעֲבָדָיו אִלּוּ לֹא הָיָה לָהֶם עָוֹן אֶלָּא זֶה שֶׁלֹּא שִׁלְּחוּ אֶת יִשְׂרָאֵל הָיָה הַדָּבָר קָשֶׁה בְּלִי סָפֵק, שֶׁהֲרֵי כְּבָר מְנָעָם מִלְּשַׁלֵּחַ, כְּמוֹ שֶׁאָמַר (שמות י' א'), "כִּי אֲנִי הִכְבַּדְתִּי אֶת לִבּוֹ וְאֶת לֵב עֲבָדָיו," וְאַחַר כָּךְ מְבַקֵּשׁ מִמֶּנּוּ לְשַׁלְּחָם וְהוּא מוּכְרָח שֶׁלֹּא לְשַׁלֵּחַ, וְאַחַר כָּךְ מַעֲנִישׁוֹ עַל שֶׁלֹּא שָׁלַח וּמַשְׁמִידוֹ וּמַשְׁמִיד עֲבָדָיו, וְזֶה וַדַּאי יִהְיֶה עָוֶל וְסוֹתֵר לְכָל מַה שֶּׁהִקְדַּמְנוּ, אֶלָּא שֶׁאֵין הַדָּבָר כֵּן.

כִּי פַּרְעֹה וַעֲבָדָיו הִמְרוּ בִּרְצוֹנָם בְּלִי הֶכְרֵחַ וְלֹא אוֹנֶס, וְהֵרֵעוּ לַגֵּרִים אֲשֶׁר הָיוּ בְּאַרְצָם, וְעָשׂוּ לָהֶם עָוֶל מֻחְלָט,

raoh to set them free if he were forced *not* to? And how could God have punished him afterward for not setting them free, then destroy him and his servants? That certainly would not have been just, and it would have contradicted everything we said.* But that is not the case.

In point of fact, Pharaoh and his servants willfully rebelled, rather than acquiescing to force or compulsion [in an earlier instance], when they oppressed the foreigners in their midst* without any justification

---

deduce an important principle from it — I.e., rather than foil our contentions, the fact that God fortified Pharaoh's heart will actually help explain them.

...who is right — See our encapsulation of this argument in the note at the end of section 8 ("in bondage").

...everything we said — For as Rambam wrote in section 2 above, "How could it ever be said that God Who is just and fair punished someone for doing something he was compelled to do and could not help but do...?"

the foreigners in their midst — I.e., the Jewish people.

whatsoever. For as it is explicitly stated, "[Pharaoh] said to his people, 'Behold, the Children of Israel [are more numerous and mighty than we]. Come, let us deal cunningly with them!' "* (Exodus 1:9–10). They did that freely and with evil intent, without any compulsion.

So God punished them for that — by preventing them from repenting and by thus allowing them to incur the sentence His judgment deemed was due them. Hence, it was their not setting Israel free previously which prevented the Egyptians from repenting.[11]

In fact, God already made this clear to Pharaoh by letting him know that if He had only wanted to have the Jewish nation set free, He would have destroyed Pharaoh and his servants, and set [the Israelites] free [then and there, on His own]. But besides wanting the Israelites set free, God wanted to punish the Egyptians for their earlier wickedness [in having oppressed them in the first place], as He told Abraham He would when He said, "I will also judge the nation that they will serve" (Genesis 15:14).

Since it would have been impossible to punish the Egyptians if they had repented, God withheld repentance from them, and they kept the

כְּמוֹ שֶׁאָמַר בְּפֵרוּשׁ (שם א' ט–י), "וַיֹּאמֶר אֶל עַמּוֹ הִנֵּה עַם בְּנֵי יִשְׂרָאֵל הָבָה נִתְחַכְּמָה לוֹ," וּמַעֲשֶׂה זֶה עָשׂוּ בִּרְצוֹנָם וּבְרוֹעַ מַחֲשַׁבְתָּם, וְלֹא הָיָה עֲלֵיהֶם בָּזֶה הֶכְרֵחַ.

וְהָיָה עוֹנֶשׁ ה' לָהֶם עַל כַּךְ שֶׁמְנָעָם מִן הַתְּשׁוּבָה, כְּדֵי שֶׁיָּבִיא עֲלֵיהֶם מִן הָעוֹנֶשׁ מַה שֶׁחִיֵּב צִדְקוֹ שֶׁזֶהוּ עָנְשָׁם, וּמְנִיעָתָם מִן הַתְּשׁוּבָה הוּא שֶׁלֹא יְשַׁלְחוּם.

וּכְבָר בִּיאֵר לוֹ ה' אֶת זֶה וְהוֹדִיעוֹ, כִּי אִלּוּ רָצָה לְהוֹצִיאָם בִּלְבַד הָיָה כְּבָר מְאַבְּדוֹ הוּא וַעֲבָדָיו וְהָיוּ יוֹצְאִים, אֶלָּא רָצָה, עִם הוֹצָאָתָם, לְהַעֲנִישָׁם עַל רִשְׁעָם הַקּוֹדֵם, כְּמוֹ שֶׁאָמַר בִּתְחִלַּת הַדָּבָר (בראשית ט"ו י"ד), "וְגַם אֶת הַגּוֹי אֲשֶׁר יַעֲבֹדוּ דָּן אָנֹכִי."

וְאִי אֶפְשָׁר לְהַעֲנִישָׁם אִם יָשׁוּבוּ, לְפִיכָךְ מָנַע מֵהֶם אֶת הַתְּשׁוּבָה וְהָיוּ

...deal cunningly with them — The Torah then enunciates just how Pharaoh and his servants oppressed the Israelites. They "set taskmasters over them to afflict them with their burdens," who had them build "the treasure cities of Pitom and Raamses"

(v. 11); they had them "serve [them] rigorously" (v. 13); they "embittered their lives with hard work involving mortar, brick, and all kinds of work in the field" (v. 14); and they ordered the midwives to slaughter Jewish firstborn males (v. 16).

Israelites in bondage.* Only then did God say, "I will now stretch forth My hand…. For indeed it was for this that I elevated you"* (Exodus 9:15–16).

9. Now, do not take us to task for saying that God sometimes punishes a person by preventing him from repenting and not allowing

מַחֲזִיקִים בָּהֶם, וְהוּא אָמְרוּ (שמות ט' ט"ו–ט"ז), "כִּי עַתָּה שָׁלַחְתִּי אֶת יָדִי וְכוּ' וְאוּלָם בַּעֲבוּר זֹאת הֶעֱמַדְתִּיךָ וְכוּ'."

ט. וְאֵין בְּךָ זָרוּת, אִם נֹאמַר כִּי יֵשׁ שֶׁה' מַעֲנִישׁ אֶת הָאָדָם בְּךָ שֶׁלֹּא יָשׁוּב וְלֹא יַשְׁאִיר לוֹ הַבְּחִירָה בִּתְשׁוּבָה, לְפִי שֶׁהוּא יִתְעַלֶּה יֵדַע

…in bondage — Let us review Rambam's argument.

He said above in section 7 that the idea that God "hardened Pharaoh's heart" was problematic. It seemed to imply that Pharaoh was compelled to keep the Israelites in captivity — even if he really didn't want to — in light of the fact that God was apparently withholding his options. That would seem to mean that God does indeed compel our actions.

Rambam's point is, though, that God compelled Pharaoh to be obstinate (and thus took away his free choice to some degree) *because* of something wrongful he'd chosen to do earlier on, which was to unjustly oppress the Israelites from the start.

Thus, God punished Pharaoh by hardening his heart afterwards, in order to prevent him from repenting for that *earlier* sin of oppression. For if Pharaoh had indeed repented for the earlier sin, he would have avoided the punishment due him for it.

So, while God does indeed sometimes prevent us from doing things — like repenting for things we have done (though that is rare) — He nonetheless doesn't compel us to do things.

I elevated you — The entire passage reads, "I will now stretch forth My hand and strike you and your people with pestilence; and you will be cut off from the earth. For indeed it was for this that I elevated you [Pharaoh] — that you would attest to My power; and to have My Name proclaimed throughout the earth."

Rambam underscores the fact that Pharaoh was placed in a position of power to demonstrate *God's* power. Now, while God's power to control the forces of nature is normally accepted, as was evidenced by the ten plagues, it also clearly refers to God's power to withhold someone's free will under special circumstances.

What's unique about that is that, while His power to control nature *seemed* to be immediate and directly linked to what was happening just then in Egypt, we discovered above that the ten plagues (like all miracles) were in fact set in motion in the course of creation. Thus, what appeared to be spontaneous actually wasn't. In contrast, God's control of Pharaoh's (and others') free will, which isn't at all manifest, was in fact spontaneous, paradoxically enough.

him the choice to repent.* For God knows our sins and metes out our punishments wisely and justly. Sometimes He punishes a person only in this world, and other times only in the World to Come,* and sometimes in both worlds together. Even the this-worldly punishments for sins vary. Sometimes we are punished physically, at other times finan-cially and at times, both ways at once. He might, for example, punish someone by limiting movements he usually has con-trol over, for example, paralyzing a person's hand, as He did to Je-roboam ben Nebat;* or He might blind his eye, as He did to the men of Sodom who gathered outside Lot's door.* In the same way, God might withhold a person's will to repent so that he is never inspired to do so at all, and he thus perishes a sinner.

But we are not obligated* to fathom His wisdom and understand why He would punish one person one way rather than another, any more than we are expected to know why a certain species was config-

הָעֲוֹנוֹת, וּמְחַיֶּבֶת חָכְמָתוֹ וְצִדְקוֹ שִׁעוּר הָעוֹנֶשׁ, וְהִנֵּה יֵשׁ שֶׁהוּא מַעֲנִישׁ בָּעוֹלָם הַזֶּה בִּלְבַד, וְיֵשׁ שֶׁהוּא מַעֲנִישׁ לָעוֹלָם הַבָּא בִּלְבַד, וְיֵשׁ שֶׁמַּעֲנִישׁ בִּשְׁנֵי הָעוֹלָמוֹת יַחַד. וְגַם עָנְשׁוֹ בָּעוֹלָם הַזֶּה מִשְׁתַּנֶּה, יֵשׁ שֶׁמַּעֲנִישׁ בַּגּוּף אוֹ בְמָמוֹן אוֹ בִשְׁנֵיהֶם יַחַד, כְּגוֹן שֶׁמְּבַטֵּל מִקְצַת תְּנוּעוֹת הָאָדָם שֶׁהָיָה בְחִירִי בָהֶן — עַל דֶּרֶךְ הָעוֹנֶשׁ, כְּגוֹן שֶׁיְּבַטֵּל אֶת יָדוֹ מִלִּפְעוֹל כְּמוֹ שֶׁעָשָׂה בְיָרָבְעָם, אוֹ עֵינוֹ מִלִּרְאוֹת, כְּמוֹ שֶׁעָשָׂה בְּאַנְשֵׁי סְדוֹם הַנִּקְבָּצִים עַל לוֹט, כַּךְ מְבַטֵּל מִמֶּנּוּ רָצוֹן הַתְּשׁוּבָה, עַד שֶׁלֹּא יִתְעוֹרֵר לָהּ כְּלָל וִיאַבֵּד בְּחֶטְאוֹ.

וְאֵין אָנוּ מְחוּיָּבִים לָדַעַת חָכְמָתוֹ עַד שֶׁנֵּדַע, מַדּוּעַ הֶעֱנִישׁ אֶת זֶה בְּאוֹפֶן זֶה מִן הָעוֹנֶשׁ וְלֹא הֶעֱנִישׁוֹ בְּאוֹפֶן אַחֵר, כְּשֵׁם שֶׁאֵין אָנוּ יוֹדְעִין מַה הַסִּבָּה שֶׁגָּרְמָה שֶׁיְּהֵא לְמִין זֶה צוּרָה

ured one way rather than another. The general principle is that "All of [God's] ways are just" (Deuteronomy 32:4), and that He punishes the sinner according to his sins and rewards the pious according to his piety.

Should you then ask, "Then why did He keep asking Pharaoh to set Israel free when he was being prevented from doing so? And why did the plagues continue to strike while Pharaoh was being obstinate when, as we said, his obstinacy was all part of God's punishment? God should not have needlessly asked him to stop doing something that he could not do!"

But that, too, was rooted in God's wisdom. It was meant to teach Pharaoh that God can withhold a person's free will if He wants to.

זוּ וְלֹא תְּהֵא לוֹ צוּרָה אַחֶרֶת. אֲבָל הַכְּלָל כִּי כָּל דְּרָכָיו מִשְׁפָּט וְיַעֲנִישׁ אֶת הַחוֹטֵא כְּפִי עֶרֶךְ חֶטְאוֹ וְגוֹמֵל לְעוֹשֶׂה הַחֶסֶד כְּפִי עֶרֶךְ חַסְדּוֹ.

וְאִם תֹּאמַר, מַדּוּעַ דָּרַשׁ מִמֶּנּוּ לְשַׁלַּח אֶת יִשְׂרָאֵל פַּעַם אַחַר פַּעַם בּוֹ בִּזְמַן שֶׁהוּא מָנוּעַ מִכָּךְ וְהָיוּ בָּאוֹת עָלָיו הַמַּכּוֹת וְהוּא עוֹמֵד בְּסֵרוּבוֹ? כְּמוֹ שֶׁאָמַרְנוּ, שֶׁהוּא נֶעֱנָשׁ שֶׁיַּעֲמוֹד בְּסֵרוּבוֹ, וְלֹא הָיָה לוֹ לְבַקֵּשׁ מִמֶּנּוּ לְחִנָּם דָּבָר שֶׁלֹּא יוּכַל לַעֲשׂוֹתוֹ.

הִנֵּה גַּם זֶה הָיָה חָכְמָה מִלְּפָנָיו יִתְעַלֶּה, כְּדֵי לְהוֹדִיעוֹ כִּי אִם יִרְצֶה ה' לְבַטֵּל בְּחִירָתוֹ הֲרֵי הוּא מְבַטְּלָהּ.

לְפִיכָךְ אָמַר לוֹ, אֲנִי דּוֹרֵשׁ מִמְּךָ לְשַׁלְּחָם, וְאִלּוּ שִׁלַּחְתָּם הָיִיתָ נִצּוֹל, אֶלָּא שֶׁאֵינְךָ מְשַׁלֵּחַ עַד שֶׁתֹּאבַד וְהָיָה הוּא רוֹצֶה לְהַסְכִּים, כְּדֵי שֶׁיֵּרָאֶה כְּאִלּוּ הָפַךְ דִּבְרֵי הַנָּבִיא שֶׁהוּא מָנוּעַ מִלְּהַסְכִּים, וְלֹא יָכֹל.

וְהָיָה בָזֶה מוֹפֵת גָּדוֹל וּמְפֻרְסָם אֵצֶל כָּל בְּנֵי אָדָם, כְּמוֹ שֶׁאָמַר (שְׁמוֹת

God therefore said to him,* "I am asking you to set them free, and you will be saved if you do. But I know you won't, so you will be destroyed." And Pharaoh wanted to comply [with God's order to set the Israelites free] in order to have it appear that he had overturned the prophet's* declaration that he could not, but he was unable to.*

Thus it served as a great and public wonder for all mankind, as it is

---

God therefore said to him — I.e., it is as if God said to him.

the prophet's — I.e., Moses'.

but he was unable to — That is to say, Pharaoh would have liked to have

complied with God's command that he set the Israelites free, since that would have shown that he could thwart Moses' declaration that he couldn't set them free. But Pharaoh was unable to do that — and that, too, was a lesson he had to learn.

written, "[It was for this that I elevated you,] to have you proclaim My Name throughout the earth" (Exodus 9:16), to affirm that God can punish a person by withholding his free will a particular way, and that the person would be aware of this and yet be unable to reassert his free will.*

10. King Sichon of Cheshbon was punished in the very same fashion. He had rebelled earlier on when he was under no compulsion to, so God punished him by preventing him from accommodating the Israelites, who then fought against him.* As it is said, "King Sichon of Cheshbon did not want to let us pass by him, because God, your Lord, hardened his spirit [as a consequence of an earlier sin, rather than by compulsion]" (Deuteronomy 2:30).

What has made this verse so difficult for the commentators is their assumption that Sichon was punished [i.e., defeated] for not letting Is-

ט' ט"ו), "וּלְמַעַן סַפֵּר שְׁמִי בְּכָל הָאָרֶץ," שֶׁיֵּשׁ שֶׁה' מַעֲנִישׁ אֶת הָאָדָם בַּמֶּה שֶׁמּוֹנֵעַ מִמֶּנּוּ בְּחִירַת פְּעוּלָה מְסוּיֶּמֶת, וְיָדַע הוּא בְּכָךְ וְלֹא יוּכַל לִמְשׁוֹךְ אֶת נַפְשׁוֹ וּלְהַחֲזִירָהּ לְאוֹתָהּ הַבְּחִירָה.

י. וְעַל דֶּרֶךְ זוּ עַצְמָהּ הָיָה עוֹנֶשׁ סִיחוֹן מֶלֶךְ חֶשְׁבּוֹן, כִּי לְפִי מַה שֶׁקֹּדֶם מִמֶּרְיוֹ שֶׁלֹּא הָיָה מוּכְרָח עָלָיו, הֶעֱנִישׁוֹ ה' שֶׁמְּנָעוֹ מִלְהֵיעָנוֹת לְיִשְׂרָאֵל עַד שֶׁנִּלְחֲמוּ בוֹ, וְהוּא אָמְרוֹ (דברים ב' ל'), "וְלֹא אָבָה סִיחוֹן מֶלֶךְ חֶשְׁבּוֹן הַעֲבִרֵנוּ בּוֹ כִּי הִקְשָׁה ה' אֱלֹקֶיךָ אֶת רוּחוֹ וְכוּ."

וּמַה שֶׁהוּקְשָׁה זֶה עַל כָּל הַמְּפָרְשִׁים, בְּחָשְׁבָם שֶׁסִּיחוֹן נֶעֱנַשׁ עַל שֶׁלֹּא נָתַן

...unable to reassert his free will — And what an astounding lesson that is, too! After all, it comes to illustrate the maddening prospect of a person being fully aware that he isn't in control of his actions. His plight becomes like that of those who lost their sight or the use of their limbs above, since he, too, suffers terrible frustration and chagrin. But the person whose free will has been taken from him would be more chagrined and frustrated, for a part of his very self as well as his will was being taken from him. So, while the others are suffering physically, he is suffering existentially, to the depths of his being.

fought against him — ...and defeated him. See Numbers 21:21–24: "Israel sent messengers to King Sichon of the Emorites, saying, 'Let me pass through your land; we will not enter the fields or the vineyards, and we will not drink the well waters, but we will pass by the king's highway past your borders.' But Sichon would not allow Israel to pass through his border. He gathered his people together and went to confront Israel in the desert. He came to Yahatz and fought against Israel, who then struck him with the edge of the sword."

rael pass through his land. They thus asked how he could have been punished for that, if he was compelled to, the same way they assumed that Pharaoh and his servants were only punished for not letting Israel free, which was not the case, as we explained. For God punished Pharaoh and his servants for their earlier wickedness, and did not allow them to repent in order that they be struck by the plagues [and ultimately destroyed]. Similarly, Sichon was punished for some earlier wrongdoing or injustice* in his kingdom by being prevented from accommodating the Jewish nation so that they would kill him.

In fact, God Himself expressly stated through Isaiah that He punishes some wrongdoers by preventing them from repenting and thus leaving them without free will. As He said, "Fatten the heart of this people, make their ears heavy...lest they...repent and be healed"* (Isaiah 6:10). This unambiguous verse needs no further explanation, and serves as a key to many locks.

This same principle explains Elijah's statement regarding the heretics of his age, that "You [God] turned their hearts round about" (1 Kings 18:37). For it indicates that their punishment for willingly re-

לְיִשְׂרָאֵל לַעֲבוֹר בְּאַרְצוֹ, וְאָמְרוּ, הֵיאַךְ נֶעֱנַשׁ וַהֲרֵי הוּא מוּכְרָח, כְּמוֹ שֶׁחָשְׁבוּ שֶׁפַּרְעֹה נֶעֱנַשׁ הוּא וַעֲבָדָיו עַל שֶׁלֹא שָׁלַח אֶת יִשְׂרָאֵל, וְאֵין הַדָּבָר אֶלָּא כְּמוֹ שֶׁבֵּיאַרְנוּ, שֶׁפַּרְעֹה וַעֲבָדָיו הָיָה עָנְשָׁם מֵאֵת ה' עַל מַה שֶּׁקֹּדֶם מֵרִשְׁעָם שֶׁלֹא יָשׁוּבוּ כְּדֵי שֶׁיָּבוֹאוּ עֲלֵיהֶם אוֹתָם הַמַּכּוֹת, וְהָיָה עוֹנֶשׁ סִיחוֹן עַל מַה שֶּׁקֹּדֶם מֵרִשְׁעוֹ אוֹ עֲווֹל שֶׁעָשָׂה בְּמַלְכוּתוֹ שֶׁיִּמָּנַע מִלְּהֵיעָנוֹת לְיִשְׂרָאֵל כְּדֵי שֶׁיַּהַרְגֻהוּ.

וּכְבָר בֵּיאַר ה' עַל יְדֵי יְשַׁעְיָה, כִּי יֵשׁ שֶׁהוּא יִתְעַלֶּה מַעֲנִישׁ מִקְצַת הָרְשָׁעִים בַּמֶּה שֶּׁמּוֹנֵעַ מֵהֶם אֶת הַתְּשׁוּבָה וְלֹא יַשְׁאִיר לָהֶם בָּהּ בְּחִירָה, כְּמוֹ שֶׁאָמַר (ישעיה ו' י'), "הַשְׁמֵן לֵב הָעָם הַזֶּה וְאָזְנָיו הַכְבֵּד וְכו' וְשָׁב וְרָפָא לוֹ," וְזֶה פָּסוּק מְפוֹרָשׁ שֶׁאֵינוֹ צָרִיךְ בִּיאוּר, אֶלָּא הוּא מַפְתֵּחַ לְמַנְעוּלִים רַבִּים.

וּלְפִי הַיְסוֹד הַזֶּה מִתְפָּרְשִׁים דִּבְרֵי אֵלִיָּהוּ, עָלָיו הַשָּׁלוֹם, עַל הַכּוֹפְרִים שֶׁבְּאַנְשֵׁי דוֹרוֹ (מלכים א' י"ח ל"ז), "וְאַתָּה הֲסִבֹּתָ אֶת לִבָּם אֲחוֹרַנִּית," כְּלוֹמַר, שֶׁכֵּיוָן שֶׁהִמְרוּ בִּרְצוֹנָם הָיָה

---

some earlier wrongdoing or injustice — Oddly enough, Rambam doesn't specify that earlier wrongdoing.

...repent and be healed — The entire verse reads, "*Fatten the heart of this people, make their ears heavy*, and shut their eyes. *Lest they* see with their eyes, hear with their ears, and understand with their heart, *repent and be healed.*"

belling was God's turning their hearts away from the path of repentance, and thus leaving them without the freedom or will to cast off their sin — which is why they continued being heretical. It is like God's statement that "Ephraim* is bound to idols — cast him aside" (Hosea 4:17), which means to say that since [the tribe of] Ephraim willingly bound itself to idols and came to love them, it was to be punished by being left to the ones it loved (which explains the term "cast him aside").

This is an excellent explanation for anyone who understands the subtleties involved here.

However, Isaiah's question, "Why would You have us stray from Your ways, God, and harden our hearts to the fear of You?" (Isaiah 63:17) has nothing to do with this [principle] whatsoever.* Rather, it is connected to what is said before and after it. For the prophet was bewailing our state of exile and foreignness, our dispersion, and the control other nations have over us, and thus said lamentingly, "O God — when Israel sees heretics prevailing, they will stray from the path of truth, and their hearts will incline away from the fear of You. It would be as if You had caused those fools to abandon the way of truth"* (which is

עָנְשְׁךָ לָהֶם שֶׁתָּטֶה לִבָּם מִדַּרְכֵי הַתְּשׁוּבָה, וְלֹא תַשְׁאִיר לָהֶם בְּחִירָה וְלֹא רָצוֹן בַּעֲזִיבַת הַחֵטְא הַזֶּה, וּלְפִיכָךְ הִתְמִידוּ בִּכְפִירָתָם, כְּעִין אָמְרוֹ (הושע ד' י"ז), "חֲבוּר עֲצַבִּים אֶפְרַיִם הַנַּח לוֹ." כְּלוֹמַר, הוּא נִתְחַבֵּר לָאֱלִילִים בִּרְצוֹנוֹ וְאוֹהֲבָם, עוֹנְשׁוֹ שֶׁיִּשָּׁאֵר בְּאַהֲבָתָם וְזֶהוּ עִנְיַן "הַנַּח לוֹ."

וְזֶה מִנִּפְלְאֵי הַפֵּירוּשִׁים לְמִי שֶׁמֵּבִין דַּקּוּת הָעִנְיָנִים.

אֲבָל מַאֲמַר יְשַׁעְיָה (ישעיה ס"ג י"ז), "לָמָּה תַתְעֵנוּ ה' מִדְּרָכֶיךָ תַּקְשִׁיחַ לִבֵּנוּ מִיִּרְאָתֶךָ" אֵינוֹ מִן הָעִנְיָן הַזֶּה כְּלָל, וְאֵינוֹ תָּלוּי בְּשׁוּם דָּבָר מִכָּל הָעִנְיָן הַזֶּה. אֶלָּא עִנְיַן אוֹתָם הַדְּבָרִים, לְפִי מַה שֶׁנֶּאֱמַר לִפְנֵיהֶם וּלְאַחֲרֵיהֶם, שֶׁהוּא נִתְחַנֵּן עַל הַגָּלוּת, וְגֵירוּתֵינוּ, וּפִזּוּרֵנוּ, וְהִשְׁתַּלְּטוּת הָאֻמּוֹת עָלֵינוּ, אָמַר בְּהִתְחַנְנוֹ, אֱלֹקֵי כַּאֲשֶׁר יִרְאוּ אֶת הַמַּצָּב הַזֶּה שֶׁיִּשְׁתַּלְּטוּ עֲלֵיהֶם הַכּוֹפְרִים יִסְטוּ מִדֶּרֶךְ הָאֱמֶת, וְיָסוּר לָבָם מִיִּרְאָתֶךָ, וּכְאִלּוּ אַתָּה הוּא שֶׁגּוֹרֵם לְאוֹתָם הַסְּכָלִים לָצֵאת מִדֶּרֶךְ הָאֱמֶת, כְּעִין

Ephraim — I.e., the tribe of Ephraim.

nothing to do with this principle whatsoever — I.e., it neither alludes to compulsion on God's part nor

alludes to their being punished for an earlier sin.

...the way of truth — That is, Isaiah's question, "Why would You have us stray from Your ways, God, and

analogous to Moses' statement, "All the nations that heard of Your Name will [thus] say, 'It was because God was not able…'"* [Numbers 14:15–16]). And so, Isaiah then said, "Return for Your servants' sake the tribes of Your inheritance" (Isaiah 63:17), that is, return in order to avoid a profanation of Your Name.

It is also similar to the explanation found in the Minor Prophets of the words of the seekers of truth, who were being oppressed by gentiles in exile. They are quoted as having said, "Whoever does wrong is [apparently] good in God's sight, and He [apparently] delights in them," and asking, "Where is the God of Justice?" (Malachi 2:17).

מַה שֶׁאָמַר מֹשֶׁה רַבֵּינוּ (בְּמִדְבַּר י״ד ט״ו-ט״ז), "וְאָמְרוּ הַגּוֹיִם אֲשֶׁר שָׁמְעוּ אֶת שִׁמְעֲךָ מִבִּלְתִּי יְכֹלֶת ה׳," וּלְפִיכָךְ אָמַר אַחַר זֶה (יְשַׁעְיָה ס״ג י״ז), "שׁוּב לְמַעַן עֲבָדֶיךָ שִׁבְטֵי נַחֲלָתֶךָ", כְּלוֹמַר, כְּדֵי שֶׁלֹּא יְהֵא שָׁם חִלּוּל ה׳.

וּכְמוֹ שֶׁבֵּאֵר בִּתְרֵי עָשָׂר דִּבְרֵי מְחַפְּשֵׂי הָאֱמֶת הַנִּרְדָּפִין עַל יְדֵי הַגּוֹיִם בִּזְמַן הַגָּלוּת, אָמַר מְסַפֵּר אֶת דִּבְרֵיהֶם (מַלְאָכִי ב׳ י״ז), "כָּל עֹשֵׂה רַע טוֹב בְּעֵינֵי ה׳ וּבָהֶם הוּא חָפֵץ אוֹ אַיֵּה אֱלֹקֵי הַמִּשְׁפָּט," וְסִפֵּר גַּם מַה שֶׁאָמְרוּ מֵחֲמַת קֹשִׁי הַגָּלוּת (שָׁם ג׳ י״ד-ט״ו), "אֲמַרְתֶּם שָׁוְא עֲבֹד אֱלֹקִים וּמַה בֶּצַע כִּי שָׁמַרְנוּ מִשְׁמַרְתּוֹ וְכִי הָלַכְנוּ קְדֹרַנִּית מִפְּנֵי ה׳ צְבָקוֹת וְעַתָּה אֲנַחְנוּ מְאַשְּׁרִים זֵדִים וְכוּ׳," וּבֵאֵר וְאָמַר שֶׁהוּא יִתְעַלֶּה יְגַלֶּה הָאֱמֶת וְאָמַר (שָׁם ג׳ י״ח), "וְשַׁבְתֶּם וּרְאִיתֶם וְכוּ׳."

They were also quoted as having said about the hardships of the exile, "It is [apparently] worthless serving God, and what good has keeping His ordinances done us, or our walking docilely before the Lord of Hosts? We now consider the guilty fortunate!'" (ibid. 3:14–15). But Malachi declared that God would reveal the truth when he said, "You will [eventually] return, and see the difference [between the righteous and the wrongful]"* (ibid., 18).

---

harden our hearts to the fear of You?" should be understood to mean, "Why would You Yourself apparently have us stray from Your ways, God, and harden our hearts to the fear of You by keeping us in exile and exposing us to the rule and influence of nonbelievers?"

…was not able — The entire verse reads, "Now if You will kill this nation as one man, then all the

nations which have heard of Your Name will thus say, 'It was because God was not able to bring this people into the land which He swore to them, that He slew them in the desert.' " That is, this verse also addresses how things will appear to be, rather than how they truly are.

…see the difference [between the righteous and the wrongful] — It is with good reason that we're offered

All the problematic verses in the Torah and the Scripture that seem to indicate that God compels us to sin have thus been explained without a shadow of a doubt and conclusively. This is a correct explanation for anyone who reflects well on what we have said.

We thus continue to maintain (thanks to this principle) that [despite verses that seem to indicate otherwise when read superficially] obedience or disobedience is indeed in man's own hands, and that he chooses his own actions. He does what he wants to do, and does not do what he does not want to do — unless God punished him for a sin he had committed by withholding his free will, as we explained.

Hence, since acquiring virtues or flaws is in one's own hands, it is imperative and proper for one to bestir himself to acquire virtues, for there is no external inspiration that can inspire him to do so. As it is

וְכָל אוֹתָם הַפְּסוּקִים הַקָּשִׁים שֶׁבַּתּוֹרָה וּבַמִּקְרָא, שֶׁנִּרְאָה מֵהֶם שֶׁה' מַכְרִיחַ עַל הָעֲבֵירוֹת כְּבָר בֵּאַרְנוּ עִנְיָנָם בְּלִי סָפֵק, וְהוּא בֵּאוּר נָכוֹן לְמִי שֶׁמִּתְבּוֹנֵן הֵיטֵב.

וְנִשְׁאַרְנוּ לְפִי הַיְסוֹד שֶׁבְּיָדֵנוּ שֶׁהַמִּשְׁמָעוֹת וְהַהֶמְרִי בְּיַד הָאָדָם, וְהוּא בְּחִירִי בְּמַעֲשָׂיו, מַה שֶׁרוֹצֶה לַעֲשׂוֹת עוֹשֶׂה וּמַה שֶׁרָצָה שֶׁלֹּא לַעֲשׂוֹת לֹא יַעֲשֶׂה, אֶלָּא אִם כֵּן הֶעֱנִישׁוֹ ה' עַל חֵטְא שֶׁחָטָא שֶׁיְּבַטֵּל מִמֶּנּוּ הָרָצוֹן, כְּמוֹ שֶׁבֵּיאַרְנוּ.

וְכֵן שֶׁקְּנִיַּת הַמַּעֲלוֹת וְהַמִּגְרְעוֹת בְּיָדוֹ, וּלְפִיכָךְ חוֹבָה וְרָאוּי לוֹ שֶׁיִּזְדָּרֵז וְיִשְׁדֵּל אֶת עַצְמוֹ בִּקְנִיַּת הַמַּעֲלוֹת, כֵּיוָן שֶׁאֵין לוֹ מְעוֹרֵר חִיצוֹנִי שֶׁיְּעוֹרְרֵהוּ

here an analogy between our state of exile and the fact that certain individuals lose their free will. After all, our free will has been taken from us, too, in exile. Thus, we suffer the same frustration and humiliation as the person whose very being was taken out of his control.

There is another point to be made, as well. Some of the misguided and lamentable Jews quoted here apparently express the notion that it seems that we haven't free will after all, and that mitzvah observance is thus absurd (see section 2 above). In utter frustration, they declare, "Whoever

does wrong is good in God's sight, and He delights in them," "Where is the God of justice?'" and "It is worthless serving God, and what good has keeping His ordinances done us?" So why observe mitzvot? — apparently, everything is preordained.

But as the prophet indicates, there'll be a time when God will bring on the great Redemption, and we will "see the difference between the righteous and the wrongful" — we'll see for ourselves that our moral choices and our mitzvot have made a difference in our beings, and that Divine justice will indeed prevail.

said in the ethical teachings of this tractate,* "If I am not for myself, then who will be for me?" (*Pirkei Avot* 1:14).

11. There is just one more thing to mention briefly to complete this chapter. Though I had not originally intended to mention it, I must do so anyway, and it is God's foreknowledge. I must mention it because it forms the basis for the opinion of those who think that we are compelled to obey or disobey, and that we do not have free will, since our wills actually hinge upon God's will.

What leads them to believe that is the following line of reasoning: God either knows [from the outset] that a certain person will be righteous or wrongful or He does not. If you argue that God knows, then you are forced to say that that person is compelled to be so, since God already knew [which he would eventually be] beforehand. Otherwise, His knowledge would be inaccurate. And if you argue that God does not already know that beforehand, then you are forced to say some terribly odd things that would topple walls.*

אֲלֵיהֶן, וְהוּא אָמְרָם בְּמוּסָרֵי מַסֶּכְתָּא זוֹ (אבות א' י"ד), "אִם אֵין אֲנִי לִי מִי לִי."

יא. וְלֹא נִשְׁאַר בְּעִנְיָן זֶה אֶלָּא דָּבָר אֶחָד שֶׁרָאוּי לְדַבֵּר בּוֹ מְעַט, כְּדֵי שֶׁיִּשְׁלַם עִנְיָן הַפֶּרֶק, וְאַף עַל פִּי שֶׁלֹּא רָצִיתִי לְדַבֵּר בּוֹ כְּלָל, אֶלָּא שֶׁהֱבִיאַנִי הַהֶכְרֵחַ לְכָךְ, וְהוּא יְדִיעַת ה' אֶת הָעֲתִידוֹת, לְפִי שֶׁזּוֹ הִיא הַטַּעֲנָה שֶׁטּוֹעֲנִין עָלֵינוּ בָּהּ אוֹתָם הַחוֹשְׁבִים שֶׁהָאָדָם מוּכְרָח עַל הַמִּשְׁמָעוֹת וְהַהֶמְרִי וְשֶׁכָּל פְּעוּלוֹת הָאָדָם אֵין לוֹ בְּחִירָה בָּהֶן כֵּיוָן שֶׁרְצוֹנוֹ תְּלוּיָה בִּרְצוֹן ה'.

וּמַה שֶּׁהֱבִיא לִידֵי סְבָרָא זוֹ הוּא שֶׁהֵם אוֹמְרִים, הָאִישׁ הַזֶּה יָדַע ה' שֶׁיִּהְיֶה צַדִּיק אוֹ רָשָׁע אוֹ לֹא יָדַע? אִם תֹּאמַר, יָדַע, הֲרֵי נִתְחַיֵּב, שֶׁיְּהֵא מוּכְרָח עַל אוֹתוֹ הַמַּצָּב שֶׁיְּדָעוֹ ה' מִלְּפָנֵי כֵן, וְאִם לֹא הֲרֵי תִּהְיֶה יְדִיעָתוֹ בִּלְתִּי נְכוֹנָה. וְאִם תֹּאמַר שֶׁלֹּא יָדַע אֶת זֶה מִקּוֹדֶם, תְּחַיֵּב עִנְיָנִים מוּזָרִים עֲצוּמִים וְיֵיהָרְסוּ חוֹמוֹת.

---

this tractate — I.e., *Pirkei Avot*, which as we recall, *Shemoneh Perakim* is an introduction to.

...things that would topple walls — The argument is as follows. There are only two logical alternatives: either God knows what is going to happen before it happens or He doesn't. It follows, then, that if you say that He knows that someone is going to be righteous, then that person is already so, since his nature was manifest beforehand in God's eyes. How could he then be said to be free enough to choose to be righteous? The decision

So, listen to what I have to say, and reflect upon it well, for it is undoubtedly true.

As has already been explained in theology, i.e., metaphysics,* God does not "know" by means of [what we refer to as] "knowledge," or "live" by means of [what we refer to as] "life," since that would make Him and His knowledge separate entities, the way we and our knowledge are (for we are distinct from what we know, and what we know is distinct from us; the two are separate entities).[12]

Also, if God knew by means of "knowledge,"* then there would necessarily have been a [primordial] plurality, and there would thus have been many "first beings": God Himself, the [primordial] knowledge by means of which He had come to know, the [primordial] life by means of which He had come to live, the [primordial] ability by means of which He had come to be capable, and so on, touching upon all His attributes.*

וְלָכֵן שְׁמַע מִמֶּנִּי מַה שֶׁאֲנִי אֹמֵר, וְהִתְבּוֹנֵן בּוֹ מְאֹד, שֶׁהוּא הָאֱמֶת בְּלִי סָפֵק.

וְהוּא, כְּבָר נִתְבָּאֵר בְּמַדָּעֵי הָאֱלֹהוּת, כְּלוֹמַר, מַה שֶׁאַחֲרֵי הַטֶּבַע, שֶׁה' יִתְעַלֶּה אֵינוֹ יֹדֵעַ בְּדֵעָה, וְלֹא חַי בְּחִיּוּת, עַד שֶׁיִּהְיֶה הוּא וְהַמַּדָּע שְׁנַיִם כְּאָדָם וִידִיעָתוֹ, לְפִי שֶׁהָאָדָם זוּלַת הַיְדִיעָה וְהַיְדִיעָה זוּלַת הָאָדָם, וַהֲרֵי הֵם שְׁנַיִם.

וְאִילוּ הָיָה ה' יֹדֵעַ בְּדֵעָה הָיְיתָ מְחַיֵּיב הָרִבּוּי, וְהָיוּ הַנִּצְחִיִּם רַבִּים, ה', וְהַדֵּעָה שֶׁבָּהּ הוּא יֹדֵעַ, וְהַחַיִּים שֶׁבָּהֶם הוּא חַי, וְהַיְכֹלֶת שֶׁבָּהּ הוּא יָכוֹל, וְכֵן כָּל תָּאֲרָיו.

---

has already been played out.

On the other hand, if you posit that God *doesn't* know what is going to happen beforehand, and thus everyone is indeed free to be righteous or not, you've allowed for free will, but then logic would force you to say things that would undo many fundamentals of the faith, most especially the assumption that God is perfect and omniscient. Thus, it would be absurd as well as heretical to claim that God doesn't know things beforehand.

metaphysics — What we translate as "theology" is literally "the science of Godliness." Rambam's use of the term "metaphysics," which we take to be the study of events and things outside of objective human experience, actually refers to Aristotle's *Metaphysica* (Aristotle's renowned work on metaphysics, which discusses causation, form, and matter, the existence of mathematical objects, God, and other abstruse concepts).

by means of "knowledge" — I.e., if God could only be said to know things by means of what we refer to as "knowledge."

...touching upon all His attributes — We'll do our best to express these

I have thus offered you an argument that is easy and likely to be understood by the masses. But the best arguments available to abrogate this claim [i.e., that God and His knowledge, His state of being, His ability, and so on, are separate entities] are stronger yet and definitive.

וְהִזְכַּרְתִּי לְךָ הוֹכָחָה פְּשׁוּטָה הַקְּרוֹבָה לַהֲבָנַת הַמוֹנֵי הָעָם תְּחִלָּה, כִּי הַהוֹכָחוֹת וְהָרְאָיוֹת הַמְבַטְּלוֹת דָּבָר זֶה הֵם חֲזָקוֹת מְאֹד וּמוֹפְתִיּוֹת.

Since it is clear that God is [indistinguishable from] His attributes, and His attributes are [indistinguishable from] Him, we say that He is the Knowledge, the Knower, and the Known;[13] Life,

הִנֵּה נִתְבָּאֵר, שֶׁהוּא יִתְעַלֶּה תָּאֳרָיו, וְתָאֳרָיו הוּא, עַד שֶׁאוֹמְרִים, שֶׁהוּא הַדֵּעָה, וְהוּא הַיּוֹדֵעַ וְהוּא הַיָּדוּעַ, הוּא הַחַיִּים, וְהוּא הַחַי, וְהוּא הַמַּמְשִׁיךְ לְעַצְמוֹ אֶת הַחִיּוּת וְכֵן שְׁאָר הַתְּאָרִים.

וְעִנְיָנִים אֵלּוּ קָשִׁים, אַל תַּחְשׁוֹב שֶׁתְּבִינֵם בִּשְׁלֵימוּת בִּשְׁתַּיִם שָׁלֹשׁ שׁוּרוֹת מִדְּבָרַי, אֶלָּא יִהְיֶה לְךָ מִזֶּה יְדִיעָה בִּלְבַד.

the Living Being, and the One Who bestows Life upon Himself, and so on, touching upon all His attributes.

These are difficult ideas, so do not expect to understand them thoroughly with the two or three lines I might offer. Just let this serve as a point of information.

---

rather mysterious ideas.

We "acquire life" (i.e., come alive) at birth, and acquire knowledge throughout life. Thus, life and knowledge are added onto us; they and we are "separate entities," in Rambam's words. They also change us. After all, I'm one way alive and another not yet alive, just as I'm one way knowing something and another way not yet knowing something.

God, on the other hand, cannot be said to have had anything added to His Being or to have changed. After all, if anything had to have been added on to Him or if He had to have changed, then He would have been imperfect and at a loss at first, which is absurd.

Also, there would have to have been a primordial entity called "knowledge" from which He could have culled His knowledge, as well as primordial entities called "life," "ability," and so on, from which He would have drawn His life, ability, and so on. And they would have had to have existed along with God from the first. Those are the other "first beings" Rambam refers to. Obviously, those other primordial, coexistent entities could not have existed, otherwise God wouldn't have been the First Entity.

So, while God certainly "lives" and "knows," we do not experience the life and knowledge that He does, since our lives and our knowledge are external, incidental, and added on to ourselves, as we've shown, while His are intrinsic to His Being.

Incidentally, this great principle explains why there is no Hebrew expression "the Life of God" — as there is "the life of your *nefesh*" (1 Samuel 1:15) and "the life of Pharaoh" (Genesis 42:15), where the possessive case* and the thing it modifies* are two separate entities — for nothing can modify itself. Hence, since God's "life" is [indistinguishable from] His essence and His essence is [indistinguishable from] His "life," rather than their being two separate entities; and since one cannot modify the other, we say "God *lives*," which expresses the idea that God and His "life" are one and the same.*

12. Nonetheless, as has already been explained in metaphysics, our minds cannot fully fathom God's Being, for His Being is perfect, while our minds are imperfect; and because nothing else brought God into existence by means of which we could know Him. In fact, our minds are as unable to comprehend Him as our eyes are to endure* sunlight, though this is not due to a weakness on the part of the sun itself, so much as on the fact that the light is stronger than our eyes can bear,* as has been explained

וּלְפִי הַיְסוֹד הַגָּדוֹל הַזֶּה אֵין הָעִבְרִית מַרְשָׁה לוֹמַר "חֵי ה'," כְּמוֹ שֶׁאָמְרוּ (שמואל א א' ט"ו) "חֵי נַפְשֶׁךָ," (בראשית מ"ב ט"ו) "חֵי פַרְעֹה," כְּלוֹמַר, שֵׁם נִסְפָּח, כֵּיוָן שֶׁהַנִּסְפָּח וְהַמְּסוּפָּח אֵלָיו שְׁנֵי דְבָרִים נִפְרָדִים, וְאֵין הַדָּבָר נִסְפָּח אֶל עַצְמוֹ, וּלְפִי שֶׁחַיּוּת ה' הִיא עַצְמוּתוֹ וְעַצְמוּתוֹ חַיּוּתוֹ, וְאֵינוֹ דָּבָר אַחֵר זוּלָתוֹ, לֹא אָמְרוּהָ בִּסְפּוּחַ, אֶלָּא אָמְרוּ "חֵי ה'," הַכַּוָּנָה שֶׁהוּא וִידִיעָתוֹ דָּבָר אֶחָד.

יב. וּכְבָר נִתְבָּאֵר עוֹד בְּמַה שֶׁאַחַר הַטֶּבַע, כִּי אָנוּ אֵין יְכוֹלֶת בְּשִׂכְלֵנוּ לָדַעַת מְצִיאוּתוֹ יִתְעַלֶּה בִּשְׁלֵימוּת, וְזֶה מֵחֲמַת שְׁלֵמוּת מְצִיאוּתוֹ וְחֶסְרוֹן שִׂכְלֵינוּ, וְאֵין לִמְצִיאוּתוֹ סִבּוֹת שֶׁיּוֹדַע בָּהֶן, וְשֶׁקּוֹצֶר שִׂכְלֵינוּ מִלְהַשִּׂיגוֹ כְּקוֹצֶר רְאוֹת הָעַיִן מִלְהַשִּׂיג אוֹר הַשֶּׁמֶשׁ, שֶׁאֵין הַדָּבָר מֵחֲמַת חוּלְשַׁת אוֹר הַשֶּׁמֶשׁ אֶלָּא מִפְּנֵי שֶׁזֶּה הָאוֹר יוֹתֵר חָזָק מִן הָאוֹר הָרוֹצֶה לְהַשִּׂיגוֹ.

---

the possessive case — I.e., "the life of."

the thing it modifies — I.e., "your *nefesh*" in the first case and "Pharaoh" in the second.

...one and the same — This is all to say that there is no such expression as "God's life" in Hebrew, since that would imply that God and His "life"

were two separate entities, as a consequence of the fact that one modifies (and is thus unequal to) the other. Instead, we say "God lives," and avoid that dilemma.

to endure — Lit., to comprehend.

than our eyes can bear — Lit., than our eyes are willing to comprehend.

many times before, precisely and clearly.*

It follows from all this that we cannot comprehend God's knowledge in all its fullness whatsoever, since He is [indistinguishable from] His knowledge and His knowledge is [indistinguishable from] Him.

This is a very wondrous notion, and it eluded them* to the day of their death. For while they knew that God's Being in all Its inherent perfection could never be fathomed, they nonetheless tried to fathom and fully grasp His knowledge. But this is impossible, for, if we could understand His knowledge, we could fathom His Being, since they are one and the same. Indeed, grasping Him perfectly encompasses grasping Him in His Being, which consists of His knowledge, His ability, His will, His "life," and all His other wondrous attributes.

But as we have already explained, it is utterly foolish to think that anyone could ever fathom His knowledge. What we know is that He "knows," just as we know He "exists."

וְדִבֵּר בְּעִנְיָן זֶה הַרְבֵּה, וְהֵם כֻּלָּם דְּבָרִים נְכוֹנִים וּבְרוּרִים.

הַיּוֹצֵא מִכָּל זֶה שֶׁגַּם לֹא נֵדַע יְדִיעָתוֹ, וְלֹא נֵדַע הֵיקַּפָהּ בְּשׁוּם פָּנִים, כֵּיוָן שֶׁהוּא יְדִיעָתוֹ וִידִיעָתוֹ הוּא.

וְעִנְיָן זֶה נִפְלָא הוּא מְאֹד, וְהוּא שֶׁנֶּעְלַם מֵהֶם וְאָבְדוּ, לְפִי שֶׁהֵם יָדְעוּ שֶׁמְּצִיאוּתוֹ יִתְעַלֶּה בִּשְׁלֵימוּת כְּפִי שֶׁהוּא אֵינָה נִתֶּנֶת לְהַשָּׂגָה, וְחִפְּשׂוּ לְהַשִּׂיג אֶת יְדִיעָתוֹ עַד שֶׁתִּהְיֶה תַּחַת הֲבָנָתָם, וְזֶה בִּלְתִּי אֶפְשָׁרִי, לְפִי שֶׁאִילּוּ יָדַעְנוּ אֶת יְדִיעָתוֹ, הֲרֵי הִשַּׂגְנוּ מְצִיאוּתוֹ, כֵּיוָן שֶׁהַכֹּל דָּבָר אֶחָד, לְפִי שֶׁהַשָּׂגָתוֹ בִּשְׁלֵימוּת הוּא שֶׁיּוּשַׂג כְּפִי שֶׁהוּא בִּמְצִיאוּתוֹ מִן הַיְדִיעָה וְהַיְכֹלֶת וְהָרָצוֹן וְהַחַיִּים וְזוּלַת זֶה מִתְּאָרָיו הַנִּפְלָאִים.

הִנֵּה כְּבָר בֵּאַרְנוּ, שֶׁהַמַּחְשָׁבָה בְּהַשָּׂגַת יְדִיעָתוֹ סִכְלוּת בְּהֶחְלֵט, אֶלָּא שֶׁאָנוּ נֵדַע שֶׁהוּא יֹדֵעַ, כְּמוֹ שֶׁאָנוּ יוֹדְעִים שֶׁהוּא מָצוּי.

...precisely and clearly — That is to say, there are three essential reasons why we cannot comprehend God Himself: 1) because His Being is of a whole other order of being than our own, which we can neither fathom nor orient ourself in; 2) because He hasn't any antecedents, which we might study and draw inferences from about Him; and 3) because a truly comprehensive analysis — to say nothing of an actual experience — of His Being would be as impossible for us to bear as an actual, near-at-hand experience of the sun.

it eluded them — I.e., those who hold that no one has free choice, in light of the fact that God knows everything beforehand.

And if we should be asked what is the nature of God's knowledge, we must say that we cannot fathom that, any more than we can fully fathom Him. In fact, anyone who would try to fathom His knowledge has already been rebuked with the statement, "Can you unearth the deep things about God? [Can you determine the Almighty's purposes?]"* (Job 11:7).

It is clear in light of all we have said that man's actions are in his own hands, and that he is free to be either righteous or wrongful without God compelling him in either direction. It therefore follows that there be mitzvot, instruction, and precautions, as well as reward and punishment.

וְאִם יִשְׁאָלוּנוּ, הֵיאַךְ הִיא יְדִיעָתוֹ? נֹאמַר שֶׁלֹא נַשִּׂיג אֶת זֶה, כְּשֵׁם שֶׁאֵין אָנוּ מַשִּׂיגִים מְצִיאוּתוֹ בִּשְׁלֵימוּת. וּכְבָר מָחוּ בְּמִי שֶׁחָשַׁב לְהַשִּׂיג יְדִיעָתוֹ יִתְעַלֶּה וְאָמְרוּ לוֹ (איוב י"א ז'), "הַחֵקֶר אֱלוֹק תִּמְצָא."

הִנֵּה נִתְבָּאֵר מִכָּל מַה שֶׁאָמַרְנוּ שֶׁפְּעוּלוֹת הָאָדָם מְסוּרִים לוֹ, וּבְיָדוֹ לִהְיוֹת צַדִּיק אוֹ רָשָׁע בְּלִי שׁוּם הֶכְרֵחַ מֵאֵת ה' עַל אֶחָד מִשְּׁנֵי דְרָכִים אֵלּוּ, וּלְפִיכָךְ נִתְחַיֵּב הַצִּוּוּי, וְהַלִּמּוּד, וְהַהִתְכּוֹנְנוּת, וְהַשָּׂכָר וְהָעוֹנֶשׁ, וְאֵין בְּכָל זֶה שׁוּם סָפֵק. אֲבָל אוֹפֶן יְדִיעָתוֹ יִתְעַלֶּה וְהַשָּׂגָתוֹ לְכָל הַדְּבָרִים תִּקְצַר בִּינָתֵינוּ מִכָּךְ כְּמוֹ שֶׁבֵּיאַרְנוּ.

זֶהוּ כָל מַה שֶׁרָצִינוּ לְסַכֵּם בְּעִנְיָן זֶה, וּכְבָר הִגִּיעָה הָעֵת שֶׁאַפְסִיק אֶת הַדְּבָרִים כָּאן, וְאַתְחִיל לְפָרֵשׁ מַסֶּכְתָּא זוֹ אֲשֶׁר לָהּ הִקְדַּמְנוּ פְּרָקִים אֵלּוּ.

All of this is undoubtedly so, but our intellects are too limited to grasp God's way of knowing and comprehending everything, as we explained.

This then sums up what we meant to offer about this. It is now time to conclude, and to begin our commentary to this tractate,* for which these chapters serve as an introduction.*

...**the Almighty's purposes** — The text continues with the idea that even though God's Being and understanding are "as high as the sky...deeper than the netherworld," "longer than the earth, and broader than the sea," nonetheless, "when He sees wickedness, shall He take no notice of it?" (v. 8–11). This alludes to the idea that God is indeed aware of our actions despite the unfathomable nature of His Being and knowledge, and He does indeed hold us accountable for our actions.

this tractate — I.e., *Pirkei Avot*.

for which these chapters serve as an introduction — Herein ends *Shemoneh Perakim*. May God grant us the wherewithall to abide by its reasoned dictates, and to draw from its great wisdom.

Synopsis

1. While one might be predisposed to a virtue or flaw from birth, and thus find it easier to act one way or another, no one is ever born inherently lofty or flawed. This said, anyone can learn how to counter his disposition.

2. This is said to underscore the fact that one is free to act any way he sees fit. Though one might be predisposed in a certain direction, he is nonetheless never compelled to do anything. Otherwise, mitzvot would be worthless, since one would not be free to do or not do whatever he wanted; education would be for naught, since one couldn't help but do one thing or another; reward or punishment would be unfair, since one couldn't help but live out his fate; and it would be worthless to take precautions or make preparations.

3. The truth is that one is granted the freedom to act as he sees fit, and nothing impels a person one way or the other. As a consequence, our actions are open to judgment, it matters whether we study or not, and it makes sense for us to take precautions.

4. Some people think certain things are "meant to be," like whom a person marries and how a person who robs acquires his money. But that is not so, since those things touch upon mitzvot and sins, and are thus subject to one's free will.

5. The only things one cannot choose to affect are certain natural phenomena, like his height, the weather, and the like. Hence, since one is otherwise free, he should mourn for his sins, which he committed of his own volition, and repent for them.

6. Other natural phenomena like gravity, the laws of nature, and the like (which do not touch upon man's actions) are also beyond our control. Their effects were implanted from Creation, and they thus follow the course laid out for them then, rather than acting out of divine compulsion moment by moment, as some think. As such, one's natural ability to act on his own without anything compelling him to was implanted from Creation, too. God consequently provided mankind with instructions as to how to be good, and it's our responsibility to be as virtuous as we can, since we are free to.

7. Sometimes, though, the Torah seems to suggest that God compels bad behavior, as when He informed Abraham that his descendants would be enslaved by the Egyptians, and when He told

Moses that some Jews would serve idols after entering Canaan. But those were simply statements of fact, not direct assignments to particular Egyptians or Jews, for each individual acted as he saw fit in the circumstances. Otherwise, any warnings against profaning the Sabbath and serving idols would mean that some people would necessarily profane the Sabbath and serve idols. Still and all, the idea that God "hardened Pharaoh's heart" is problematic.

8. In point of fact, what Pharaoh and his court did wrong from the start — and of their own volition — was to oppress a foreign nation (Israel) in their midst for no reason. God punished them for that by not allowing them to repent, which then set the stage for their not setting the Jewish nation free, and then for their being punished.

9. It is important to realize that this, too, is an instance of God's wise and just ways. For there are times when God punishes us for our misdeeds and rewards us for our good deeds here, in this world (either physically or financially); other times when He does so in the World to Come but not here (by preventing us from repenting); and yet other times when He does so in both. Nonetheless, we do not have the capacity to understand why one person is punished one way and another person another way. Pharaoh's punishment also served as a sign to everyone that God can utterly withhold a person's freedom to act a certain way.

10. There were several other instances in which God removed a person's ability to repent, including the one involving King Sichon of Cheshbon, one encompassing the entire Jewish nation at a certain point, and one involving certain heretics. Nonetheless, as a rule, unless God punishes a person by taking away his free will, a person himself chooses to either acquire virtues or settle for flaws. Thus, one should take it upon himself to acquire those virtues, for only he can impel himself to.

11. We will now explain God's foreknowledge in light of our freedom of choice. "Since God already knows whether a person will be righteous or wrongful beforehand," some argue, "that person is forced to be righteous or wrongful." But this is based on a basic misunderstanding of the idea of God "knowing." God doesn't know things the way we do, so we cannot speak about His knowledge in terms of His "coming" to know something. God's knowledge is a veritable part of His Being. Otherwise, He would have to have

acquired a piece of knowledge; and that piece of knowledge would have to have existed from the very beginning for Him to have had acquired it later. That would mean that there were several entities before anything was created (i.e., God, His knowledge, and all the other traits attributed to Him), which by definition is impossible.

12. *Nonetheless, we cannot the fathom the nature of God's Being or His knowledge whatsoever. All we know is that He "knows" and He "exists." We must understand, though, that our behavior is in our hands alone, and God never compels us to behave one way or the other.*

SUPPLEMENTARY NOTES

Introduction

1. Rambam explains in the introduction to his Commentary on the Mishnah that Rabbi Yehudah HaNasi placed *Pirkei Avot* in *Seder Nezikin* because that particular order, which concerns itself with torts and personal or property damages, is addressed to judges, who especially need the sort of counsel given in *Pirkei Avot*.

For as he put it there, judges need to be ethical and civil. If they are not, they will harm both themselves and others. That being the case, it is best for them to avoid distractions or leisure, and to overcome their need for pleasure or any inclination they would have to control others. This necessity encompasses many of the qualities promoted in *Shemoneh Perakim*.

Interestingly enough and certainly not by accident, Rambam points out that judges would also do well to always strive for consensus and compromise between litigants. That alludes to the sort of balanced behavior favored in this work (see chapter 4). For we achieve balance in our behavior by taking both extremes into consideration and arriving at a balanced synthesis. This is much the same as consensus and compromise.

Rabbi Yehudah HaNasi — Rabbeinu HaKadosh, "our Holy Master" — epitomizes the sort of individual this work is encouraging us all to be. He was pious and of noble character. Reaching the heights of wisdom and honor as well as of humility and meekness, he rose above all petty desires, and he truly feared God (Rambam, Introduction to his Commentary on the Mishnah).

2. There will prove to be many important things to learn from *Pirkei Avot*. Interestingly enough, though, Rambam starts out by claiming he'll only be offering us insights into what *Pirkei Avot* says about character and how we may be encouraged to strive for goodness and avoid wrong, and adds that he will be spelling out certain ideas and terms (Commentary on *Pirkei Avot* 1:1). Yet as we'll see in our next two notes, he will actually be offering much more.

3. If we follow the wording here, we notice something quite interesting. After starting the first paragraph off with a short statement about *Pirkei Avot*, Rambam then mentions that he "decided to expand on the subject."

It apparently became clear to him that since *Pirkei Avot* is difficult to live up to, though easy enough to understand, and since it leads to personal perfection and true good fortune, that he could no longer settle for the sort of straightforward explanation he'd apparently planned. He'd have to "offer even more."

4. This paragraph is more than a little mysterious — and tantalizing. It also points to much to come.

The idea that it is "not easy for most of us to abide by" what is said in *Pirkei Avot* alludes to Rambam's forthcoming thesis that some people would not be expected to follow its dictates, because *Pirkei Avot* is, for the most part, directed toward the pious, and not everyone is or can be pious (though everyone can take much of *Pirkei Avot* to heart and apply it to his life).

His statement that *Pirkei Avot* "fosters great perfection" also resonates with what we'll be discussing later on. In point of fact, Rambam spoke about the idea of achieving perfection by taking *Pirkei Avot* to heart earlier on in his writings (see his introduction to his Commentary on the Mishnah). His claim that *Pirkei Avot* also fosters "great perfection and true good fortune," alludes to the World to Come. For Rambam said explicitly later on in his writings that Torah study in general (which obviously includes the study of *Pirkei Avot*) leads us to perfection and enables us to earn a place in the World to Come (*Moreh Nevuchim* 3:27). So we would do well now to elaborate on Rambam's concept of perfection as well as his explanation of the World to Come.

The Hebrew term for perfection is *sheleimut*, which can also be translated as "wholeness" or "fullness." Rambam indicates that the aim of *Pirkei Avot* is to instruct us in how to achieve *sheleimut* by encouraging us to be ethical and to rectify our deeds by pursuing personal and intellectual virtues (Commentary on *Pirkei Avot* 5:2).

At one point Rambam lets us know, though, that not everyone is constitutionally "cut out" to achieve utter *sheleimut*, as we indicated above (see *Moreh Nevuchim* 1:34). At another point, he reveals that ultimately one's degree of *sheleimut* corresponds to his degree of closeness to God (ibid. 3:18). Furthermore, there are two sorts of closeness to Him — the kind achieved by acting in a Godly way in this world (ibid. 1:54), and the one achieved by understanding Him as He really is (see 5:1 below, *Moreh Nevuchim* 1:59). At yet another point, Rambam assures us that there isn't a single mitzvah that doesn't bring one closer to *sheleimut* or that doesn't inhibit something that would prevent one from achieving it (*Iggeret Teiman*).

Nonetheless, he goes on to reveal that there are actually four orders of *sheleimut*.

The first hinges upon one's material circumstances (what he owns and what its quality, quantity, and worth are). This order neither touches upon one's essential being, nor is it especially noble.

The second hinges upon one's physical circumstances (his health, strength, constitution, etc.). It too is neither essential nor especially noble.

The third order of *sheleimut* hinges upon one's social circumstances (his character and how he interacts with others). While this class is certainly more noble than the earlier ones and is the very thrust of most of the mitzvot, Rambam holds (surprisingly enough, considering the gist of this entire work!) that it too doesn't touch upon one's essential being, since it only comes into play in society and doesn't involve one's very being. (Like material and physical *sheleimut*, social *sheleimut* says nothing about a person himself, so much as about the person in relation to things and to other people.)

This prioritizing certainly gives us pause and provides us with a far deeper insight into this work as a whole. It suggests that *Shemoneh Perakim* serves as a sort of preparatory text toward the fourth, highest level of *sheleimut*, which concerns itself with one's personal perfection and the ability to achieve true humanness, which is rooted in having arrived at a true understanding of God (*Moreh Nevuchim* 3:54).

As to the World to Come, it is important to know that it is an entirely spiritual experience. Most of our Sages understand it to be the state to which the world itself will evolve at the End of Days, after the Messianic Era. Rambam seems to understand it to refer to the Afterlife (*Hilchot Teshuvah* 8:8). A close reading of that text can lead one to surmise, though, that Rambam in fact subtly equated the afterlife with the End of Days. As a matter of fact, his son, Avraham ben HaRambam, whom most scholars declare faithfully transmitted the teachings of his father, explicitly equates it with the End of Days in his *Milchamot Hashem*.

In either case, it will be a completely spiritual experience, far above our ken and beyond our grasp (*Hilchot Teshuvah* 8:6–7): a perpetual, deep, abstract, clear, and unambiguous encounter with God, as we'll soon see. Rambam points out elsewhere that we physical beings cannot fathom the delight of the World to Come any more than the blind can fathom the delight of color, the deaf can fathom the delight of sound, or fish can fathom the delight of fire.

For the only out-and-out pleasure we know of is the kind connected to eating, drinking, and the like. We cannot imagine much of anything else being delightful — with few exceptions.

After all, many of us work extraordinarily hard to achieve many intangible things like honor, respect, or revenge. Nevertheless, as a rule, intangible, immaterial, and more spiritual things are beyond us (Commentary on *Perek Cheilek*). And we'll certainly have no need for bodily satisfaction in the World to Come (*Hilchot Teshuvah* 8:6), any more than we'd need to have any self-interests served.

Be that as it may, the World to Come is "a form of life without death; goodness without evil," where "the bodiless, ministering angel-like souls of the righteous...bask in God's glory by comprehending and grasping the truth of God," and thus enjoy a state of being that is "unfathomably, incomparably, and unparalleledly greater" than anything we know of (*Hilchot Teshuvah* 8:1–2, 6).

In the end, what we're being promised here in this first section of the work is that *Shemoneh Perakim* will provide us with an understanding of the plain meaning of *Pirkei Avot* along with its psychology and ethics, as well as a peek into the sort of rigorous spiritual excellence offered to all who fulfill its promise.

5. Interestingly enough, Rambam says that divine inspiration is actually more a stepping-stone to true and full prophecy than a degree of it (*Moreh Nevuchim* 2:45). That would suggest that piety is more accurately a preamble and a prerequisite to prophecy rather than a direct lead into it as the phrase "piety leads to prophecy" would seem to suggest.

Prophecy will be discussed at some length in chapter 7 below.

6. It's important for our purposes here to point out that Rambam considers prophecy to be the epitome of human perfection (*Moreh Nevuchim* 2:36).

7. We'll discuss character, piety, and prophecy at length later on. For now, though, we need to introduce other details relevant to them.

Rambam classified human beings into eight categories: "wrongdoers," "boors," "the unlearned," "the typical," "sages," "the righteous," "the pious," and "prophets" (Commentary on *Pirkei Avot* 5:6).

While we might define "wrongdoers" as perhaps inveterate, bred-in-the-bone evil people, Rambam defines them as indulgent people who tend to extremes (Commentary on *Pirkei Avot* 5:9). We'll discuss Rambam's ideas of right and wrong, as well as indulgence and extremes, later on.

While we might describe "boors" as crass, coarse, or even vulgar simpletons, Rambam is a bit kinder. He certainly sees them as unpolished and neither personally nor intellectually mature, but he also doesn't take them to be bad or particularly flawed. He seems to see them as the sort of people we'd call "the salt of the earth" — neither sophisticated nor accomplished, but not bad (Commentary on *Pirkei Avot* 5:6). He describes "the unlearned" as people who have achieved certain virtuous character traits, but none of the intellectual ones (Commentary on *Pirkei Avot* 5:6) — good, but not particularly well-educated people.

Rambam next speaks of "*golems*," which we translate as "typical" people. A more literal — albeit indelicate — translation might be "clods" (see Commentary on *Pirkei Avot* 5:6). Traditionally, a golem is a living, clay humanoid that certain great and holy individuals were allowed to create during particular crises in Jewish history. (Many have heard of the golem of the great Maharal of Prague, for example.) Nonetheless, Rambam uses the term to refer to people who are comprised of an admixture of some virtuous character and intellectual traits, and some flawed ones (Commentary on *Pirkei Avot* 5:6) — people who aren't bad per se, but who haven't achieved their human potential, either. Which is to say — many of us.

We'll allude to this category later on, since it reflects who we are. We'll return to "the pious" and "prophets," as well, because they reflect who we can be.

"Sages" are characterized as people who have managed to achieve more than a few personal virtues, and certainly several intellectual ones (Commentary on *Pirkei Avot* 5:6).

Rambam goes into great detail about how sages are meant to carry themselves, apparently because he expects us all to strive for that level (if not beyond). Sages must conduct themselves in a comely and correct manner when they eat and drink, speak, walk, dress, or conduct business, and even in their most private and intimate moments (*Hilchot Dei'ot* 5:1). In general, they must only express anger about issues that truly merit it; to desire only the things their bodies needs to live on, and no more; to work only enough to have what it takes to get by; and never to act either silly or mournful, but rather happy and welcoming (ibid. 1:4). They're to be neither boisterous nor loud, but cordial, complimentary, and peaceable (ibid. 5:7). And they're to be neither arrogant nor diffident, but humble (ibid. 1:5).

Specifically, they're to only eat what's good for their health, certainly not excessively — one or two dishes in the course of a meal, and no more (ibid. 5:1). They're to eat meat only once a week, on Sabbath eves (ibid., 10). They should eat in their own homes rather than elsewhere, unless absolutely necessary and for a mitzvah, in order to avoid demeaning themselves before the eyes of the unlearned, and they're only to drink wine to help digest food (ibid., 2–3).

They're only to be intimate with their spouses once a week, and never to be frivolous or coarse about it, or to be drunk, lethargic, or sad in the course of it (ibid., 4). They must conduct themselves discreetly in all realms (ibid., 6). Their clothes are to be attractive and clean, but neither extravagant or shabby — somewhere in between (ibid., 9). They're only to speak about things that touch upon wisdom or kindness (ibid., 7).

We'll find that Rambam's point is that we "wrongdoing," "boorish," "unlearned," and "typical" people should strive to be sages first, then go on from there to be pious and even veritable prophets — if we can.

8. The Jewish philosophers Rambam drew upon include Rav Saadyah Gaon, Ibn Gabirol, Rabbeinu Bachyah ibn Pakudah, Rabbi Yehudah HaLevi, Rabbi Avraham ibn Ezra, and others. Non-Jewish philosophers include Socrates, Plato, Aristotle, Alexander of Aphrosias, Ibn Sina, al-Gazzali, Ibn al-Zaig, and others.

Rambam's admiration for Aristotle is well known, and he cites him quite readily at different points, including in his commentary to *Pirkei Avot* (1:6). He referred to him as "the preeminent philosopher" (*Moreh Nevuchim* 1:5), and said that he'd attained a level of understanding almost on par with prophecy, the ultimate human reach (*Iggeret Ibn Tibbon*). In fact, Rambam cited him a number of times in his *Moreh Nevuchim* (see 2:17, 19, 24). Nonetheless, there were times when he rejected Aristotle's reasoning altogether and denigrated his opinions (see *Moreh Nevuchim* 2:15, 18, 22).

9. Or as he put it elsewhere, "Don't judge a wine by its flask" (Commentary on *Pirkei Avot* 4:22).

See *Hilchot Kiddush HaChodesh* 17:24, where Rambam also cites non-Jewish secular sources (in order to calculate the onset of the new moon). In *Hilchot Sanhedrin* 2:1, he indicates that members of the Sanhedrin had to be well-versed in the kinds of non-Torah material that would help them to arrive at decisions.

Rambam cited many non-Jewish sources in *Moreh Nevuchim*, from Greek to Arab, either gleaning from them or refuting. He even cited works composed by idolaters (whose opinions he described in *Moreh Nevuchim* 3:30 as "unhealthy") in his determination to offer the historical nexus of the mitzvot (see ibid., 29).

All of these are instances of subjects that are otherwise forbidden to study but permitted in order to comprehend God (see 5:4 below, and 5:6, where such actions will be described as is "a sin in a certain sense," since they're forbidden if we don't need them in order to comprehend God).

To understand Rambam's advice to "accept truth from whoever utters it," Jewish or not, it is important to note that he avers on two separate occasions that though there were Jewish scientists and philosophers in antiquity, their writings were lost or suppressed as a consequence of the exigencies of exile and persecution, or they were only known by the elite who kept it hidden (see *Hilchot Kiddush HaChodesh* 11:3 and *Moreh Nevuchim* 1:71, 2:11; also see *Moreh Nevuchim* 2:8).

An obvious possible implication of this is that Rambam himself (certainly one of the elite) was privy to those writings, and he set out to allude to although not to cite those ancient teachings in the course of his writings — perhaps even couching them in the words of non-Jewish scientists and philosophers.

10. We find it curious that Rambam considers citing a source as being "unnecessarily wordy." But he said the same in his *Sefer HaMitzvot*, which served as an introduction to his magnum opus, *Mishneh Torah*, and held to it. Yet he expended hundreds upon hundreds of words to explain the beauty of silence (Commentary on *Pirkei Avot* 1:16)!

11. Continuing our thoughts in note 9 above, we'd also add that in his *Ma'amar Odot Derashot Chazal*, Avraham ben HaRambam praised our Sages' own admiration of truth despite its source. He cited as an example their acquiescence to the opinion of non-Jewish scholars in *Pesachim* 94b.

Interestingly enough, Rambam himself quoted the Sages as saying outright in that context that "the scholars of the other nations have defeated the Sages of Israel," though this statement is not found in our text of the Talmud. Nonetheless, Avraham ben HaRambam went to great pains in his work to show just how right the gentile scholars were, based upon the discussion there in the Talmud.

Also interesting is the fact that in his edition of Avraham ben HaRambam's works, Rabbi R. Margolios cites the authors of *Akeidat Yitzchak* and *Nechmad V'Na'im*, who both indicate that according to the great Tycho Brahe, the sixteenth-century Danish astronomer, the Talmudic Sages were right, and shouldn't have acquiesced to the others' opinions! But as Rabbi Kapach indicates in his note 8 to *Moreh Nevuchim* 2:8, none of this is relevant to reality as we know it today, since it is based on ancient, limited astronomy. So, in point of fact, neither side was correct.

Apparently, the lesson we're to draw from all this is that material truth is no more static than material phenomena, while transcendent truth, which the Sages would never have accepted from anyone outside the realm of divine, Torah-based revelation, is static and unchanging.

Chapter 1: The Human Nefesh and Its Capacities

1. With few exceptions, we purposely didn't translate the term *nefesh* in this work. It is usually translated as either "soul" or "spirit." And indeed, Rambam himself equates it with the spirit of life found in all animate objects, as well as with the immortal soul (*Moreh Nevuchim* 1:41), but that is clearly not its meaning in this context. After all, he's about to point out that the *nefesh* encompasses five different spheres of physical, emotional, and mental activity. Hence, he obviously isn't speaking about anything otherworldly.

Interestingly enough, he also equates the *nefesh* with human will and consciousness (ibid.). Thus, the best translation for *nefesh* in this work would be "the self," which is a ponderous and awkward term. Thus, except for when it just didn't fit, we simply wrote "when one...," "one is...," etc., when referring to the *nefesh*. There were times we were forced to simply say "the *nefesh*," and other times when we translated it differently, depending on the context. But all in all, it denotes one's self, one's very being.

Rambam himself clearly uses the word in this way when he writes of ancient Sages who wrote notes "to their *nefesh*," i.e., to themselves, before the Mishnah was redacted (Introduction to his Commentary on the Mishnah).

2. Rambam reintroduces the three-*nefesh* system that he mentions here but rejects it in several other instances (e.g., at the end of section 2 of this chapter). At one point (*Moreh Nevuchim* 3:12), he seems to indicate that, unlike humans, animals do indeed have three *nefashot*. It seems that their three *nefashot* would best be translated as "the natural, the dynamic, and the nonmaterial" (rather than "the spiritual," as we translate it here, which has other connotations that are irrelevant to animals).

But at another point (ibid. 3:46), he mentions the three *nefashot* in a human context, yet he changes it somewhat by referring to human *desire* rather than human nature, and he refers to them there as capacities, rather than parts, of the *nefesh*.

3. There's an interesting analogy to the various and often contradictory components of the one *nefesh* elsewhere in this chapter, having to do with one of the *nefesh*'s own components — the intellect. It is pointed out at the end of this chapter's fourth section that one's intellect encompasses many different capacities, including "the capacity to reason, speculate, acquire knowledge, and differentiate between good and bad actions," and that some of those capacities themselves can be broken down into a wealth of subcapacities, listed there (see Kapach's note 21 to *Moreh Nevuchim* 1:53). The functions of the intellect — which is just one of the *nefesh*'s components — thus serves to illustrate the *nefesh*'s own multifunctionality.

Rambam illustrates how one thing can thus do and produce a number of different, even conflicting, functions elsewhere in his writings, as well. He points out that fire, for example, can melt some things, solidify others, and cook, burn, whiten, and blacken yet others. Someone not knowing the nature of fire would think that six different entities were at work: one that melts, another that solidifies, etc. But of course, fire is the one source (or "cause") for all those effects (*Moreh Nevuchim* 1:53). In very much the same way, the *nefesh* is the source of and impetus behind our various personal components.

In contrast, in section 3 below, Rambam uses an analogy that is applicable here, too. He cites "three dark rooms," "the first of which was...illuminated by sunlight, the second by moonlight, and the third by candlelight." His point is that, while all three rooms were indeed "illuminated," they were nonetheless illuminated by three different sources and generators of light.

The opposite is true of the *nefesh*. The one *nefesh* "illuminates" (i.e., animates) our stomachs, lungs, hearts, and so on, in physical ways, our senses in sensual ways, and our intellect, imagination, and emotions in emotionally and mindfully responsive ways.

We can draw an analogy between the oneness of the *nefesh* — despite its various capacities — with God's oneness despite His many functions in the world. As Rambam puts it, "Those who truly know God don't consider Him to have many attributes. They believe that the various qualities attributed to Him, including His might, greatness, power, perfection, goodness, etc., all refer to His [one] essence" (*Moreh Nevuchim* 1:20).

The point again is that our entire being, which is so complex and often beveled at oblique angles, is, nonetheless, driven and powered by the one *nefesh*, one self, which expresses itself in so many different ways.

4. It's important to know that Rambam is raising the idea of character and self-improvement here because he believes that the aim of *Pirkei Avot* (to which *Shemoneh Perakim* serves as an introduction) is to instruct us in how to improve ourselves, i.e., our *nefesh* (Introduction to his Commentary on the Mishnah; Commentary on *Pirkei Avot* 5:2).

5. The term used for "character" here and throughout this work is *middot*. It's usually taken to refer to our personal attributes, qualities, and overall disposition. It literally means "dimensions" or "measurements," and was used to refer to the dimensions of the Holy Temple, for example in Tractate *Middot*. However, when speaking about character and disposition elsewhere, Rambam uses the term *deiʼot* (see *Hilchot Deiʼot*), which we're told means "viewpoints" or opinions arrived at about things after lengthy consideration (*Moreh Nevuchim* 1:50). Why the change of terms, and why does Rambam specifically use *middot* here?

Apparently his point is that our dispositions and characters are *products* of our thoughts about and perceptions of things. While we're certainly born with some opinions of reality, we retain them when we find that they agree with our perceptions of things, and reject them when they don't. He also seems to be implying that one could "measure" (i.e., analyze and then come to know) another's perceptions of things by using his or her disposition as a barometer.

6. Interestingly enough, Rambam speaks elsewhere about the opposite situation. He cites different instances of "illumination" — actually, revelation — all originating in the same source, yet manifesting themselves differently.

As he points out, revelation originates in a single source — God's "flow" (*Moreh Nevuchim* 2:36), which is to say, in an instance of the Divine Mind calling upon and imbuing itself into a human mind. Yet different "illuminated" souls experience that "flow" differently. Some experience an intense, extended instance of it only once in their lives, or sporadically; others experience it again and again, and for a long time; and still others never experience illumination per se, only an offshoot of it, and only once in a while at that. Moses experienced it glaringly, boldly, and undeniably, again and again (*Moreh Nevuchim*, Introduction).

Perhaps there are two lessons to be drawn from these two instances of illumination (i.e., one source illuminating various ways versus various things illuminated by various sources). First, while we're all unique, multifarious manifestations of the One Source, our own beings are themselves sources of multifarious, unique manifestations. And second, manifestation seems to function in an hourglass-shaped way, since it begins expansively on-high, then narrows down and concentrates itself upon a single *nefesh*, and then widens ever more expansively throughout the diverse being which each one of us is.

7. In fact, the concept of analogy is very important to Rambam. He contends that part of our confusion with Torah stems from the fact that we simply don't realize that it often uses analogies (see *Moreh Nevuchim* 1:46). To be sure, the Torah is forced to use analogies, because it addresses a wide variety of people — the simple and the sophisticated; those with great faith and those without. Thus, the only way to address them all cogently enough for each to grasp what it says is to use terms that speak to some one way, and to others in other, analogous ways. But we often lose sight of that.

For example, the Torah promises us various delights in the afterlife should we live a virtuous life. The mistake most of us make is in drawing analogies to the sensuous, palpable worldly delights we know of, when in fact the Torah is referring to the sort of diaphanous, very subtle and fine spiritual delights the soul revels in. Now, it would be best if we'd all long for the delights of the spirit in the afterlife and serve God on so high a level. Nonetheless, the fact that some of us serve God in the hope of some sort of trinket or bauble in the afterlife is all right, too. Because in the end, they, too, would have served God and brought goodness into the world (see Commentary on *Perek Cheilek*).

We actually can't really be faulted for less than lofty motivations to serve God, since many of us can't grasp spiritual delights any more than the blind can grasp the delight of colors, the deaf can grasp the delight of sound, or fish can grasp the delight of fire — because it's utterly out of our realm. Indeed, the only delights we know of center around eating, drinking, and the like; and anything apart from that doesn't exist (let alone delight), as far as we're concerned. Nonetheless, we're assured that spiritual delights are unending and beyond anything we know of, and that those who attain them now want nothing more to do with mere physical delights than a king in his grand palace would want to have anything to do with things that made him happy as a little boy (see Commentary on *Perek Cheilek*).

Nonetheless, our point is that Torah addresses both "readers," if you will, the one who understands the kind of spiritual delight the Torah is actually referring to, and the one who would settle for the analogous kind of delight he knows on earth.

In point of fact, the Torah actually uses many analogies, as Rambam goes to great pains to underscore. It uses the term "good" (*tov*), for example, to refer to what is commonly accepted as morally good (*Moreh Nevuchim* 1:2), or to refer to the fulfillment of a goal (ibid. 3:13). It uses the term "man" (*adam*) to refer to either Adam, humankind, or to what we'd refer to as "the common man" (ibid. 1:14). It uses the term "place" (*makom*) to refer to a particular location, or to a person's personal stature or standing (ibid. 1:8). And it uses the term "heart" (*lev*) to refer to the actual physical heart, or to thought, opinion, or reason (ibid. 1:39).

The Torah also uses analogies to describe God (see ch. 8 below). He is said to be "alive," but He is certainly not alive the way we mortal, vulnerable, dependent beings are. He is said to have "knowledge," but His knowledge is nothing like our own. He's said to "see" and "hear," but He certainly doesn't have eyes and ears or any other body part. He really can't be said to be "strong" or "weak," for that matter, since those are relative terms, and God's nature is unchanging and unaffected by external circumstances (*Moreh Nevuchim* 1:35), yet He's described in such terms in the Torah. At bottom, it would be best to say that God is not just quantitatively different from us, He is also *qualitatively* different.

The esoteric truism of analogous terms is not only applicable to the Torah; it's also applicable to our understanding of the world and of life itself. It touches upon how we relate to each other as people and what we expect of others, for example. So while one person might, for example, consider and expect a "good" person to be ethical and dependable, another might expect someone depicted as "good" to be merely competent and friendly.

8. This is the first of several references to the practice of medicine in *Shemoneh Perakim*. As is well known, Rambam was a physician himself (and quite a prestigious one at that), so his mention of medicine is neither insignificant nor coincidental.

At one point he cites the practice of medicine in a most superficial manner as being just one of the various mechanical skills to which the intellect is capable of applying itself. As he puts it in section 4 of this chapter, "The intellect encompasses the human capacity to reason, speculate, acquire knowledge, and differentiate between good and bad actions. Now, some of its functions are practical, and others are speculative. The practical ones are either mechanical or conceptual.... The mechanical include the capacity to acquire skills like carpentry, agriculture, *medicine*, or navigation."

Yet here in the text, he gives medicine more status by acknowledging that it enables us to appreciate the nature, workings, and import of the most physically vital aspect of our being — digestion. As he puts it, "The makeup of these seven capacities [of the digestive system]...[is] relevant to the art of medicine and has no place here."

Interestingly, at another point, he lauds the choice of a medical career (in seeming contradistinction to what we pointed out two paragraphs back) by saying, "The practice of medicine has a very large role in [acquiring the] virtues, knowing God, and comprehending what is true bliss. Studying and pursuing it is thus one of the greatest forms of [divine] service. It is not like weaving or carpentry [for example], because it enables us to put purpose into our actions and make our actions truly human — things that foster virtues and [the realization of] many truths" (5:2).

Perhaps the richest and most fluid way Rambam refers to the practice of medicine is as a source of metaphor. It is used in that sense throughout chapter 3, where he says, for example, that "the *nefesh* can be healthy or ill, just as the body can be" (3:1), and where he points out that since "a person would go to a doctor when he realized he was ill....likewise one whose *nefesh* is ill should go to a sage who can heal the *nefesh*" (3:2).

He does the same at various points in chapter 4. In section 7 there, he likens people who ill-advisedly emulate the ways of the pious to "some fool who knew nothing about medicine, who saw expert practitioners giving cathartics to dangerously ill patients, ... and through this they were healed and their lives were quite dramatically saved," who would thus "start to take them...and become ill instead."

In that chapter's tenth section, Rambam advises us that "it is important for a healthy individual to constantly scrutinize his character, to weigh his actions, and to gauge his disposition every single day and to quickly treat himself..." the way a doctor would when he notices a subtle change in his constitution. For the latter wouldn't "ignore [the illness] or allow it to take hold to the point where he would need the strongest medicines available."

Finally, in the second section of chapter 5, Rambam counsels that one should only "favor more appetizing things for medical reasons, for example if his appetite was weak he would whet it with well-seasoned and sweet foods, or if one suffers from melancholia he could ward it off by listening to poems and music, by strolling in gardens and among fine buildings, or by sitting beside attractive works of art and the like, in order to settle his spirit and ward off his melancholia."

9. Rambam discussed the uniqueness of the sense of touch elsewhere. His point there was that not only is it the only sense not centered in a particular organ, it is also the only "objectionable" one. This is for two reasons: first, because it's the only one we have that is utterly animalistic rather than distinctively human (*Moreh Nevuchim* 2:36); and second, because it's the one that has us crave food, drink, and intercourse, which we should always approach with moderation (ibid. 3:8). In fact, both ideas are derived from Aristotle (*Nicomachean Ethics* 3:10), as Rambam readily acknowledges.

As Aristotle put it, while animals see, hear, taste, and smell for functional reasons alone (i.e., to hunt, find shelter, defend themselves, etc.), we humans often use our sense of sight, hearing, and smell to enjoy more refined, lofty things like art, music, and fine scents, while our sense of taste, and especially our sense of touch, are limited to animalistic needs.

In fact, Aristotle went on to say that our sense of touch is especially animalistic because touch (or the feel of things) is the dominant drive in taste (i.e., appetite) and sexuality. (Which would explain why we enjoy eating, for example — because it immediately and concretely gratifies the tongue, taste buds, and the belly.) As an illustration, Aristotle cited a certain glutton's prayer for his neck to be as long as a crane's so that he might enjoy the foods he loved that much longer.

But Rambam could be said to have other reasons to find the sense of touch "objectionable" — based especially on the fact that it is the only one that "functions throughout the body rather than in a specific organ," as he put it here.

The ubiquitousness of the sense of touch is a sign of two personal flaws: intemperance (see 4:2, 3) and imbalance (see 4:3, 4, 8, 9, 10; 7:2). It is a sign of commonness and frequency, while the best of traits are unique and rare (5:6; see Introduction to Commentary on the Mishnah). It also runs counter to his idea that we should concentrate all of our goals and deeds toward one end alone (ch. 5).

10. While we translate the term used here (*dimyon*) as "the imagination," it is usually translated as "the imaginative faculty" or "the creative mind." It can also be translated as "intuition" or even "instinct," depending on Rambam's use of the term. So it would do us well to explore Rambam's understanding of *dimyon*. We'll discover just how important a concept *dimyon* is to Rambam in the process, as well as unearth some of its strengths and weaknesses.

Rambam says at one point that when we function through our *dimyon*, we look at things "in their composite state" rather than deduce their true nature, and we accept them for what they seem to be (i.e., we take them at face value). Why is this? Because the *dimyon* can't transcend the physical and tangible (i.e., it cannot see beneath the surface) [*Moreh Nevuchim* 1:73].

In fact, Rambam's first illustration of that is found in 1:3, where he points out that "we also use analogous terms to refer to humans' and other creatures' senses, even though a human being's senses are not like a horse's, [just like] no one species' senses are like any other's. For every species which has a *nefesh* has one unique to itself, with functions that are necessarily different than any other's. [Nonetheless,] *some people equate the two functions* and think they are identical, but this is not so." The word for "equate" there is related to *dimyon*. His point is that on the surface of things, the senses of human beings and those of animals seem to be one and the same, but in fact they're not. (Compare this point with our note on p. 32 ["produces a phantasm"], where we speak of an iron ship that seems to be sailing in midair.)

Rambam avers in that same citation that most living things have a *dimyon*, but this is apparently a case of *dimyon* as instinct or reflex. As Rabbi Yosef Kapach explains it (in his note 39 to *Moreh Nevuchim* 1:73), Rambam is referring to instances in which an animal who had been struck once or twice by his master would know enough not to approach him when his master had his staff in his hand, for he could easily imagine his master striking him again with it.

As another example of *dimyon* as instinct or reflex Rambam cites a mother's love for her child. He points out that this is not an intellectual response, but rather a *dimyon*-based (i.e., reflex- or instinct-based) one (*Moreh Nevuchim* 3:48).

There happen to be instances in Rambam where *dimyon* does indeed refer to intuition and higher imagination, when it has to do with prophecy, in which it plays an extensive part. We'll discuss prophecy in general and the *dimyon*'s place in it in more depth in 7:2.

It's important to note, though, that despite its central role in prophecy, and notwithstanding its function in everyday life and human productivity, Rambam also tends to downplay the *dimyon*. He equates it with the *yetzer hara* (humankind's baser instinct, its pull away from the Divine, its inherent ability to morally and spiritually delude itself), and thus takes it to be either the root cause of all personal flaws, or in some way connected to them (*Moreh Nevuchim* 2:12). He points out, in fact, that Adam and Eve's calamitous mistake was a consequence of their following the dictates of their *dimyon* rather than reason (ibid. 1:2).

But Rambam's disdain for the *dimyon* doesn't just lie in its connection to our baser instincts rather than to pure reason, which is our essential humanity (as we'll see later in the chapter). He also seems to eschew it because it functions involuntarily and passively, rather than deliberately (*Moreh Nevuchim* 1:47) — unlike the rational mind.

Rambam alludes to this facet a number of times: when he characterizes "imaginings" as things "that [just] come to mind" (see Ezekiel 20:32; *Moreh Nevuchim* 3:51); when he cites the fact that one of *dimyon's* functions is to imitate (rather than create), and the fact that it works best when the senses are at rest and inactive (*Moreh Nevuchim* 2:36); and most especially, when he notes later on in our work that free will — that most important of human boons — doesn't function in the imagination (see 2:1).

11. Rambam's use of these three particular examples of absurdity and phantasm is seemingly ironic in light of things he has said elsewhere.

At one point he accepts the idea that angels are depicted in the Torah as having wings, since that description appeases the imagination's mistaken idea that anything that flies would have to have wings (*Moreh Nevuchim* 1:49), when angels actually don't have wings. Yet in the text here he degrades the idea of anything flying without wings or other "natural" means of self-propulsion.

He says in our text that it's ludicrous to conceive of "an individual whose head is in the heavens while his feet are on the ground." Yet we're told that "Adam extended from the ground to the heavens" (*Chagigah* 12a), and Rambam probably understood this to refer quite fittingly to Adam's spiritual stature (see *Moreh Nevuchim* 1:8).

And while he belittled the notion of "an animal with a thousand eyes" here, he nonetheless explained the eyes in Ezekiel's prophetic vision of *ofanim*, angels whose "whole body, backs, hands, wings, and wheels *were full of eyes all around*" (Ezekiel 10:12), as representing properties or qualities (*Moreh Nevuchim* 3:2).

We contend, though, that this isn't a contradiction. What it does is serve to further explain the difference between imagination and reason, as spoken of in the previous note, and between reason and prophetic vision.

Most of us, who depend on our reason, take things at face value and can't grasp the idea of nonphysical phenomena, so we use our imaginations to add wings onto angels to explain their ability to fly. Yet we can accept the absurd notion of a lifeless entity like an iron ship propelling itself upward without wings, simply because we can equate it with actual, discernible birds that "float" in the air. Prophets, on the other hand, whose grasp is rooted in the imagination, can envision a human being vast in "size" (i.e., in spiritual and intellectual stature) or a creature with many "eyes" (i.e., with many properties and qualities), which our reason simply couldn't allow for.

12. The Mutakallimun were members of a sect of Arabic religious thinkers and dialecticians who tried to reconcile Islamic ideology with Aristotelian philosophy, and arrived at some very seriously flawed notions (see *Moreh Nevuchim* 1:71–76).

13. I.e., that we should take the *conceivable*, or "what may or may not be so," as seriously as we take the actual (see *Moreh Nevuchim* 1:73, tenth proposition; also see *Moreh Nevuchim* 1:49 and 3:15).

"After all," as we'd put it today, "who knows — it just might be!" In fact, we apparently take that very much to heart in modernity. A contemporary advertiser crows, "We believe that if it can be imagined, it can be done!" in keeping with this very old error in logic. But often, as the expression goes, "reality beckons," and we come to realize that *not* everything that can be imagined can be — other than virtually (see our note on p. 32 ["produces a phantasm"]).

On the other hand, the Mutakallimun also maintained that what *can't* be imagined *can't be*. And that, of course, stifles our faith in all things invisible and spiritual.

They also maintained positions that strike us as odd. They claimed, for example, that once something is conceived to be possible, it can then either stay the way we conceive it to be or change, regardless of whether that change makes sense. And so, while they agreed that "earth moves toward the center while fire turns away from the center, and that fire heats while water cools," they reasoned that that's only so by dint of habit, and that we could equally logically allow for a deviation of that habit where "fire would cool and move downward and still be fire, and water would heat and move upward and still be water" (*Moreh Nevuchim* 1:73).

Rambam's translator and student, Rabbi Shmuel Ibn Tibbon, in his *Biur MeHaMilot HaZarot* (at the end of his translation of *Moreh Nevuchim*), thus characterized the Mutakallimun as a "class of so-called sages who were actually without wisdom, who used their imaginations to assess things rather than reason or actual reality." He also accused them of lapsing into rhetorical fancy, as one might expect of a class of thinkers whose name is derived from the Arabic term for "word."

14. Apparently not only do our various body parts serve our emotions, but our senses do, too, as we'll learn at the beginning of the next chapter. And though we'll touch upon whether our imagination and our intellect also serve our emotions when we discuss free will, in short: sometimes they do and sometimes they don't.

Rambam addresses the centrality of the heart at various junctures. He points out that while the procreative organs, for example, are vital for the maintenance of the human race, they're less vital to us personally; the digestive system, on the other hand, which includes the heart, is vital for our own personal existence. Other parts, like our hands and feet, are subordinate, since their primary function is to help in digestion (i.e., to acquire and prepare food), while yet other parts, like our hair and skin, are less important (*Moreh Nevuchim* 1:72; also see ibid. 1:46).

As such, both the heart and the emotions sit at the center of our beings. The heart does so, because it keeps us alive (and coincidentally sits at the "center" of our bodies, as the ancients saw it — i.e., at the approximate center of the upper, more "noble" part of the body), and the emotions sit at the center of our beings because our body in general and our senses are subservient to them.

He points out some other things about the heart that consequently touch upon our emotions as well, when he speaks of the reciprocal relationship between the heart and the other organs. He indicates that the heart, which rules over the entire body, nonetheless derives as much from the other organs as they do from it (*Moreh Nevuchim* 1:72). So for example, while the kidneys are fed by the heart, it's also true that they cleanse the heart's blood. The same might be said about the emotions. For while the emotions grant our various body parts their drive and vim, those same body parts also act as the emotions' tools, and grant them their richness and function. Thus there's a reciprocal relationship there, too (see *Moreh Nevuchim* 3:12).

15. The idea that the intellect allows us to "differentiate between good and bad actions" also touches upon free will, as we'll find. However, as Rambam indicates at one point, the ability to differentiate good from bad isn't the ultimate human intellectual function, but rather the *pen*ultimate one, second to the ability to reason (see *Moreh Nevuchim* 1:2).

16. The "immutables" refers to the so-called "essential forms" which Rambam describes as "permanent" and "stable" (see *Moreh Nevuchim* 3:8). We'll be discussing "form" as well as "matter" at the end of this chapter.

17. In much the same vein, Rambam says elsewhere that something is termed "good" only when it fulfills its life purpose (*Moreh Nevuchim* 3:13). That seems to extend the point made here in the text, that one fulfills his life's purpose when he acquires reason.

Yet at the very beginning of chapter 4, Rambam uses the term "good" in reference to the balanced character traits we are to strive for. Apparently, then, we have to realize two life goals: acquiring reason and acting in a balanced way. In fact in his introduction to his comments on the Mishnah, Rambam underscores the fact that one only achieves true human perfection after perfecting both his intellect *and* his character.

Nonetheless that doesn't seem to be the case at first. Because he starts off by saying there (in the introduction to his Commentary on the Mishnah) that humankind has a single purpose — to comprehend abstract concepts and to understand truisms with clarity. Continuing in that vein, he says that only knowledge allows one to evolve from "potentially human" to "actually human." Yet then most significantly, almost in midsentence, he adds that one must perfect his character, as well.

One must learn to subdue his desires, he offers, because physicality acts as a great barrier to the acquisition of reason (*Moreh Nevuchim* 3:10), and because in fact, a person who can't subdue his desires is nothing more than "an animal in human form" (as he puts it in *Moreh Nevuchim* 1:7), who is *incapable* of acquiring reason. Such a person is depicted as a speck of mere "matter floating alone upon the sea of hyle" (i.e., the great sea of formless, primordial matter the Greeks referred to).

So, indeed, achieving our life purpose hinges on growing intellectually *and* personally.

(Rambam reiterates the point later on when adding that the world's ultimate purpose, in fact, is to allow for the existence of such a "learned person with good character" [Introudction to his Commentary on the Mishnah], but he adds something that's both astounding and telling. If indeed we're to strive to actualize ourselves intellectually and personally, and if the world serves as an environment in which such a person could live and thrive; and yet, as he put it there, *only one person in a generation merits being a fully actualized human* — what, then, is everyone else's role in this world, he asks? The answer is that the rest of us act to service, assist, and attend to that individual! After all, Rambam reasons, if everyone was a scholar and a philosopher, the world would go to ruin, and humankind would be undone in short order. For if everyone spent the amount of time it takes acquiring the sort of knowledge and character needed to be a fully actualized person, none of the world's work would get done.)

But Rambam decided not to go on with the discussion here. For as he put it at the very end of the section, "This is not the place for a discussion about form and matter, or about the different degrees of reason and how to acquire them," or about using that to reach perfection. For "it is not necessary for what we want to say about character," which comprises the thrust of this book. It's more appropriate to speak of abstract matters and intellectual perfection elsewhere, as he says.

18. As we indicated in our note on p. 37 ("reason is its 'form'"), Rambam says that our defining spirit and life-force lies in our ability to reason. But that should give us pause. Are we then defined by our ability to speculate abstractly and the like, as described? Have we no soul? As we'll explain shortly, the answer hinges on the fact that there are different "degrees" of reason, and the highest of those is what we'd refer to as the soul, as we'll soon see.

Reason seems to differ both quantitatively and qualitatively, according to Rambam. Which is to say that, while some of us have more reason than others, others have a whole other order of it. The sort of analytical reason described in our note on p. 37 ("reason is its 'form'") is only one type. It is part of one's intellect (after all, as Rambam pointed out above in the text, "the intellect encompasses the human capacity to reason, speculate, acquire knowledge," etc.).

But the higher order of reason — which Rambam in fact refers to as one's immortal soul (see *Moreh Nevuchim* 1:70) — is called one's "active reason" and "Godly capacity," as opposed to one's ability to reason analytically, which is called one's "potential reason" (Introduction to Commentary on the Mishnah) or "hylic reason" (see note above for the meaning of "hyle") (see *Moreh Nevuchim* 1:72). It's one's "active" reason that realizes transcendent and lofty truths, which his "potential" or analytical reason can't (Introduction to Commentary on the Mishnah).

A person's ability to reason analytically offers us the potential to *actually* reason, i.e., to achieve the above-cited "active reason," described as mankind's ultimate *sheleimut* (perfection) [*Moreh Nevuchim* 1:2], his essence (ibid. 1:1), his actual connection to God (ibid. 3:51), and the mechanism by which he comes to know and commune with Him (see Introduction to Commentary on the Mishnah; *Hilchot Yesodei HaTorah* 4:8–9; *Hilchot Teshuvah* 8:3; *Moreh Nevuchim* 1:68, 3:8). In point of fact, Rambam's famous son and disciple Avraham ben HaRambam described the experience of joining one's active reason to God's own as *deveikut* (attachment), a common term for the sort of mystical adhesion to the Divine that has been practiced by Kabbalists (*Milchamot Hashem*).

(We find some evidence for Rambam's own formula for *deveikut*. He says at one point that God acts as the "form" of the world, so to speak — since the world only exists because He does, and as a consequence of His continuously bestowing it with existence [*Moreh Nevuchim* 1:69]. As such, when we think of the world abstractly — i.e., when we focus on its "form" separate from its "matter" — we thus become "one" with, i.e., commune with or attached onto, Him [see ibid., 68].)

As Rambam put it at another point, what remains behind after death isn't the spirit implanted in a person at birth. For while the latter is potential, the immortal soul is realized (ibid., 70); and while the latter is inborn, the former is not (ibid., 72) and is bestowed upon us in its raw form from the Divine Intellect instead (ibid. 3:8).

Thus Rambam's argument at the beginning of this section, that "if the *nefesh* never achieves its form, then its aptitude to achieve it would have been for naught, and its existence worthless" seems to be this: Unless we advance from the physical, emotional, and intellectual to potential reason, then onto active reason, our uniquely human ability to do just that would have been in vain, and we'd thus prove to be less than fully human (see *Hilchot Yesodei HaTorah* 4:8; *Moreh Nevuchim* 1:71, 3:51; and *Hilchot Teshuvah* 8:1).

19. For as we indicated before, Rambam's aim in *Shemoneh Perakim* is to help us improve our *nefesh* (i.e., ourselves) (Introduction to Commentary on the Mishnah; Commentary on *Pirkei Avot* 5:2) by achieving personal, character-based *sheleimut* rather than the sort of ultimate *sheleimut* referred to in the discussion just above (see our supplementary note 4 to Rambam's Introduction for a discussion about the various levels of *sheleimut*).

20. This last paragraph is yet another indication that *Shemoneh Perakim* was intended for a "popular" audience (see our note to Rambam's Introduction on p. 32 ("sailing in the air") for our discussion of how he addresses two sorts of audiences here). Suffice it to say, though, that there are quite a few other instances where Rambam addresses himself to a specific readership.

He'll indicate in 8:11 below that the metaphysics he'd presented was so difficult that this work's readers couldn't hope to "expect to understand them thoroughly," and that they were better off just letting what he'd said "serve as a point of information." At another point there, he also said even less ambiguously, "I've thus offered an argument that's easy and likely to be understood by the masses. But the best arguments available to abrogate this claim are stronger yet and definitive." (Those ideas were in fact treated at length elsewhere [see *Hilchot Teshuvah* 5:5, *Moreh Nevuchim* 3:19–21].) At another point he expressed that he was addressing readers who'd already delved into philosophy, and had a clear understanding of the makeup of the *nefesh* and its capacities — the contents of this chapter (ibid. 1:68). And at one point he admitted that he prefers addressing the "one in tens of thousands" to addressing the masses (*Moreh Nevuchim*, end of *Tzivah*).

Chapter 2: The Capacity of the Nefesh to Disobey and Where Its Virtues and Flaws Are Found

1. While it is true that obedience and disobedience touch upon our senses and emotions, and that they play themselves out in those theatres, Rambam says elsewhere that they are actually *rooted* in either our imagination (*Moreh Nevuchim* 1:2) or in our ability to reason (ibid. 3:8).

He indicates that our imaginations (i.e., fantasies) provoke us to disobey, and to satisfy our passions in untoward ways; while reason encourages us to obey, and to satisfy our passions in reasonable ways. We nonetheless have the capacity to have reason rule over our imaginations (i.e., to use reason to argue against fantasy), and thus to regulate our desires, and we're to depend on nothing other than reason (i.e., nothing lesser and external) to do that (Commentary on *Perek Cheilek*). He adds as well that a person's spiritual status is, in fact, determined by his ability to exercise that option (*Moreh Nevuchim* 3:8).

Thus, his point here in the text seems to be that this process is bolstered and implemented by our senses and emotions (and our intellects, as we'll see).

2. We'll now address Rambam's perspective on Torah and mitzvot as a whole.

Rambam contends that the Torah serves two essential purposes: that of bettering and enhancing the "body" (i.e., each individual's as well as society's physical well-being, as we'll see), and of bettering and enhancing the individual *nefesh*. He also contends that while bettering and enhancing the *nefesh* is ultimately more significant, bettering and enhancing the body always comes first, since the individual (or society) can never improve on a *nefesh*-level while suffering physical discomfort, hunger, thirst, or torment (*Moreh Nevuchim* 3:27).

(The term "bettering and enhancing" will sometimes prove to be cumbersome, but the original term used in the Hebrew, *tikkun*, implies both, rather than just one. It's not a familiar nor often-enough used term to simply refer to in Hebrew, as we do in the case of *nefesh*. Nonetheless, see our note on p. 28 ["what would then heal it"], where we discuss *tikkun* somewhat.)

He speaks to both an individual's and society's well-being because the two are essentially interdependent. After all, it's obviously essential for people to have enough food, lodging, sanitation, health, children, and sleep (*Hilchot Dei'ot* 3:3), and these all require other people (*Moreh Nevuchim* 3:27), which thus pleads the case for the importance of society.

Rambam thus initially encourages us to accede to the general good and defer to the society-related mitzvot rather than do what we'd perhaps prefer doing to achieve piety, as well as to strive for the sort of lofty character traits this book will eventually be addressing, for the good of society as a whole (*Moreh Nevuchim* 3:27). For in point of fact, in the end, that would be for our own individual good as well.

He then addresses the betterment and enhancement of the individual's *nefesh*, and offers that this also involves improving character (see 1:2 above, and Commentary on *Pirkei Avot* 2:1). Yet it also involves a lot more. Aside from deferring to the character-based mitzvot specific to this task (which we'll examine shortly), it also embraces engaging in active and constant reflection, becoming knowledgeable, arriving at possibly mistaken personal convictions after considering the alternatives (*Moreh Nevuchim* 1:50), and eventually arriving at proper convictions (ibid. 3:27).

All in all, though, the Torah's aim is to better and enhance mankind and the individual for *two* reasons: so that there be justice and civil interaction for the sake of a well-functioning society, i.e., for the sake of the (individual and public) "body," and so that each individual earn a place in the World to Come, i.e., for the sake of the individual *nefesh* (*Moreh Nevuchim* 3:27).

We'll thus now focus on the means of bettering and enhancing the *nefesh*, and on the point of doing that — to earn a place in the World to Come.

The *nefesh* is bettered and enhanced by engaging in the sort of mitzvot that are more likely to touch upon one's inner being, like fearing God (ibid. 3:24, 52), and uprooting idolatry and everything associated with it from one's heart (ibid., 29, 37). Other mitzvot in that category touch upon drawing near to and comprehending God, loving Him by way of arriving at correct perspectives about His Being, and engaging in the sorts of mitzvot that would help you to abandon mundane desires and only yearn for what is necessary. Others help one become refined and adaptable rather than stubborn and rude; instill in him purity and holiness (*Moreh Nevuchim* 3:33, 48; also see *Hilchot Issurei Bi'ah* 22:19-21); teach him to engage in God-related rather than worldly things (*Moreh Nevuchim* 3:51); and foster personal virtues (which is the thrust of *Shemoneh Perakim*; see Commentary on *Pirkei Avot* 5:13).

Now onto a discussion of the aim of a perfected *nefesh*, which touches upon the acquisition of a place in the World to Come and other things (see supplementary note 4 to the Introduction for a depiction of the Rambam's conception of the World to Come itself).

As Rambam puts it, whoever acts in accordance with the Torah and "comes to understand it clearly and correctly" (i.e., comes to arrive at the proper moral and metaphysical perspectives) will merit a place in the World to Come "that corresponds to his deeds and wisdom" (i.e., the metaphysical counterpart of his or her spiritual standing in this world) [*Hilchot Teshuvah* 9:1].

There are worldly rewards to observing the Torah as well, including presence of mind, soul satisfaction, and well-being. But these are only promised to those who observe the Torah in the proper spirit and with devotion (ibid.). Nonetheless, one shouldn't observe Torah with that end in mind (or in order to avoid the joyless and dire consequences due those who transgress it), because one would thus be serving God with an ulterior, self-serving motive.

One would do best to observe Torah in love (see below), as well as in the spirit of "pursuing the truth simply because it is the truth" (i.e., because Torah's mandates and perspectives are rooted in the truth of the universe, as revealed by God Himself) and "because good will ultimately come of it" (i.e., because the ultimate aim of the world will be achieved in the end by Torah means, and those who observe it will play a part in that) [ibid. 10:1-2].

The sort of love referred to above is rooted in the love of God. Because after all, "when a person loves God appropriately" (i.e., knowing what it means to love God, for most of us have a rather murky impression of what "loving God" is, at best), he or she "observes the mitzvot from love as a matter of course" (ibid., 2), and thus earns a place in the World to Come.

In sum, as Rambam put it elsewhere, the pious will achieve perfection by fulfilling all the details of the mitzvot, and repeating them continually (*Moreh Nevuchim* 3:52).

3. Rambam speaks about the imagination working in our sleep in two other, antithetical instances. In one instance, he cites the fact that prophets — who prophesied while in a dream state (*Hilchot Yesodei HaTorah* 7:2) — did so by means of the following process: an "emanation" (i.e., a stream of communication) would descend from God to the prophet's reasoning ability; and it would descend again to the prophet's imagination, where it would then play itself out (*Moreh Nevuchim* 2:36). In another instance, he points out that when ordinary people dream, our thoughts *ascend upward* from our imaginations to our reasoning abilities (ibid., 6).

What is interesting is the fact that Rambam also explains that our dreams go from the imagination to our reasoning abilities by means of angels, and that they're transported from the lowest degree of angel (*ishim*, who communicate directly to prophets [*Hilchot Yesodei HaTorah* 2:7]) to a higher degree of angels (*keruvim*) as they ascend (*Moreh Nevuchim* 2:6).

This is easily explained by means of Rambam's assertion elsewhere that bodily functions are all referred to as "angels" (*Moreh Nevuchim* 2:6). As such, we can explain his use of "angel" in such an unexpected way by the fact that the Hebrew word for angel (*malach*) can also be rendered as "messenger," "courier," or "relayer," as in a relayer of electric signals from the brain outward.

But perhaps what is most fascinating is the fact that all this goes a long way to explain Rambam's understanding of the verses that read, "And [Jacob] dreamed, and behold a ladder sat upon the earth. The top of it reached to Heaven, and behold, angels of God were *ascending and descending* upon it. And, behold, God stood over it" (Genesis 28:12–13). For Rambam says that the angels refer to prophets, and he makes much of the fact that the verse refers to both ascending and descending (*Moreh Nevuchim* 1:15; but see *Hilchot Yesodei HaTorah* 7:3 and *Moreh Nevuchim* 2:10, where he places it in another context). It is probably legitimate to infer that he is contrasting the upward movement of our everyday dreams with God's messages descending upon the prophet by means of the very same venue, in reverse.

4. Rambam cites the role that longings play in this phenomenon in another context. He seems to contend there that we are *not* prodded to action by ideas (or fantasies) alone. After all, he says, we often imagine things which we're permitted to pursue but we simply don't. What prods us on are, in fact,

our longings (*Moreh Nevuchim* 2:4). Yet this seems to fly in the face of our contention in the note at this point in the text that "our 'longings...personal bents, desires and even our personality'...are all based on ideas...which prod us onto action."

It is important to note that Rambam mentions the fact there that we're "moved to act *either by instinct or reason*." We might then posit that while it is indeed true that we are *very often* prodded on by our instincts, we nonetheless have it within us to be inspired to act by means of reason.

5. We'll now present evidence from other sources for our assertion that Rambam would more likely refer to those who delve into Godliness as wise.

At one point, Rambam does indeed allow for different denotations of the Hebrew word for wisdom, *chochmah*. He acknowledges that it sometimes denotes expertise in the arts and handicrafts; that at other times it signifies having virtuous character traits; that in a more unfavorable sense it now and again designates cunning and subterfuge; and finally — and most significantly for our purposes — it also denotes expertise in the things that lead to the knowledge of God (*Moreh Nevuchim* 3:54). However, we'll illustrate that the latter is, nonetheless, the most significant use of the word in his eyes.

Rambam expands upon the idea he expresses in the text at this point of "remote and immediate" causes of things elsewhere. The points made there will illustrate just how much value he placed on knowing God as an element of true wisdom.

He declares (in *Moreh Nevuchim* 1:69) that "everything but God owes its origin to the following four causes: its matter, form, agent (i.e., instigator), and its ultimate purpose or aim. And these can be either remote or immediate." Rambam then illustrates the notion of causes in general by offering a chair as an example.

He points out that a chair is typically comprised of wood (which is its matter), it stands up and is of a certain shape (which is its form), it was made by a furniture maker (who is its agent) in order for someone to sit on it (which is its ultimate purpose).

More relevant to our concerns, Rambam then illustrates causation in the case of a human being. He depicts man as being comprised of a body and a *nefesh* (which is his matter), he's able to enunciate and reason (which is his form), he was created by God (Who is his Agent). But for what reason? So as to comprehend abstract ideas, he points out. But is that his ultimate purpose? No. He's to comprehend abstract ideas so as to thus come to know God — which is his purpose and aim.

He also elaborates upon the "remote" and "immediate" causes of things in another, more day-to-day vein, which we'd illustrate thusly. Suppose a person broke his arm. The process might be as follows: a breeze might have come about through the natural, Divinely created course of events, which might then have evolved into a storm. The storm might then cause a heavy tree branch to break off, which could then land on a nearby wall that would then topple. A stone from that wall could then fly through the air, strike the person's arm, and break it.

According to Rambam's understanding, the stone itself would be the immediate cause of the person's broken arm, the fallen tree branch would be a more remote cause, the wind would be an even more remote cause, the natural course of events that brings about a breeze would be a further-yet remote cause, while the ultimate cause would be God's creation.

From here, Rambam touches upon the purpose and aim of all things, but what is most illuminating for our purposes is his analysis of the ultimate purpose and aim of the creation of mankind.

As he lays it out, we're forced to ask why man has to work so hard his whole life long in order to earn a living. Why does he have to earn a living? In order to stay alive. Why is he alive? In order to learn things and perfect his personality. Why would he have to do that? In order to be able to comprehend abstract ideas. And finally, why does he have to do that? *In order to comprehend God.* For while man's immediate (i.e., self-apparent) purpose and aim is to earn a living, *his most remote (i.e., ultimate) purpose and aim is to comprehend God* (from *Milot HaHigayon*, as cited in *Rambam La'Am*, vol. 18, pp. 163–164, note 16).

It's thus clear that knowing God's ways and role in the world is true wisdom, for a truly wise person would dwell at length on what touches upon his ultimate purpose and aim in life, which is to comprehend God.

Parenthetically, we'll also cite the following statement from this same source, because it further underscores Rambam's God-centered view of purpose and meaning, and hence wisdom. He points out that the further back one goes to find the cause of things, the sooner he'll come upon God. And the further *out* one goes to find the aim of things, the sooner he'll come upon God as well. For God is at the beginning (i.e., He's the Primary Agent) and at the end (i.e., the Ultimate Aim), the very first and the very last; cause of all causes, aim of all aims.

6. This could also be translated as "as well as any *data* one has acquired," according to Ibn Tibbon, Rambam's translator and student, in his *Biur MeHaMilot HaZarot* (which is often found at the end of Hebrew versions of *Moreh Nevuchim*, though the term is incorrectly listed under the letter *samech* rather than *sin*, as it should be).

7. While Rambam cites the fact that there are both character *and* intellectual virtues and defects, we'll see that he'll spend far more time discussing those of character. He apparently does this because character improvement is the thrust of *Shemoneh Perakim*, as we'll discuss in the following two supplemental notes.

8. In chapter 1:4 above, Rambam refers to our emotions as personal "incidentals." We expanded on that somewhat in our note on p. 34 ("and many other such incidentals of the *nefesh*"), but the idea calls for explanation in the context of free will.

Rambam says the following about free will in section 2 of chapter 8 below: "Your actions are in your own hands, no one compels you to do anything, and nothing other than yourself ever inclines you toward a character virtue or flaw.... For if you were compelled to act the way you do, then all the Torah's imperatives and prohibitions would be for naught and worthless, since you would not be free to do as you wish.... The whole idea of reward and punishment...would be utterly unfair."

So, if my free will largely plays itself out in my emotions, and free will is such a vital principle of the faith, then how can my emotions be said to be "incidental" to my being? They would seem to be essential.

We would also do well to recall Rambam's statement at the end of the first chapter to the effect that *reason* is our essence, and that anyone who hasn't actualized his ability to reason (see 1:5 above) hasn't reached his or her full potential (as we indicated in our notes there). That would seem to denigrate emotions — and thus free will — even further.

But once again, we take heart from Rambam's statement at the conclusion of that section that "while there is much to say about form and matter, still and all *this isn't the place for it.*"

Why isn't *Shemoneh Perakim* the place for such a discussion? Because "it is not necessary for what we want to say [here, in *Shemoneh Perakim*] about character," which is this work's thrust. For as we pointed out in supplementary note 17 to chapter 1, *Shemoneh Perakim* is meant to instruct us in how to improve our character — i.e., our emotional selves (see 2:3). In point of fact, our emotional life *is* incidental to our true beings, which is our ability to reason (see our note on p. 34 above ["and many other such incidentals of the *nefesh*"]). Still, not only do we have it within us to freely and consciously grow emotionally, we're *enjoined* to do just that. But why? In order to undo the emotional imbalances that befuddle our abilities to reason and achieve wholeness. And therein lies the significance of our emotions.

It is also important to recall that free will (i.e., our emotions — see in our note on p. 34 ["and many other such incidentals of the *nefesh*"]) plays an essential role in arriving at reasoned personal convictions, as well (see the statement at the end of section 1 to that effect).

We'll delve further into the interrelationship between character and reason in the following note.

9. We'll take this opportunity to touch upon Rambam's view of character per se, as well as the relationship he finds between character and intellect — or better yet, the convictions a person would arrive at with his intellect. We'll discuss his perspective on specific personality traits in chapter 4.

The first point to be made is the one we offered in supplementary note 5 to chapter 1, which is that, while Rambam evidently holds that our characters are often products of our thoughts and perceptions, some of our traits are clearly inborn. We'll discuss the issue of "nature versus nurture," or inborn rather than acquired character traits, in chapters 3 and 4.

That not withstanding, Rambam's analysis of character is based on the great variety of human personalities. He points out that people run the gamut from being enraged to even-tempered, egomaniacal to meek, voracious to easily satisfied, miserly to squandrous, licentious to noble, cruel to merciful, cowardly to courageous, etc. (*Hilchot Dei'ot* 1:1). In fact, he says at another point that people can be so disparate that they sometimes seem to be "of different breeds." For one person can be cruel enough to kill his youngest in anger, while another can be so tender-hearted that he couldn't swat a fly (*Moreh Nevuchim* 2:40), and while some people can face down lions, others are incapacitated by the sight of a mouse (ibid., 38).

Though he doesn't touch upon it, it is safe to say that Rambam certainly recognized that the very same person can be wretched one moment and tender the next, depending on circumstances. We can only assume that he didn't mention this because at another point he mentions that one is to be judged by the majority of his actions (see *Hilchot Teshuvah* 3:1–2 on relative moral assessment).

As to the relationship between character and convictions, Rambam perceived a profound connection between the two. Yet in a number of places, he underscores the importance of consciously acting out of — i.e., expressing character traits that are *based on* — sound convictions (*Moreh Nevuchim* 1:5, 42; Commentary on *Pirkei Avot* 4:27). Elsewhere he indicates that a person would have to purify his character *before* he could ever hope to arrive at sound convictions (*Moreh Nevuchim* 1:5, 34; see ibid. 3:8).

The solution to this seeming contradiction seems to lie in the fact that Rambam apparently perceived there to be a dynamic, reciprocal relationship between one's character and his convictions. Nonetheless, based on our statements in the previous supplementary note vis-à-vis the secondary nature of emotions, we'd say that Rambam apparently contends that a honed and balanced personality necessarily precedes true and reasoned convictions.

10. Rambam's statement here — that all we can say of a digestive system or imagination is that it functions well or not, rather than that it performs morally well or not — reminds us of an observation he makes elsewhere. He points out that it's incorrect to say that the fact that the world is round is either a good or a bad thing — it's actually either true or false — for one cannot legitimately make a value judgment about a natural phenomenon; one can only assess its veracity. Thus the capacity to make value judgments

is centered in what he refers to as "conventional" or "self-evident" wisdom; whereas statements of fact (i.e., what is true as opposed to what is false) are centered in and can only be arrived at by means of reason (*Moreh Nevuchim* 1:2).

His point there is that the ability to arrive at truth is far loftier than the ability to proffer conventional wisdom, much the way that the ability to consciously use one's emotions and character for higher purposes is far loftier than allowing them to act on their own.

But Rambam seems to be making another point here as well. In section 3 of chapter 6 below, he illustrates the difference between acts that are universally and conventionally taken to be "bad" (like murder, theft, abuse, etc.), and those that are only bad because Torah declares them to be so (like the eating of meat and milk together, desecrating the Sabbath, and the like). He seems to be saying that while conventional perceptions of good and bad are rather inferior in comparison to data arrived at by reason, still and all, the analysis of the Divinely inspired "authority-based" mitzvot (as he puts it in 6:3), which subsequently leads to acquiescence, touches upon reason as well, so that the entire process could even be said to *transcend* reason. For after all, authority-based mitzvot are rooted in prophetic revelation.

11. Rambam said in 1:2 above that "the digestive system encompasses the processes of ingestion, retention, digestion per se, excretion of waste, growth, procreation, and metabolism."

Interestingly enough, he discusses excretion and ingestion in another, contradictory context. He likens excretion to bravery in that, like excretion, bravery is also rooted in a powerful human impulse to reject something harmful (*Moreh Nevuchim* 2:38). Similarly, he likens ingestion to the accumulation of knowledge (ibid. 1:30). Extending the metaphor, we might liken retention to miserliness, digestion to the processing of information, growth to spiritual progress, procreation to creativity, and metabolism to making choices.

We might resolve the apparent conflict by saying that, while the digestive system automatically processes what comes into the body from the outside and contributes something of itself back into the world, the *nefesh* should consciously and willingly act as an intermediary between the inner and outer self, and determine what should come in and what should go out.

Chapter 3: Diseases of the Nefesh

1. The issue of character traits we develop later on in life — either because we mimic others who have them, or because we adopt them of our own volition — comes up elsewhere (see *Hilchot Dei'ot* 1:2). Rambam maintains, of course,

that we would do well to adopt and choose good character traits. But he adds that we can best reinforce good learned traits by continuously studying works that foster and encourage them, especially once we have acquired the sorts of traits they encourage (Commentary on *Pirkei Avot* 3:11). This is assumedly because we would resonate with these traits more once we have acquired them, and because we have already invested our time and energies into their advice.

2. There are a number of points to be made here. First, that Rambam is using the terms "healthy" and "ill" here analogously, in ways discussed in supplementary note 7 to chapter 1. He himself pointed that out elsewhere, when he said outright that "health" is an analogous term used to describe equilibrium, both physiological and emotional (see *Moreh Nevuchim* 3:10).

Second, the term used for "benevolent" in the phrase "a healthy *nefesh* and its parts are predisposed to doing good, *benevolent,* and pleasant things" could legitimately be translated as "pious." In that case, the phrase would be implying that people who are healthy in their beings would do the sorts of things that pious people would do. The implication would of course then be that pious people are, by definition, morally healthy.

And thirdly, it is important to note that Rambam defined the *nefesh* as the sum total of various emotional, intellectual, and sensual, *as well as* physical, components in chapter 1. Yet he seems to be distinguishing between the *nefesh* in its entirety and the body with his statement here that "the *nefesh* can either be healthy or ill *just as the body can be.*" But it seems Rambam is once again indicating that he'll be concentrating on the *nefesh*'s *emotional* capacity from here on, since that is where character and free will are most relevant for our purposes here. As we said previously, his goal in *Shemoneh Perakim* is to help us heal and rectify our character rather than our intellect.

He does make the point elsewhere, though, that one can have "unhealthy" personal convictions as well, and would thus be ill in his *nefesh* as far as that is concerned (*Pirkei Moshe B'Refuah*, Discourse 25; *Moreh Nevuchim* 3:46).

Interestingly enough, though, there seems to be a difference between treating character-illness and treating conviction-illness. For when we're character-ill and would need to change our ways, we're told in chapter 4 that we would have to radically shift course, then radically reverse our ways again to a limited extent. It's said in section 4 there, for example, that if "we were to encounter someone who is disposed toward allowing himself very little.... We would not order him to [merely] act generously.... We would order him to practice being *extravagant* again and again, many times over.... We would then discourage him from being extravagant and tell him to be [merely] generous — no more and no less — all the time."

Yet when it comes to changing our convictions, we're discouraged from making radical changes, and told to proceed step by step, since "it's impossible to go from one extreme [outlook] to another instantaneously" (*Moreh Nevuchim* 3:32). He makes a point of saying, for example, that those who wrongly observe God's mitzvot for self-serving purposes, which is certainly an incorrect personal conviction, would have to be taken by the hand, so to speak, and taught how to serve God out of love, step by step (*Hilchot Teshuvah* 10:1). And we're *never* told to go back to an ideational "middle path," since ill convictions can only be cured by (eventually) adopting their diametric opposite (*Moreh Nevuchim* 3:46, see there for examples).

Lastly, the reference to "the health or illness of the body" here in conjunction with moral well-being hearkens somewhat to a statement Rambam made to the effect that, if we could only control our digestive systems (the way we can control our emotions), we'd be a lot healthier on a physical level as well (*Moreh Nevuchim* 1:72).

3. Much of this is restated in *Hilchot Dei'ot* (2:1), though with a couple of discrepancies.

Unlike here, Rambam points out there that *the extent* to which one would go to seek out odd or harmful foods depends on the seriousness of his or her physical illness, just as the extent to which one would go to avoid pursuing righteousness depends on the seriousness of his or her character illness.

Another discrepancy lies in the fact that Rambam cites a verse there that reads, "Woe to those who call evil good, and good evil; *who consider darkness as light, and light as darkness*; who consider bitter as sweet, and sweet as bitter!" (Isaiah 5:20), and another verse that characterizes such individuals as "those who abandon the paths of uprightness, to walk *in the ways of darkness*" (Proverbs 2:13).

Apparently his point is that the more ill one is, the more "in the dark," i.e., cut off from the truth, he or she is as well. For healthy behavior is as much a product of correct information and convictions (as we indicated) as is a healthy choice of food.

Notice, though, that Rambam uses a similar verse at the end of this chapter, "The ways of wrongdoers are like darkness" (Proverbs 4:19). One would think that he would have done better bolstering his point with a verse of this nature earlier on, the way he did in *Hilchot Dei'ot*.

4. In another sense, though, the word *perish* in this phrase is an analogous term here, meant to imply that such a person will surely remain imperfect the rest of his life and never achieve his potential (based on *Moreh Nevuchim* 3:13, where Rambam explains "good" to mean the fulfilling of one's purpose, and ibid. 3:10, where he explains how death implies "bad").

5. We find it curious that at the beginning of this chapter, Rambam defines individuals with ill *nefashot* as people who "are predisposed to doing bad, harmful, and disgraceful things," while he refers to them here and at the end

of section 2 as people who "continue pursuing pleasure." Apparently, then, there is also a connection between the pursuit of pleasure and the well-being of one's *nefesh*, but how far does it go? Am I only truly *nefesh*-healthy when I indulge in as little sensual satisfaction as I can?

Rambam brings up the connection between one's moral well-being and abstinence in *Hilchot Dei'ot*. He offers there that we are to pursue balance in our character (which we'll return to shortly) and says, for example, that we would do well to only express anger when it is justified, to limit our working hours, to never lapse into extremes of behavior, to be generous but not overly so, to be happy and not maudlin, and so on (themes that will repeat themselves later on in *Shemoneh Perakim*). Then he offers that we are also only to long for the sorts of material things that the body needs to exist and no more, suggesting that we are indeed to practice a degree of abstinence (*Hilchot Dei'ot* 1:4). He adds that doing without a lot of extraneous things makes a person happy (ibid. 2:7).

Nonetheless, we must factor in things Rambam says in chapter 4 below that touch on this latter point as well. He says in sections 6–8 there that certain especially pious individuals would go to an extreme once in a while and would be austere, but for a good reason, but some well-meaning but ill-advised people saw them acting that way and did so as well. Rambam condemns this and says there that "the Torah...wants us to live normally and to follow a balanced path: to eat and drink what is permissible in balanced measure; to cohabit in ways permitted in balanced measure; etc."

This being the case, we would suggest that the reason why Rambam presents us with both perspectives on *nefesh* well-being in this chapter is to slowly draw us into the fray of chapter 4, which struggles with the theme of just how pious and abstentious a person is to be — or how equibalanced — while yet living in the world.

Chapter 4: Treating Diseases of the Nefesh

1. Interestingly enough, Rambam defines good and bad very differently elsewhere. People, places, and things are said to be "good" when they're suited to their objectives (*Moreh Nevuchim* 3:13). As such, we would deem a doctor whose temperament, skills, and knowledge were on par with his patients' health objectives a "good" doctor, because he was well-suited for his medical objective.

Similarly, people, places, and things are said to be "bad" when they either lack something or they deprive us of things (ibid., 10). As such, we'd deem a doctor whose temperament, skills, and knowledge were *not* on par with his patients' needs a "bad" doctor, because he was lacking in one or more of those requirements, and he deprived us of health.

Yet, in light of the fact that Rambam also defined "health" as a state of equilibrium, and "illness" as a state of disequilibrium (ibid.), we'd thus determine that his overall point is that our deeds are both "good" and "healthy" when our dispositions are in a state of equilibrium as he describes it here in the text, and that this best suits our ultimate objective, which is perfection.

As an aside, Rambam defines *avor*, a cognate of the Hebrew term for "sin," *aveirah*, as denoting going too far, beyond the usual limits (ibid. 1:21), i.e., as going to an extreme.

2. See our first note to chapter 3 ("doing bad, harmful, or disgraceful things") for a discussion of inborn versus learned traits, as well as supplementary note 1 there.

3. Rambam addresses stinginess and extravagance elsewhere (which we'll touch upon in more detail in section 4 below). Rather than discussing them in relation to being stingy or extravagant toward others, as we might expect, he speaks of it in terms of self-abnegation versus self-indulgence. He warns us not to fast and deny ourselves food in order to avoid spending money (*Hilchot Dei'ot* 1:1); or to lust after riches on the one hand, or be lazy and avoid work, on the other (ibid. 2:7).

4. As Rambam put it, it wouldn't do to be riotous or merry, nor unhappy and mournful, either. It would be best to be quietly happy (*Hilchot Dei'ot* 1:4), since mirth and light-headedness lead to licentiousness (ibid. 2:7), while sadness leads to its opposite, since it discourages interaction with others (based on ibid. 2:7).

5. Rambam equates contentment with true wealth, in that the content person feels he has everything he needs and doesn't yearn for anything else (see 7:2 below). He also draws a distinction between the content and people who are never satisfied with what they have (*Hilchot Dei'ot* 1:1). At a certain point he focuses on contentment as a primary example of a character virtue (Commentary on *Pirkei Avot* 2:12).

6. The question of why it is so important to rectify one's disposition is discussed elsewhere. Rambam points out that bad traits like anger, hostility, envy, sarcasm, the pursuit of wealth or glory, the pursuit of food, and so on make a deep impression in one's being, and so are even more threatening to one's spiritual stature than bad deeds like promiscuity, robbery, or theft (*Hilchot Teshuvah* 7:3). That's probably because the latter are offshoots and consequences of the former. For as he implied above at the very beginning of this chapter, bad dispositions (like anger, hostility, envy, etc.) foster bad deeds (like promiscuity, robbery, or theft).

7. We'll now delve somewhat into Rambam's path of equibalance, known

popularly as "the golden mean" (a phrase that actually arose in the sixteenth century). As he defines it, following the path of equibalance means exhibiting a trait that lies halfway between the two possible extremes (*Hilchot Dei'ot* 1:4). In different contexts, he refers to it as "the way of the upright" (ibid., 4, 6) and "the way of the wise" (ibid., 4, 5), and he contrasts it with the ways of the pious (see *Hilchot Dei'ot* 1:5, Commentary on *Pirkei Avot* 5:6).

There's no doubt that Rambam's presentation of this concept was affected by Aristotle's own in the latter's *Nicomachean Ethics*. Nonetheless, Rambam often disagrees with Aristotle's stance in that work, and we'll find that he doesn't owe his ideas to Aristotle at bottom, for there are many traditional Jewish sources that offer the very same perspective as Aristotle's. As such, we contend that Rambam chose to use a "modern" medium to express a traditional idea, much the way contemporary rabbis might use, say, computer jargon to explain traditional sources. (While Aristotle was, of course, not contemporary with Rambam, his writings were very fresh on the minds of Rambam's contemporaries, and were considered "modern.")

Rambam himself cited verses that sum up the path of equibalance. For example, he offers the verse in Proverbs 4:26–27, "Make the path of your feet even, and let all your ways be firm. Do not turn to the right hand or to the left; [and thus] remove your foot from evil" (*Hilchot Dei'ot* 2:7), and the verse in Ecclesiastes 7:16–18, "Do not be excessively righteous, nor make yourself overwise; why should you destroy yourself? Do not be excessively evil nor foolish; why should you die before your time? It is good to take hold of this, but do not withdraw your hand from that, either. For one who fears God performs them all" (*Hilchot Dei'ot* 3:1).

There are two early nonscriptural sources that Rambam doesn't cite that make similar statements. The first is the Jerusalem Talmud, which states: "The ways of the Torah can be likened to two roads, one of which is fiery, and the other of which is snowy. Follow one and you'll be burned to death, and follow the other and you'll perish in the snow. What should you do? Walk between the two extremes" (Jerusalem Talmud, *Chagigah* 77a). The second is the *Tosefta* which states, "It is incumbent upon man to go between the extremes and incline neither to this side or that" (*Tosefta, Chagigah* 2). Similarly, the widely read and influential Rabbi Yehudah HaLevi, who lived one hundred years before Rambam, wrote, "The Torah has not charged us with [asceticism]. We are to take the moderate path instead — to provide each of our body's and *nefesh's* capacities its due portion equally, provided we do not do it to an excess" (*Kuzari* 2:50, 3:1–7. See *Kol Yehudah* there for illustrations; also see *Chovot HaLevavot* 3:3, 9:3; and *Rambam La'Am*, vol. 18, pp. 168–169 [note 9] for other illustrations).

But perhaps the greatest explications of the utterly Jewish and Torah-based root of this principle can be found in section 8 of this chapter, and in

Moreh Nevuchim 3:46, where Rambam illustrates the principle in the context of mitzvot and other impeccable Torah-based viewpoints.

8. Most medieval thinkers followed the theory of the so-called "four bodily humors." They believed that the human body was comprised of four rudimentary, potent elements called "humors" — blood, phlegm, and yellow and black bile. Illness was due to an irregularity in one or more of them. Rambam's use of the term *lethargy* at this point in the text alludes to that system, and not to the relatively innocuous lethargy we cite today as a character fault.

Along the same lines, see Rambam's remarks in 5:2 about melancholia having to do with black bile, as we point out in our note there, and his statement elsewhere that certain antisocial and unfavorable traits, for example an obsession with money or lewdness, meanness, and the need to remove oneself from society and live in a desert or a desolate place, are all rooted in diseased black bile (Commentary on *Pirkei Avot* 2:14).

Apparently his point is that there *are* certainly biological (or genetic) bases for behavior, which simply cannot be denied. Nonetheless, we have free choice and needn't blame everything we do — for bad or for good — upon our makeup.

What is perhaps most interesting about this statement in the text is the fact that certain people might be *ascetic*, hence more inclined toward piety, as a consequence of their physiology.

9. One might think that a person would be encouraged to be extravagant in his offering of charity when repenting of his ways, for example. But as Rambam says, "Among the things one can do for *teshuvah* is to...give charity *according to his means...*" (*Hilchot Teshuvah* 2:4). He also said that anyone who claimed to be a prophet would surely prove to be a false one if he commanded people to disperse all their money to the poor (*Iggeret Teiman*).

10. Rambam's statement here that balance is "what we should strive for and the direction in which our actions should head" seems definitive and universal, but it is actually not. There are certain balanced and moderate traits one *shouldn't* exhibit. It's not good enough to simply be humble; one should be meek (*Hilchot Dei'ot* 2:3), simply because humility is too close to arrogance, i.e., it's "halfway there already," so to speak, and a person might thus come to lapse into it (Commentary on *Pirkei Avot* 4:4). (Note as well, though, that Rambam described humility as a balanced trait in section 2 of this chapter, and presented meekness as an extreme, which would seem to advocate for humility. But in fact he wasn't suggesting one or the other there, only offering insight.)

And Rambam also deems anger as an extremely bad temperament which one should go to extremes to avoid by not even expressing it when it is justified (see *Hilchot Dei'ot* 1:4, 2:3).

11. The difficulty of the process of self-improvement is not to be denied. In fact, Rambam likens it to "wrestling" with oneself (Commentary on *Pirkei Avot* 2:6). He nonetheless points out that while change often takes years to actualize (see *Moreh Nevuchim* 3:51), it will eventually become easy for you to act as you'd choose (*Hilchot Dei'ot* 1:7).

12. Once again, we're born with certain predispositions, we easily adapt to others, there are others we determine it would do us well to adopt, and there are others yet that are supplied to us by our backgrounds and surroundings, as is Rambam's point here (see *Hilchot Dei'ot* 1:2, 6:1).

It's important to note, though, that both our dispositions *and our convictions* can be thus affected. Because it is simply our nature to be pulled one way or the other by external influences (*Hilchot Dei'ot* 6:1; see *Moreh Nevuchim* 2:23), aside from inner drives. As such, we're advised to circumvent problems before they arise by dissociating ourselves from sinful people and choosing to befriend the righteous and learned. In fact, if we find ourselves living somewhere where everyone around us is sinful, we're told to completely isolate ourselves (*Hilchot Dei'ot* 6:1). We'll discuss this latter admonition later on, when we reflect upon piety.

13. We're informed that the person going to the other extreme in order to rectify his personality would have to practice that other extreme "for a long time" (*Hilchot Dei'ot* 2:2). Similarly, we're told that our invalid (and extreme) convictions can be rectified along the same lines as well (*Moreh Nevuchim* 3:46; but see our supplemental note 2 to chapter 3).

14. The idea of implanting a virtuous trait by repeating it again and again is cited elsewhere in the context of offering charity. Rambam submits that it is far better to give many poor people relatively small donations than to give one poor person a single generous donation, since you would foster the trait of generosity sooner by practicing it often (Commentary on *Pirkei Avot* 3:18).

Rambam also offers an alternative method of improving one's character: taking vows upon oneself not to practice something inappropriate. For example, vowing not to eat meat for a year or two if one is a glutton (*Hilchot Nedarim* 13:23; see Commentary on *Pirkei Avot* 3:16). While that is also an example of going to one extreme in order to expunge another, it is also a more rigorous, perhaps more promising method for certain individuals, since people tend to take vows very seriously.

15. He goes on to say there that people are more likely to "go from asceticism to [mere] temperance than from indulgence to [mere] temperance." That is to say, people are more likely to allow themselves *more* than less, which is clear. His advice then is that we'd have to tell "an indulgent person to engage in asceticism longer than we'd tell an ascetic person to engage in indulgence."

This is so because if someone who was striving for piety were disposed toward indulgence, we'd tell him to be more ascetic (as one would expect). But if he were disposed toward asceticism — which one might think is a *good* trait for piety — we'd nonetheless tell him to be *somewhat* indulgent. That is to say, we'd advise him to practice the sorts of Torah-sanctioned "indulgences" Rambam cites in section 8, where he says, "The perfect Torah which perfects us...wants us to live normally and to follow a balanced path: to eat and drink what is permissible in balanced measure; to have intercourse in ways permitted in balanced measure; to develop the world in a just and honest way, rather than live in caves or on mountaintops; not to wear sackcloth or coarse wool; and to thus never strain, deplete, or afflict our bodies."

Along with that, however, goes the caveat that we "place a single goal before [our] eyes all the time" when we seek piety and "indulge" in the ways indicated — "to comprehend God Almighty as much as a human being can.... [To] know Him and direct all [our] actions, movements, and utterances to that end" (5:1 below; see note 21 below).

He then says that, "We would oblige a cowardly person to practice daring longer than we would oblige a daring person to practice cowardice," and that "we would train a meek person to exhibit boastfulness longer than we'd train a boastful person to exhibit meekness," but he doesn't explain why. Apparently it is because prophets, and hence pious individuals, had to be bold and forthright (see the first degree of prophecy in *Moreh Nevuchim* 2:45).

He sums it all up best, perhaps, by his statement that "One who goes *a little* beyond temperance is pious, but an utter ascetic is a sinner" (Commentary on *Pirkei Avot* 5:13).

16. There's some confusion as to Rambam's stance on humility versus meekness. In section 2 above, he describes humility as a balanced trait (and hence desirable), and meekness as an extreme. Thus we're told here in the text that the pious would "tend to be...somewhat more humble than meek."

Yet at a certain point in his writings, Rambam states that we're to strive for outright meekness (*Hilchot Dei'ot* 2:3); and that while the wise would be (merely) humble, the pious would be meek (ibid. 1:5). Then he says that we're commanded, in fact, to follow the middle path and be humble (ibid., 6).

So is someone on the path to piety to be humble or meek?

The answer seems to lie in the expression that Rambam uses to describe the actions of the pious. He says they would tend to be "*somewhat* more humble than meek," and thus tend toward the more balanced trait of humility, but only somewhat so. They did so "in order to safeguard themselves" — to guard themselves against lapsing into the extremes of piety we are warned about. (In point of fact, that would be a pious instance of "going beyond the letter of the law," since the normative halachah requires us to be meek, as we indicated above.)

At one point Rambam even quantifies the degree of humility versus meekness such individuals are to strive for. He says that, "If there were, for example, 64 degrees between arrogance and utter meekness, then you should go 63 degrees toward meekness, but no more" (Commentary on *Pirkei Avot* 4:4).

As such, we'd draw a bar graph thusly:

-32	-31	0	32
Meekness	Suggested level	Humility	Arrogance

17. Rambam is careful to underscore the fact that only *some* pious individuals would go to such extremes, and *only once in a while*, since his overall point is that we are not to go to extremes, other than to treat an illness of the *nefesh*. Nonetheless, he does spend some time at other junctures celebrating seclusion.

He cites four good reasons to seclude oneself: as in the instance cited in the text, in order to avoid unwholesome company (*Hilchot Dei'ot* 6:1); in order to think deeply and concentrate (*Moreh Nevuchim* 3:51); in order to draw closer to God (ibid.); and in order to foster courage (*Moreh Nevuchim* 3:32), i.e., confidence and self-sufficiency.

His point all in all is that sometimes extremes like seclusion and the like are indeed called for, to avoid sin. For example, he suggests "especial holiness" (i.e., extra caution and piety) in the face of sins like theft and illicit sexuality (*Hilchot Issurei Bi'ah* 22:19–20).

18. We'll now offer Rambam's overall explanation and apparent depiction of piety.

All in all, one's piety is determined by his intellectual pursuits, his personal qualities (see *Moreh Nevuchim* 3:18, Commentary on *Pirkei Avot* 2:10, 11), and his pursuit of truth (Commentary on *Pirkei Avot* 4:7).

Though he doesn't spell it out, it seems Rambam would depict someone who strives for piety as an individual indeed in pursuit of truth, who comes to long for a deep and intense relationship with God as a consequence of that pursuit. This person would then strive for both deeper-yet intellectual insight and moral rectitude. He'd apparently come to realize that, as Rambam presented it, a person can be neither morally nor intellectually lofty as long as his passions and "humors" are inflamed, nor could he have the sort of intense relationship with God that someone striving to be pious would like. Furthermore, he'd come to know that the more tempered his passions and humors, the purer he would be (*Moreh Nevuchim* 3:51).

As such, he'd likely go to one extreme or another by being more ascetic than most, as well as more daring, tender-hearted, and humble; and to perhaps even resort to fasting, denying himself sleep, food, intercourse, comfort, and human contact, as is depicted in our text — all in order to arrive at piety, and to safeguard himself from the people and things that would dissuade him from having the sort of relationship with God he seeks.

For as Rambam put it in *Hilchot Tumat Ochlin* (16:12), "The ancient pious ones...were referred to as 'abstainers'.... [For] the ways of piety [entailed] separating oneself from people, not coming in contact with them or eating and drinking with them. For abstention brings one to bodily purity [free of] wrongful deeds, and bodily purity brings one to holiness of *nefesh*...and *nefesh* holiness enables one to conform to the ways of the Divine Presence" — and to thus cleave unto Him to the degree aspirants would want to.

But again Rambam's point is that the sorts of extremes spoken of in the last paragraph do not depict Jewish piety, which is characterized by a reasonable, even-handed pious quest for closeness to God by means of the qualities He has implanted within us. For as he noted elsewhere, "Should you think that envy, lust, honor, and similar things are bad traits that remove a man from the world, and that one should thus remove himself from them and go to the opposite extreme and not eat meat, drink wine, marry, live in an attractive house, or dress in fine clothes, and dress in sackcloth and hard wool and the like instead, like gentile priests do — you would be wrong" (*Hilchot Dei'ot* 3:1).

In fact, Avraham ben HaRambam even used the term "the *Jewish* pious" (whom he referred to as "the disciples of the prophets") and contrasted them with those who express "piety" by remaining celibate, fasting often, or wearing coarse wool (*HaMaspik L'Ovdei Hashem*).

19. Rambam subsequently offers a regime for maintaining health. He focuses there upon avoiding the sorts of things that harm the body, like lack of exercise, eating to excess or eating harmful things, and the like (see *Hilchot Dei'ot* 4:1).

Interestingly enough, besides counseling us to "eat and drink what's permissible in balanced measure," Rambam also advised us not to go to *intellectual* extremes, and likened doing so to eating too much honey (i.e., "too much of a good thing") and vomiting as a consequence (*Moreh Nevuchim* 1:32; see ibid. 1:31 as well).

20. Rambam decried the sorts of beyond-the-pale, burdensome restrictions of the ancient pagans at various points (*Moreh Nevuchim* 2:39; 3:29, 47). At the same time, though, he was sure to point out that the mitzvot certainly aren't meant to lead to gluttony or lewdness (ibid. 2:39).

He also underscored the fact that despite the fair-mindedness and balance of the mitzvah system, there are always certain more carnal, excitable people who object to any and all restrictions, and have a hard time adhering to them (ibid. 2:39).

21. The discussion here of appropriate and inappropriate piety, as well as doing things for God's sake rather than for one's own, forms a bridge between this chapter and the next one.

As we indicated in note 18 above, Rambam objected to subjecting oneself to extremes of self-denial at a certain point in *Hilchot Dei'ot* (3:1), which is the work that most parallels *Shemoneh Perakim* when it comes to character improvement. What is most interesting for our discussion here is the content of the entry immediately following the one we cited in note 18, *Hilchot Dei'ot* 3:2–3. It addresses the issue raised in the next chapter of *Shemoneh Perakim* — doing everything for God's sake.

As Rambam puts it at the beginning of chapter 5, "It is important to... place a single goal before your eyes all the time, which is to comprehend God Almighty as much as a human being can. Which is to say, that you know Him and direct all your actions, movements, and utterances to that end, so that nothing you do is arbitrary or tends to thwart that goal. So, for example, when you eat, drink, sleep, have intercourse, awake, move about, or rest, let your only aim be your health. But let your goal in being healthy be to remain robust and well enough to acquire the knowledge and the personal and intellectual virtues you would need to reach that goal."

This closely parallels his terminology in *Hilchot Dei'ot* 3:2–3, where he writes that a person should "adjust [his] heart and actions to comprehend[ing] God. One's resting, rising, speaking, and indeed every other action, should be toward this end.... When one eats and drinks, he shouldn't do so for its sake alone...but should eat and drink for the sake of his bodily health... [in order for] his body to be perfect and strong enough for him to be pious and to comprehend God."

The point seems to be, then, that while one should be balanced in his ways and make use of worldly things as God would have him, he should nonetheless use those things for truly pious rather than just pedestrian and self-serving reasons.

22. We're also taught that the reason we're thus restricted is to discourage the idea that our whole purpose in life is to eat, drink, and have intercourse (*Moreh Nevuchim* 3:35). All in all, then, we're apparently being asked to wean ourselves from our natural, worldly tendencies to indulge ourselves and concentrate on rank physicality, toward a higher, God-based perspective on human potential and personal motivation.

23. We're also taught that the reason we're thus enjoined to be so charitable is because "one who is rich today may be poor another day...[just as] one who is poor today may be rich another day" (*Moreh Nevuchim* 3:35). In contradistinction to the previous note, in this instance, we're being asked to be more worldly in certain instances, if you will, and to thus keep the exigencies of life in mind, *as well as* to foster the sort of higher, God-based perspective we cited above.

24. Rambam offers a number of cogent explanations of what God hopes for us to derive from fulfilling His mitzvot. The apparent temerity of suggesting that anyone could explain God's thoughts and intentions has vexed many ever since, despite the logic and reasonableness of Rambam's assumptions.

Be that as it may, his explanations can be found in his *Moreh Nevuchim*, in chapters 35–49 of the third section.

25. See notes 6 and 10 above about the perils of anger.

26. After all, as Avraham ben HaRambam points out, we're not to be so sensitive that we couldn't endure the thought of animals being slaughtered for the sake of food or the wicked being justifiably punished (*HaMaspik L'Ovdei Hashem*).

27. Rambam indicates that we have flaws and we sin for two reasons: either because we simply don't know the right thing to do, or because we're driven by our passions (*Moreh Nevuchim* 3:36), which is to say, because we're either intellectually or personally imperfect. The solution lies, then, in the conscious pursuit of wisdom and righteousness (see *Hilchot Teshuvah* 6:5).

28. The question of how Moses could express anger of all things, which is such a negative trait, is quite a legitimate and perplexing one. After all, as Rambam himself pointed out, a sage should neither yell nor raise his voice, but should always prefer peace, and should only contend with someone with a cool head (*Hilchot Dei'ot* 5:7), and that acting otherwise is indeed a profanation of God's Name — *though it is not a sin per se* (see below) on his part (*Hilchot Yesodei HaTorah* 5:11).

The only plausible answer seems to be that Moses intended to instruct and reprimand his people for their shortcomings, so he *expressed anger outwardly* in order to indicate how serious he was about the matter, but didn't actually *experience* it in his heart, which is perfectly appropriate for a leader and teacher (see *Hilchot Dei'ot* 2–3).

In fact, this is corroborated by the words of the people, as Rambam expresses it at the end of the next paragraph in the text. For they acknowledged that Moses "certainly hasn't any personal flaws," and explained his actions to mean that he was "only expressing anger at [them]" rather than actually being angry.

And since the sort of profanation of God's name that Moses was guilty of wasn't in fact a sin, as we indicated above, the word *sin* in the text ("But what was his sin?" and "What sin did he commit, anyway?") is simply an analogous term.

29. A very telling, overarching statement about improving one's personality is the following one, from Rambam's *Hilchot Teshuvah* (7:3):

"Do not think that one would only have to repent for concrete sins, like promiscuity, robbery, or theft. For just as a person has to repent for such sins, he also has to divest himself of all his bad traits and repent for anger, hostility, envy, sarcasm, the pursuit of wealth or glory, the pursuit of food, etc.... For those sorts of sins are even more serious than the concrete ones. Because when a person is steeped in them, it is very difficult for him to lay them aside."

Chapter 5: Using All of One's Personal Capacities to One End

1. We turn now to the grand and recondite notion of comprehending God. Rambam makes a particularly comprehensive statement about the subject at several points, indicating the following.

At bottom, we have one, single, solitary purpose in life, which is to comprehend abstract notions so as to know the truth for what it is. (Everything else we do merely serves to keep us alive and comfortable, and is not essential to our beings.) The *greatest* abstract notion we can comprehend is that of God's being, along with everything associated with that (Introduction to Commentary of the Mishnah; see *Moreh Nevuchim* 3:8).

We'll discuss the idea of God's being and makeup shortly. But allow us now to delve somewhat into some more specific reasons of why we're to comprehend God, and the benefits of doing that.

A more "practical" reason to comprehend God is based on the fact that one cannot really be said to *believe* in Him unless he comprehends Him (see *Moreh Nevuchim* 1:50). Other reasons and incentives are based on the fact that one could never achieve one's potential without comprehending Him (*Moreh Nevuchim* 1:54); furthermore, the more one comprehends Him, the closer he is to Him (ibid., 18), and the more he pleases Him (ibid., 54).

Rambam points out that not only is the knowledge of God to permeate our lives — it will in fact influence our ultimate destinies, as well. Each one of us will be engrossed in the pursuit of it in the Messianic Era (*Iggeret Teiman* 4), and everyone's standing in the World to Come will in fact be rooted in his knowledge of God (see Commentary to *Perek Cheilek*).

At a certain juncture, Rambam equates knowing God with loving Him, and he seems to equate the sort of love he's referring to with being absorbed in the thought of Him (*Moreh Nevuchim* 3:51, 52; *Hilchot Tefillah* 10:6), much as one might be absorbed in the thought of a person he loves (see ibid. 10:3). But we'll touch upon the love of God and its relationship to knowing Him in supplementary note 11 below.

Now, what are we in fact to comprehend about God? This work isn't the place to offer anything other than a rudimentary explanation of Rambam's ideas on the subject. Thus, the following is a representative sampling of his thoughts (based primarily on *Hilchot Yesodei HaTorah* 1:1–7).

In short, we're to understand that God existed before everything else and created it all; that His existence is a prerequisite for the existence of everything else; that He would continue to exist even if nothing else did, for He is utterly self-reliant and unique; that He is eternal; that He is one in a unique sense (see *Moreh Nevuchim* 1:57 as well); and that He is utterly incorporeal (see *Moreh Nevuchim* 1:28 as well), and thus undergoes none of the things corporeal beings undergo. We're also to understand that He provides everything for His creations, and that He influences Creation moment to moment (*Moreh Nevuchim* 3:54).

Needless to say, there's a plethora of ramifications to each and every one of those statements which deeply affect reality as we know it. The individual in pursuit of piety would be expected to consider as many of those ramifications as he is able, as well.

Rambam lays especial importance on being able to *negate false qualities in God*. He says at a certain point, in fact, that the more (human, corporeal, material) qualities you can negate in Him, the better your understanding of Him (*Moreh Nevuchim* 1:59; see ibid. 1:56–60 for the full discussion of negative attributes).

2. Rambam makes the point that while there is a lot we can understand about God in His relationship to the world, we will nonetheless never be able to grasp Him Himself (ibid. 1:58–59).

3. Much of what follows in this chapter about using mundane drives and capacities in the service of God corresponds with what Rambam said in *Hilchot Dei'ot* 3:2. There he suggests that we earn a living in order to afford the things we need, rather than to amass wealth (or to define ourselves as anything other than as individuals in pursuit of piety, we might add). We're to eat and drink for health's sake, despite the taste or texture of healthy things, rather than to satisfy our palate. And we're to have relations only to maintain our health or to have children, rather than to merely satisfy our desires (see *Moreh Nevuchim* 3:8 as well).

4. The following is the gist of Rambam's *Hilchot Teshuvah* 9:1. It presents us with a uniquely metaphysical reason to abjure from physical satisfaction and the pursuit of wealth.

Since it is known that the reward for observing mitzvot and the goodness we merit by following God's path for us, as enunciated in the Torah, is life in the World to Come, and that the punishment to be meted out to the wrongful who abandon the ways of righteousness, as enunciated in the Torah, is spiritual banishment, why, then, are we told throughout the Torah that if we obey, we'll enjoy such and such, and if we don't, that such and such will happen to us, all of which are in this world (like satiety or famine, war or peace, self-rule or subjugation, in-dwelling or exile, success or failure, and all other such matters enunciated in the covenant)?

In fact, all of those things are true, and will continue to be so: When we observe the mitzvot of the Torah, we enjoy all the goodness of this world, and when we transgress, we suffer all the bad things cited. Yet, all that goodness isn't the ultimate reward for observing the mitzvot, nor are all those punishments the ultimate ones for transgressing the mitzvot.

The answer is that God gave us the Torah, which is a tree of life. Whoever follows what is written in it and comes to understand it clearly and correctly will thus merit a life in the World to Come that corresponds to his deeds and wisdom.

We're also promised by the Torah that if we observe it happily and with soul-satisfaction, and delve into its wisdom at all times, then all the things that would prevent us from observing it (like illness, war, famine, and so on) will be eliminated; and that God will grant us all the good things that would make us stronger yet in our observance (like satiety, peace, prosperity, and so on), in order for us not to have to spend our days placating our bodily needs, but be free instead to delve into the wisdom as well as do the mitzvot that will earn us a place in the World to Come.

But the Torah is also letting us know that if we willfully abandon it and busy ourselves instead with the passing fancies of the day, the True Judge will revoke all the goodness of this world which enabled us to scoff, and will bring bad upon us, so as to prevent us from possessing the World to Come, and to enable us to be lost in our wickedness.

So the import of all of the blessings and curses enunciated there is accordingly that if you serve God happily and keep to His ways, He will bring upon you all those blessings, and keep the curses away, in order for you to be free to pursue the wisdom of the Torah, to engage in its study, and to consequently merit life in the World to Come, to enjoy the good of the world that is all good, as well as length of days in a world that is endless. You will, as a consequence, merit two worlds: a good life in this world, which will then bring you to life in the World to Come.

But if you do not acquire wisdom or engage in good deeds here, how will you ever merit it? If you abandon God and instead wallow in food, drink, promiscuity and the like, He will bring all those curses upon you, and withhold all the blessings. And your life will be so consumed with terror and fright that you will have neither the presence of mind nor the well-being to do the mitzvot. As such, you'll lose life in the World to Come, and will have thus lost two worlds. For when a person is preoccupied in this world with illness, war, or famine, he neither engages in wisdom nor performs mitzvot by means of which he merits life in the World to Come.

5. Rambam expands upon the idea of encumbrances to personal betterment in various places. In *Moreh Nevuchim*, for example, he points out that too many family concerns and the pursuit of extraneous things tend to befuddle one's mind (*Moreh Nevuchim* 1:35); that basic dishonesty, anger, sensuality, and the need for control encourage one to reject the sort of discipline required to grow in one's spirit (ibid. 2:39); and that the continued pursuit of pleasure leads to burdensome ill health, worry, and sadness (ibid. 3:33). In *Hilchot Dei'ot* he also offers a diet, exercise, and hygiene regimen (see *Hilchot Dei'ot* 4:1–21).

Rambam also provided us with general guidelines for how to serve God in the course of our more secular, everyday routines. He pointed out that we should engage in intercourse in order to produce wise and noble children, for example; and should sleep in order to be rested and healthy enough to serve God well (*Hilchot Dei'ot* 3:3). Other common daily practices which might seem to be encumbrances to one's spiritual goals also can be carried out with such intentions.

6. See our supplementary notes 8 and 9 to Rambam's introduction, where we first addressed his use of secular, often foreign knowledge. At a couple of points, in fact, Rambam asserts that one could never truly understand God or His ways in the world without first studying certain sciences, mathematics, and logic (see *Moreh Nevuchim*, Introduction, 1:5, 55; 2:23).

7. Rambam breaks all speech down into five sorts: 1) mitzvah-related speech, including Torah study and teaching; 2) forbidden speech, including false testimony, lying, and tale-bearing; 3) "unbecoming" speech, or speech that hasn't any inherent worth or merit but isn't forbidden either, such as small-talk, speaking about daily events, telling stories, relating biographies, and either debasing lofty people or praising flawed ones even on a very subtle level; 4) "preferable" speech (which Rambam refers to at this point in the text), including praising intellectual and personal virtues, quoting maxims or poems that encourage such traits and discourage the others, praising Sages and relating their commendable deeds in order to encourage others in them; and denigrating wrongdoers and their flaws in order to discourage others in them, and 5) "acceptable" speech, including discussion of business matters, or conversations about food, drink, and clothing, which should be kept to a minimum but needn't be avoided. We'd do best to concentrate upon mitzvah-related and "preferable" speech, though (Commentary on *Pirkei Avot* 1:16). But silence is especially virtuous, since it allows for quiet, awed realizations of God's presence (*Moreh Nevuchim* 3:53; see *Hilchot Dei'ot* 2:4–5).

8. At another point, Rambam indicates that it's the person who uses his *mind* to perfect himself and to delve into Godly study, and to incline toward God alone, rather than anything else, who uses his mind to learn about the world in order to understand how God works through it is on par with the prophets (*Moreh Nevuchim* 3:51); while he indicates here in our text that it's someone who uses all his personal capacities with God as his sole impetus, who pursues character virtues, and who only does things that accomplish his goal of comprehending God who's on par with the prophets.

His point must be, then, that in order to be on par with the prophets a person would have to focus his intellectual pursuits upon intellectual growth with the end of drawing close to God. Similarly, he should focus his moral and personal pursuits upon personal growth with that same end in mind.

9. Indeed, everyone is to strive for lofty traits, not just the pious. For as Rambam said, we're each commanded to "walk in God's ways," which includes being righteous, upright, and holy (*Hilchot Dei'ot* 1:6).

10. As we indicated in supplementary note 1 above, knowing God and loving Him are complementary of each other. For, as Rambam put it, the quality of one's love of God corresponds to the quality of his comprehension of Him (*Moreh Nevuchim* 3:51)

At one point, Rambam advocates being utterly absorbed in the love of God, being "as lovesick as he would be if he could not stop thinking of a woman he was in love with," being utterly fixated on Him alone (*Hilchot Teshuvah* 10:3). Yet at another point, he advocates a less rapturous, more intellectual love of God. He speaks there of coming to love Him by contemplating His great works in the world and extrapolating the divine wisdom behind all that (*Hilchot Yesodei HaTorah* 2:2, 4:12). But rather than contradicting the first prescription, this latter one seems to be a preparation for the former. For Rambam says at the second point that contemplating God's wonders and realizing His wisdom *will then lead to* an "immense passion to know the Great Name."

(We contend that "knowing the Great Name," being "as lovesick as [one] would be if he could not stop thinking of a woman he was in love with" in one's love of God, and being utterly absorbed in the love of God, all correspond to the idea of *deveikut* — attachment to the Divine — which we discussed in supplementary note 18 to Chapter 1.)

As to the idea of fearing God as a means of growing closer to Him, Rambam writes that "while we're to serve [God]...out of love...we're nonetheless not excused from fearing Him" (Commentary on *Pirkei Avot* 1:3). He also writes that the fear of God fosters wisdom and is even more precious than it (ibid. 4:4). We come to fear Him by fulfilling His mitzvot (*Moreh Nevuchim* 3:52), which is to say, by subjugating ourselves to His Will.

11. Interestingly, some people point to Rambam's delving into the books of idol worshipers (which he often did, as he indicated in *Moreh Nevuchim* as an instance of "sinning for the sake of Heaven," since he himself determined in *Hilchot Avodah Zarah* 2:2 that it is forbidden to do just that. But in fact, this is

wrong. See Rambam's commentary to *Sanhedrin* 4:10, where he indicates that it's perfectly permissible to study and know about things that are nonetheless forbidden to act upon.

A better example of sinning for the sake of Heaven would be the one Rambam himself offered in his Commentary to *Pirkei Avot* 5:18. He makes the point there that, despite the fact that audacity is discouraged in general, we're nonetheless obliged to reproach heretics audaciously; and that we'd do well to make good use of character faults when required for the sake of Heaven. For while a trait may be considered sinful in one instance, it would be considered perfectly appropriate and laudable in another.

Chapter 6: *The Difference between the Eminent Person and One Who Controls His Desires*

1. Rambam is referring here to overcoming the *yetzer hara*, the evil inclination, which we addressed in supplemental note 10 to chapter 1, defining it as "humankind's baser instinct, its pull away from the Divine, its inherent ability to morally and spiritually delude itself." We also discussed some of Rambam's insights into that phenomenon. Ultimately, though, Rambam sees the *yetzer hara* as a manifestation of our imagination, rather than of reason (*Moreh Nevuchim* 2:6, 12), that has us stray from truth (ibid. 3:22).

2. The comment offered in the text here calls for some explanation.

Aristotle's *Nicomachean Ethics* (book 7, ch. 1) is the agreed-upon source of Rambam's citations here from "the philosophers." We base our understandings of the difference between "eminence" and piety upon what is written there.

Aristotle depicted an "eminent" person there as "superhuman, heroic, and [in possession of] divine virtue"; someone "not the child of a mortal man, but one of God's seed"; and a person whose virtues are even "higher than virtue" (W. D. Ross's translation).

We contend that Rambam chose to contrast that with the Jewish notion of true Jewish piety, and to debunk the whole idea of godly, perfect, "heroic" figures.

We find further proof for that distinction in Rambam's characterization of prophets and prophecy — the ultimate reach of piety (see introduction, section 2). For he said at a certain point that, while the philosophers maintained that prophets were inherently and "perfectly pious," in point of fact, prophets had to have prepared themselves to be pious (*Moreh Nevuchim* 2:32), and they did that by controlling their desires (see *Hilchot Yesodei HaTorah* 7:1).

Some may point out Rambam's comments to *Pirkei Avot* 5:13, where he seems to equate the Aristotelian view of the "godly" man with the Torah's concept of a "messenger (or angel) of God," where he cited the subject of the verse, "and the messenger of God went up from Gilgal" (Judges 2:1) as an example of someone with a perfect character.

But Rambam cites the Sages' revelation (in *Vayikra Rabbah* 1) that that person was Phinehas the son of Elazar the Kohen (*Moreh Nevuchim* 2:42). He declared that Phinehas was a zealot, a trait Rambam declares as extreme in 7:2 below. Apparently the difference lies in the fact that Phinehas' zealotry is to be admired, though, because of the circumstances in which it was expressed (see Numbers 25:6–8), since he was following a Divine charge (*Hilchot Issurei Bi'ah* 12:4). Hence, his "sin" of zealotry would have been the type perceived as being "for the sake of Heaven" (see 5:6 above), but is nonetheless a sin. Phinehas wasn't perfect, so much as perfectly appropriate for the task at hand.

3. The statement here that "while someone who controls his desires is on par with an eminent person in many ways, but his level is decidedly lower than his because he still longs to do bad," reminds us of a statement of Rambam's about *teshuvah* (usually translated "repentance," but more accurately characterized as the process of returning to God after having forsaken Him [see *Hilchot Teshuvah* 7:6–7]).

He says that "one who has done *teshuvah* should not consider himself beneath a righteous person as a result of his past transgressions and sins.... He is just as beloved and as desired by God as if he had never sinned. Not only is that so, but he also enjoys a great merit. For he has tasted sin, forsaken it, and conquered his evil inclination.... Such a person's worth is even greater than [that of] those who never transgressed" (ibid., 4).

We can reasonably assume, then, that the person who controls his desires in our text is a *ba'al teshuvah* (a "penitent"; i.e., someone who had sinned and then returned to God), and that his piety is an end-product of his *teshuvah*.

(One shouldn't be concerned with the fact that Rambam seems to acknowledge the existence of "eminence" in his reference above to "those who had never transgressed." It is clear that Rambam is referring to people who, in theory, never had the opportunity to sin, for one reason or another. For he doesn't indicate that such a person couldn't sin [as would be said of an "eminent" person] — just that he hadn't.)

The *ba'al teshuvah*, in this context, would not be someone who led a life of sin and utter abandon his whole life long and then came to regret his low ways and to rectify himself. He is more likely to have in fact striven to do what is right and noble all along, and to have, nonetheless, momentarily come to be confounded by the body and its urgings (see *Moreh Nevuchim* 3:8).

As to the phenomenon of *teshuvah* itself as Rambam expounds it, it is ultimately rooted in the fact that everyone has his faults (*Hilchot Teshuvah* 3:1; also see 4:4 above, and 8:1 below), and in our being free to make moral decisions despite predispositions and flaws. For if everything were predetermined, there would be no process of *teshuvah*, since our actions would have always been out of our hands (see *Hilchot Teshuvah* 5:1–4; also see 8:3–10 below).

Teshuvah essentially entails acknowledging that one has sinned, no longer engaging in that sin, regretting it, and taking it upon himself never to commit it again (*Hilchot Teshuvah* 2:2–3), though there are many more things one can do to deepen his *teshuvah* and to further affix it to his heart (see *Hilchot Teshuvah* 2:1, 4–5). And while nothing utterly precludes *teshuvah* (*Hilchot Teshuvah* 4:6; see ibid. 1:4; but see ibid. 6:3 and 8:8 below), a number of things hinder it (*Hilchot Teshuvah* 1:1–4).

4. As we explained in the translator's introduction, we've depended on Rabbi Yosef Kapach's Hebrew translation of Rambam's original Arabic text. We digress from that in one significant way in this chapter. For rather than refer to the person the philosophers saw as higher than the one who controls his desires as "pious," as Rabbi Kapach did, we chose to use the term "eminent." We contend that the use of the term "pious" in this instance would be a misreading of the chapter, based on Aristotle's terminology, as we indicate in supplementary note 2 above.

We weren't alone in our rejection of the term "pious," in fact. Ibn Tibbon translated the term as "the eminent, pious person" (indicating that he was struggling for a term that somehow captured both high ethics and piety, and that alluded to a different sort of person, in light of the Greek term); Dr. Joseph I. Gorfinkle translated it as "the saintly (or highly ethical) man" in *The Eight Chapters of Maimonides on Ethics* (obviously struggling for the same reasons as Ibn Tibbon); and Rabbi Yitzchak Shilot utterly rejected "pious" in his translation in *Hakdamot HaRambam LaMishnah*.

But we return to Kapach's translation at this point in the text, and use "lofty" rather than Shilot's "better," and Ibn Tibbon's and Gorfinkle's "more praiseworthy," in order to underscore the point we soon make about the significance of "loftiness."

5. As Rambam indicated elsewhere, the Sages certainly didn't believe that there were mitzvot that served no purpose. For that would imply that God's actions could be meaningless, which is patently absurd. Instead they maintained that the apparently "meaningless" (or "non–reason-based") mitzvot do indeed have meanings which nonetheless "[are not] known to us, either due to our lack of knowledge, or to our intellectual insufficiencies" (*Moreh Nevuchim* 3:26).

Chapter 7: On the Partitions and Their Meaning

1. We'll take this opportunity to provide Rambam's insights into prophecy in general here, while we'll delve into what distinguishes Moses' prophecy from the others' in another note.

As we indicated in our first note in the text at this point ("prophets"), belief in the phenomenon of prophecy is fundamental to the Jewish faith (Commentary on *Perek Cheilek*). It's so fundamental that one who doesn't believe in it hasn't a place in the World to Come (ibid.; *Hilchot Teshuvah* 3:8). In fact, Rambam makes the point that one must believe in prophecy before he can even be said to believe in the veracity of the Torah, since the latter depends on the former (*Moreh Nevuchim* 3:45).

An essential element of the belief in prophecy was the idea that what a prophet did primarily was to ascend toward and adhere unto God in a particular fashion and to commune with Him (Commentary on *Perek Cheilek*), in order to descend and instruct the Jewish nation (see *Moreh Nevuchim* 1:15). He could also have done so for his own sake, so as to deepen his own insight; or for the sake of gentile nations as well, in order to impart wisdom to them, instruct them, or prevent them from doing wrong (*Hilchot Yesodei HaTorah* 7:7), but those were not their primary objectives. The prophets also served as a vital link in the transmission of the oral tradition as it was passed down from Moses (Introduction *to Mishneh Torah*).

Rambam tells us other things about prophecy as well. He cites the fact that the ancients also believed in prophecy, but their belief was different in its makeup than ours. Some ancients contended that a prophet was a good (though not necessarily pious) person God simply selected to prophesy, regardless of his intellect. The Greek philosophers believed that prophecy was only bestowed upon a person of moral and intellectual stature with a well-developed imagination (or, *dimyon* — see supplementary note 10 to chapter 1), but they also believed that once the person striving for prophecy completed the requirements, he was sure to achieve it. Jewish tradition, on the other hand, agrees with the need for moral and intellectual stature on the part of an aspiring prophet, but it informs us that fulfilling the requirements nonetheless doesn't guarantee actual prophecy (*Moreh Nevuchim* 2:32; *Hilchot Yesodei HaTorah* 7:5).

As to the prophets' makeup, they were exceedingly wise and learned, even-tempered (see section 2 below), healthy, above mundane concerns, of full faith, abstinent (see Introduction to Commentary on the Mishnah), and always in control of their desires (*Hilchot Yesodei HaTorah* 7:1); they had to have been born with healthy minds as well as imaginations and to have dwelt upon the mysteries of the universe with the knowledge of God in mind; and they suppressed all thoughts of power, influence, honor, or esteem (*Moreh Nevuchim* 2:36).

There were degrees of prophecy (as our text indicates) — twelve in all, though the first two were stepping-stones to prophecy, rather than actual prophecy.

Those first and lowest two are referred to as "divine inspiration" and "the spirit of holiness," respectively. The first is characterized by being moved to participate in great, principled, and important deeds, but not to prophesy verbally. The second is marked by the sense that one has been overtaken by "something" that moved him to wisdom, moral insight, or civil action.

The other degrees are distinguished as follows: the third by seeing a prophetic vision in a dream; the fourth by hearing things in a prophetic dream without seeing their speaker; the fifth by being addressed by a human being in a dream; the sixth by being addressed by an angel in a dream; the seventh by being addressed by God's voice; the eighth by having symbolic visions while awake; the ninth by hearing voices in a visionary state while awake; the tenth by being addressed by a human form in a prophetic vision while awake; and the eleventh by being addressed by an angel in a prophetic vision while awake (*Moreh Nevuchim* 2:45). The twelfth degree is unique to Moses, as we'll soon discover.

The actual experience of prophecy (as well as the sorts of recondite skills a prophet would need, spoken of in our note to the text) entailed the following:

The prophet would first sit in solitude, be happy and of a good heart, and concentrate his thoughts (*Hilchot Yesodei HaTorah* 7:4). Then he'd place himself in a frame of mind perhaps best termed as a "reason mode" or "active reason" (see supplementary note 18 to chapter 1), and conjoin it with God's "Active Reason" (Commentary on *Perek Cheilek*). An "emanation" (see next paragraph) would come upon the prophet's reason, then pass through his imagination (see supplementary note 3 to chapter 2), which could only integrate all this when the prophet's senses would be stilled and shut down (*Moreh Nevuchim* 2:36). A vision would then result, which would have the prophet shake and grow weak, and which would temporarily befuddle his mind (*Hilchot Yesodei HaTorah* 7:2). But as we indicated above, a prophet could also receive a vision in a dream state.

Interestingly enough, this "emanation" from God (from *shefa*, a "flow" or "bestowance"; an instance of "abundance" or "profusion") isn't unique to the prophetic process. It's the same Divine mechanism that was used to bring about the creation of the world and acts to maintain it (*Moreh Nevuchim* 1:69). It is also what enables us to think. Nonetheless, when this emanation from God intensively affects an individual's logical mind alone, he can at best hope to be a scholar or philosopher; he can hope to be a leader, psychic, or a wonder-worker if it intensively affects his imagination alone; while he can hope to be a prophet if it intensively affects both (*Moreh Nevuchim* 2:37).

2. Rambam discusses wisdom, strength, and wealth in tandem in another context, but in a wholly different way.

Referring to wealth and strength as we usually understand them, he says that rather than strive for them, we should strive for true wisdom, since wealth and strength aren't only less-than-lofty achievements, they're also quite removed from one's true inner being. For wisdom indeed touches upon one's inner being, imbuing one with true human perfection, and "it remains with him alone, grants him immortality, and is what truly characterizes him as a human" (*Moreh Nevuchim* 3:54).

Then, citing traditional sources, he defines wisdom as either personal loftiness — as a function of technical skill and knowhow (the way we speak of mechanical "genius") — or as as cunning and a sort of Machiavellian shrewdness. Yet he defines "true" wisdom as the knowledge of God and of His Providence, and he adds that the truly wise would use their knowledge to substantiate the truisms that the tradition transmits but doesn't explain.

By virtue of the fact that the truisms transmitted by the tradition are done so by means of prophecy alone, a point to be made is that while prophecy is indeed vital to the transmission of the Torah which instructs us in the things we'd need to know in order to achieve human perfection, nonetheless, since there have only been a few prophets of that caliber (and none in our day and age), it behooves us to pursue true wisdom in our own lives in order to become truly human.

3. Interestingly enough, Rambam declares elsewhere that Kings Solomon and David weren't on par with Isaiah, Jeremiah, and other prophets of their caliber. They only experienced "a spirit of holiness," the second-lowest degree of prophecy, as indicated above (*Moreh Nevuchim* 2:45).

We might take that to mean, then, that only lesser prophets had character faults, while others didn't. But as Rambam will illustrate shortly, even great and clearly fully inspired prophets like Elijah, Samuel, and Jacob were predisposed toward character faults as well. Hence, the point remains that prophets weren't utterly flawless.

4. It is explained that Jacob couldn't prophesy at the time because his "imagination was preoccupied" (*Moreh Nevuchim* 2:36). As we discovered in supplementary note 10 to chapter 1, the "imagination" not only plays a major role in prophecy, its Hebrew term (*dimyon*) can also be translated in various ways. As such, we'd be justified in saying that Jacob's "unconscious mind" was so utterly preoccupied with thoughts of Joseph at the time that he couldn't possibly concentrate well enough to allow for prophecy.

We'll take this opportunity to discuss the idea that prophets were flawed, which many might be disturbed by — especially when they're the likes of Solomon, David, Elijah, Elisha, and our forefather Jacob!

After all, didn't Rambam himself say above that "other than prophecy, there is no greater rank than piety" (introduction), clearly implying that prophets were more than pious? Didn't he consider prophecy to be the epitome of human perfection (supplementary note 6 to introduction), and didn't he offer that prophecy was the ultimate reach of piety (supplementary note 2 to chapter 6)? Didn't he point out that prophets had to have controlled their desires (ibid.), to have been "exceedingly wise and learned, even-tempered, healthy, above mundane concerns, of full faith, abstinent...to have dwelt upon the mysteries of the universe with the knowledge of God in mind; and [to] suppress all thoughts of power, influence, honor, or esteem" (supplementary note 1 to chapter 7)? So how could they be flawed?

His point is that, indeed, prophets did conquer their untoward impulses, and they were truly lofty, learned, and high-minded — but they weren't flawless. But unlike us, a prophet (even more so than the person being spoken of there) dedicated the whole of his being and "used all his personal capacities with God as his sole impetus," he "never [did] or [said] anything, great or small, that either would not foster a character virtue itself or encourage one"; and he "concentrate[d] upon and [thought] about every move [he made], and every action [he took]" to determine if it would draw him closer to God (5:6).

So, what made the prophets so inestimably great was the fact that they focused their entire beings on the sublime goal of drawing close to God Almighty, despite their mortal flaws.

The final point to be made is that considering the overabundance of faults most of us have (which no honest soul could deny), an otherwise lofty and flawless prophet exhibiting only two or three faults is truly a human anomaly.

(Also see the comments of Maharsha to *Horayot* 11b, where he discusses the fact that someone deemed "perfect" and utterly righteous [see Rashi's comments there] was nonetheless guilty of having sinned, underscoring Rambam's point that even the utterly righteous are not flawless.)

5. Rambam contends that our physicality impedes our ability to comprehend *anything* abstract — not just God (*Moreh Nevuchim* 3:9–10). We cannot quite understand how anything could be utterly removed from space and time, senses, emotions, and the like, as a consequence of that physicality.

6. Rambam described Moses as the most perfect of people. He credited him with having actually comprehended the truth (Commentary on *Pirkei Avot* 4:2); with having been the father of wisdom, prophecy, and Torah (ibid. 4:4); with having been God's chosen one from among humanity; and with having attained the level of angels (Commentary on *Perek Cheilek*).

We'll now offer Rambam's insights into the nature of Moses' type of prophecy as opposed to others'.

Moses' prophetic process was qualitatively different than others'. Whereas the other prophets received their prophetic visions either in a dream or in an unconscious trance, Moses received his prophecies in a waking, conscious state and on his feet. Whereas the other prophets would grow morbidly faint when they prophesied, shivering and becoming frightened by the encounter, Moses experienced none of that. Whereas the others couldn't prophesy at will and would often have to wait for days or even years for a prophecy — or might not ever prophesy again — Moses could prophesy at any time. Whereas the others received their prophecy through the agency of an angel and an allegorical vision, Moses envisioned clearly and literally. And whereas the others had to attune their thoughts and otherwise prepare themselves for prophecy, Moses was always attached to God, and thus never had to prepare himself for prophecy (*Hilchot Yesodei HaTorah* 7:6; Commentary on *Perek Cheilek*).

7. Our forefather Abraham, for example, was so "familiar" with God that he was certain enough that it was God Himself who appeared to him in a dream to tell him to offer up Isaac as a sacrifice (see Genesis 22:1–19) that he headed off to do just that as soon as he awoke (*Moreh Nevuchim* 3:24).

8. Moses asked to understand two different things about God, as Rambam explains elsewhere: God's essence and His attributes. God denied him knowledge of His essence, since "No man will see Me and live" (Exodus 33:20), i.e., no living, material human being could ever hope to understand God Himself, who is above and beyond all materiality. But He did promise to let Moses know all of His "attributes."

Rambam defines God's attributes as His actions in the world — what He does and how He does it. And, as Rambam put it, God let Moses know "the nature of all things, their relation to each other, and how they are managed by God, both in general and in particular" (*Moreh Nevuchim* 1:54). Thus, his point is that Moses was shown how God manifests Himself in the world and interacts with it. While that is a nearly boundless revelation, it is not the ultimate one. Since God is not only intimately and utterly, profoundly connected to the world, He is also transcendent of it (see *Moreh Nevuchim* 1:56–60, for example). It's His transcendence that can never be experienced by any human being still "fixed in matter," as Rambam put it earlier. Hence, Moses was denied that. The implication, of course, is that Moses was granted it after his death, in the afterlife.

Chapter 8: On Human Nature

1. As Rambam says elsewhere, free will is actually self-evident and unambiguous, and would seem to require no justification whatsoever (*Moreh Nevuchim* 1:51). He is apparently suggesting that it seems clear that man is beholden to no one for his actions (after all, who moves our arms, feet, etc., but us?). Deeper thought, though, might suggest otherwise. After all, some would reason, doesn't God command my destiny (while others would attribute that to "gods" or "the fates")? Rambam will thus go to great pains to illustrate just how free our will actually is.

2. The belief in astrology, which Rambam cited at the beginning of this section, is rooted in an age-old dilemma.

As Rambam pointed out, the ancients felt that the world didn't seem to follow an ordered, systematic course of events. After all, some perfectly righteous individuals suffered terribly for no apparent reason, while some thoroughly wicked people were healthy and comfortable (*Moreh Nevuchim* 3:16). That seemed to be unfair and to raise questions about God's interactions with the world. But they arrived at a faulty conclusion as a result of their reasoning.

After all, they reasoned, God (who is by definition fair and beneficent) is either aware of the world's goings-on or unaware of them. If He is aware of everything, yet His actions don't seem to be "good and beneficent," the ancients concluded that one of two things were true: either His wishes can be thwarted by circumstances or forces beyond His control (which they realized is absurd); or, despite the fact that he is perfectly aware of everything and fully capable of managing everything, He considers it beneath Himself to "enter the fray," so to speak (*Moreh Nevuchim* 3:16), and allows other entities to hold sway, like the stars and constellation. But that is where they were wrong.

Rambam offers elsewhere, though, that in truth God isn't responsible for some people seeming to suffer unfairly. Human adversity and pain is rooted in three things: 1) the fact that we're subject to deterioration and death, and open to the influence of natural processes and change; 2) the fact that *other people* — not God — sometimes do us harm; and 3) the fact that we do ourselves harm (*Moreh Nevuchim* 3:12).

3. See Rambam's statement that "everyone should...consider himself, as well as all the world, half-meritorious and half-culpable all year long. And he should believe that if he were to commit just one sin, he would incline himself and the entire world toward guilt and bring about destruction; and, contrarily, that if he were to perform just one mitzvah, he would incline himself and the entire world toward merit, and bring on salvation and redemption. As it is written, 'A righteous man is the foundation of the world' (Proverbs 10:25), which is to say that the righteous themselves incline the world in the direction of merit, and rescue it" (*Hilchot Teshuvah* 3:4).

4. As Rambam puts it, "God's providence will necessarily function more so over someone who enjoys...a greater portion of [His] 'emanation' [i.e., God's outpourings of divine essence] than others.... [In fact,] it is the degree of emanation...that has the prophet speak, guides the actions of the prophets, and perfects the knowledge of the pious" (*Moreh Nevuchim* 3:18) — irrespective of their own will!

In fact, the state of being we refer to as "beyond free will" in our note to the text seems to corroborate the fact that God alone "created everything there is" (*Hilchot Yesodei HaTorah* 1:1). For it indicates that He created every moment there is, every action taken, even every decision arrived at.

The "beyond free will" state might also be what Rambam is referring to rather mysteriously in his discussion of a state of mind that is neither reason nor imagination, but is aware of and apparently *beyond* both (*Moreh Nevuchim* 3:15), since that discussion immediately precedes one about divine providence.

5. Interestingly enough, Rambam equates correct viewpoints with "life" and harmful ones with "death" (*Moreh Nevuchim* 1:42). His point then seems to be that while we are free to arrive at any conclusions about the true nature of things we see fit, a wrong decision may lead to serious, even "life"-threatening consequences (i.e., consequences that threaten our personal viewpoints).

6. Much of what is discussed in this chapter is expanded upon in *Hilchot Teshuvah*, chapters 5–7. In addition to citing, "Behold, I have placed before you today life and goodness, death and evil...therefore choose life" there (see *Hilchot Teshuvah* 5:3), Rambam cites other verses as well.

The first one is, "Behold, I have presented to you this day a blessing and a curse" (Deuteronomy 11:26), which is followed by, "[You will receive] a blessing if you obey the mitzvot of God, your Lord, which I am charging you with today; and you will be cursed if you disobey the mitzvot of God, your Lord" (ibid., 27–28). That is again to say that the choice is ours, so we'd be wise to therefore "choose a blessing."

The other verse cited is, "O, that there were such a heart in them always! That they would fear Me and observe all My mitzvot" (ibid. 5:26), which indicates that God does indeed allow us the free will to follow His mitzvot or not. After all, though the quote clearly indicates that He prefers that we do, He nonetheless doesn't compel us to.

7. Despite our explanation of it in the note to the text there, the juxtaposition of free will and Torah study is curious and unexpected here in the text. It alludes to something vitally important about free will, as we'll see. Before we explain that, though, we'll present Rambam's explanation of what is usually referred to as divine providence, which we'll use the Hebrew term for — *hashgachah* — instead, since it encompasses a number of ideas together, including divine attention, compulsion, control, and providence.

Since perfectly righteous people sometimes suffer terribly and wicked people sometimes live good lives, it seemed to the ancients that God left the world under the charge of lesser forces, like the constellations (see note 2 above). Rambam's contention is that man isn't at all under the control of the constellations — or of anything else. He's free to do as he'd like, depending on his circumstances.

But that raises other questions: What role, then, *does* God play in the world if man is free to act at will? And what about personal responsibility? As we'll find, that all touches upon *hashgachah*.

Rambam first provides us with four classical perspectives on *hashgachah* and then offers his own, which is actually an amalgam of a number of them (see *Moreh Nevuchim* 3:17).

The first perspective actually denies *hashgachah* and claims that everything is subject to happenstance. That easily explains the suffering of the righteous.

The second claims that divine *hashgachah* oversees and controls certain more exalted things, but that it leaves other, lesser things — like mankind — to chance. That also explains the suffering of the righteous.

The third maintains that everything and everyone is under the direct and absolute control of *hashgachah* and is directly subservient to divine "will, intentions, and governance," and that nothing happens by chance. The ramifications of this perspective, Rambam points out, is the idea that *everything* is foreordained, that man is consequently unable to choose his own actions, and that the Torah's requirements that we do one thing or another — as well as the whole notion of personal responsibility — are absurd, since man is compelled to do everything he does. That explains the suffering of the righteous as well, but sheds a sinister, black light upon God's "justice."

The fourth perspective asserts that man is free to act as he wills, according to his circumstances, and that divine requirements and mitzvot are thus viable and reasonable. It also asserts that all rewards and punishments are just and equitable, and that, while people do indeed suffer despite their righteousness at times, God is nonetheless fair, but His decisions are based on an opaque and nebulous higher and deeper "wisdom" than what we can comprehend. That last point also explains the suffering of the righteous, albeit only obliquely.

The fifth perspective, which Rambam underscores as the Torah's own, is that man is free to act as he wills, depending on his circumstances, and that as a consequence, he's responsible for his actions (and that divine requirements and mitzvot are again thus viable and reasonable). Accordingly, whatever happens to him is a direct consequence of his choices, and is rooted in an objective, equitable, and *revealed* system of divine justice, rather than some unfathomable wisdom. Agreeing with this perspective, Rambam adds that despite man's free will, *hashgachah* is quite real nonetheless — that God does indeed interact with the world, but that the degree of His interactions with a person and His subsequent *hashgachah* depends upon that person's moral and intellectual standing. We'll get back to this point shortly

But that again raises the issue of divine justice in light of the suffering of the righteous. In response to that, Rambam thus attributes our perceptions of divine *in*justice to our not being privy to the actual workings of divine justice

— or of the true makeup of anyone's heart. As a result, people who *appear* to be righteous suffer, while others who *appear* to be bad do not. But all is not as it appears to be.

As he puts it elsewhere, "The determination of [a person's moral standing] is not based on the number of offences or merits [he accrued], so much as on their relative value. For there are some merits that compensate for several offences...and there are some offenses that compensate for several merits.... But such a determination can only be made by the All-Knowing God, for He alone knows the relative worth of our merits and offences" (*Hilchot Teshuvah* 3:2). Also see this chapter's section 9, which reads: "God [alone] knows our sins and metes out their punishments wisely and justly. Sometimes He punishes a person in this world, other times in the World to Come [which we cannot determine], yet other times, He punishes Him in both...."

Now, Rambam makes another point (cited in supplemental note 4 above) that goes very far to explain the juxtaposition of free will and Torah study at this point in the text.

He explains that God's *hashgachah* is a product of His "emanation" (i.e., the outpourings of His divine essence) [*Moreh Nevuchim* 3:17; see end of supplementary note 1 to ch. 7], and that the more divine emanation a person experiences (depending on his degree of prophecy, as well as on his character and intellect), the more *hashgachah* — i.e., the more divine attention, compulsion, control, and divine providence — he'll be subject to.

He then offers a curious statement, which is that this greater degree of *hashgachah* even "*has the prophet speak, guides the actions of the righteous, and perfects the knowledge of the pious*" (*Moreh Nevuchim* 3:18). This indicates that God does indeed compel certain actions. He sometimes compels prophets to speak, the righteous to act, and the pious to realize certain things.

Now, since prophets, the righteous, and the pious — who are most conversant in Torah — are thus most manifestly affected by *hashgachah* and thus subject to divine control indeed, Rambam's point therefore seems to be that God's *hashgachah* is directly linked to one's Torah knowledge, and that the more Torah one knows, the greater his experience of *hashgachah*. Thus, Torah study is mentioned at this point in the text to encourage us in our interactions with God, and to afford us a means of enjoying divine providence, as well.

That relationship between Torah study — as well as observance — also explains other references to the fact that we'll enjoy divine *hashgachah* if we study and truly live by the tenets of the Torah. See supplementary note 4 to chapter 5, and supplementary note 2 to chapter 2 for citations.

8. Rambam alluded to this idea in a more arcane manner with his statement that, "The soul is utterly nonmaterial and nondependent on materiality.

There is no doubt that when it separates [from the body at death], it returns to its origin and from the 'quarry' from which it came" (*Ma'amer HaYichud*, ch. 2).

9. As Rambam explains, they held that God Himself creates "accidents" (incidental properties of things) each and every moment of a thing's existence. And thus, as soon as He no longer wants that accident to go on, it ceases. So, for example, when a person writes something using a pen, it's not he who is moving the pen — God is creating each instance of the pen's movement Himself, since movement is an accident (incidental property) of the pen (*Moreh Nevuchim* 1:73, sixth proposition).

10. In fact, Rambam explained that what prophets were actually doing when they "predicted" miracles was merely conveying God's message to the people about when the event was going to come about, rather than warning them about something that was just then being set in motion (see *Moreh Nevuchim* 2:29).

11. A person would have had to commit either a thoroughly heinous sin or a great number of sins (*Hilchot Teshuvah* 6:3), or to have caused many others to sin (*Hilchot Teshuvah* 4:1; Commentary on *Pirkei Avot* 5:16), inclined someone away from the path of goodness onto the path of evil, seen his child become more and more wicked and not protested, or have said to himself either, "I'll sin now and repent later," or "I can sin and always be atoned for by Yom Kippur" (*Hilchot Teshuvah* 4:1) to have had his free will withheld from him.

12. The difference between our existence and knowledge and God's is not just a difference of magnitude or degree, because that implies that we're similar to God to some degree, which isn't true. His existence and ours as well as His knowledge and ours only share the same name, with nothing else in common between them (*Moreh Nevuchim* 1:56).

It's like the difference between our human capacities and other beings' capacities. For as Rambam said earlier on, "A human being's senses are not like a horse's [just like] no one species' senses are like any other's. For every species which has a *nefesh* is unique to itself, with functions that are necessarily different from any other's" (see 1:3 above). God and we are separate orders of being. (Also see *Moreh Nevuchim* 3:20's "There is no more commonality between our minds and God's than there is between our selves and His Self.")

There is another point to be made about the difference between God's knowledge and ours. God's knowledge could be said to be wholly "conceptual," while ours could be said to be "experiential" (as well as conceptual).

As Rambam puts it, when an artisan makes something, his knowledge of the myriad and various movements involved in the workings of that very thing is not based on his observations of them as they go on. On the contrary, the object itself and its movements are all a product of his knowledge and skill. For when an artisan conceives of something, he can be said to "know everything about it" beforehand in his mind, and to then see to it that his concept is concretized. We only learn about the object step by step, however, in the process of time, and from the outside in.

Similarly, God conceives of the world in His "mind" and thus knows it fully from the outset, and then He concretizes it, while we only come to understand the world in the process of time and from "the outside in" (see *Moreh Nevuchim* 3:21).

13. Our knowledge is usually in the potential state. We actualize it when we strip things of their matter and dwell on them abstractly, i.e., when we concentrate on a thing's "actuality." At that point, our actualized mind and the actualized entity are said to meld together and become one. God's knowledge, on the other hand, is always "actualized" rather than "in potential." It then follows that He, His "knowledge," and what He "knows" are one and the same. Hence, He's always the Knowing (i.e., the subject under study), the Knower, and the Known all in one (*Moreh Nevuchim* 1:68).

ABOUT THE AUTHOR

A student of the late Rabbi Aryeh Kaplan, ordained by Rabbi Shraya Deblitzky of Bnei Brak and by Rabbi Leibel Tropper of Monsey, New York, and a leader in Jewish outreach, Rabbi Yaakov Feldman was the founder and director of Machon Binah in California, the director of other outreach organizations in New York, and a Hillel director at the State University of New York at Purchase.

Rabbi Feldman has translated and commented on *Chovot HaLevavot* (*Duties of the Heart*) by Rabbeinu Bachyah ibn Pakudah (Jason Aronson Publishers), *Mesillat Yesharim* (*The Path of the Just*) by Rabbi Moshe Chaim Luzzatto (Jason Aronson Publishers), and *Shaarei Teshuvah* (*The Gates of Repentance*) by Rabbeinu Yonah (Rowman and Littlefield Publishers). He has completed a translation of Rabbi Yehudah Ashlag's *Hakdamah L'Sefer Zohar* (*An Introduction to the Zohar*) with original comments; a translation of Rabbi Moshe Chaim Luzzatto's *Ma'amar HaGeulah* (*A Discourse on Redemption*) with original comments; an original work based on Rabbi Moshe Chaim Luzzatto's *Derech Hashem* (*The Way of God*); as well as nonliteral, popular reworkings of both *Shaarei Teshuvah* and *Chovot HaLevavot*, which are all awaiting publication.

He has served on or chaired several boards of directors, including Ohr Ki Tov and Jewish Family Service of Rockland County, as well as the Clergy Committee of Nyack Hospital and the Ethics Committee of United Hospice of Rockland. He serves as chaplain at Good Samaritan Hospital of Suffern, New York, and is a past chaplain of United Hospice of Rockland and Westchester Medical Center.

Rabbi Feldman currently offers two classes at www.torah.org, entitled "Spiritual Excellence" and "Ramchal," which are read by thousands of people each week. He has also written articles for Jewish journals, magazines, and newspapers, as well as children's stories. He lives with his wife, Sara, and their children in Spring Valley, New York.